A VAST ILLUSION

A VAST ILLUSION

Time According to
A COURSE IN MIRACLES

Second Edition

KENNETH WAPNICK, Ph.D.

Foundation for "A Course in Miracles"

Foundation for A Course in Miracles
951-296-6261 • *www.facim.org*   "
41397 Buecking Drive
Temecula, CA 92590

Printed in the United States of America

Portions of *A Course in Miracles* ©1975, "Psychotherapy: Purpose,
Process and Practice" ©1976, "The Song of Prayer" ©1978, *The
Gifts of God* ©1982, used by permission of the Foundation for Inner
Peace.

Cover: from a painting by Dot Bottcher

Second Edition, 1993

Library of Congress Cataloging-in-Publication Data

Wapnick, Kenneth
     A vast illusion : time according to a Course in miracles / Kenneth
Wapnick. --2nd ed.
                    p.   cm.
     Includes bibliographical references.
     ISBN 0-933291-09-4
     1. Course in miracles. 2. Time--Religious aspects--Christianity.
I. Title
BP605.C68W365   1993
299'.93--dc20   93-41757

CONTENTS

Preface.. vii
Introduction.. 1

PART I: THE ORIGIN AND NATURE OF TIME

Introduction.. 5
Chapter 1: The Metaphysics of Time............................ 7
Chapter 2: Commentary on Various Texts 27
Chapter 3: Commentary on "The Little Hindrance"......... 57
Chapter 4: Commentary on "The Present Memory"......... 85

PART II: THE PLAN OF THE ATONEMENT - THE MIRACLE

Introduction.. 123
Chapter 5: The Plan of *A Course in Miracles*................. 125
Chapter 6: The Miracle 135
Chapter 7: Guilt: The Ego's Use of Time 197
Chapter 8: The Holy Spirit's Plan 225

PART III: THE END OF TIME

Introduction.. 251
Chapter 9: The Real World 253
Chapter 10: The Second Coming 269
Chapter 11: The Last Judgment 281
Chapter 12: God's Last Step 301

Appendix – Charts 327

Index of *A Course in Miracles* References 331

Preface to Second Edition

For this new edition, the book has been retypeset and some minor editorial revisions made. Other changes occurring in this edition are associated with the publication of the second edition of *A Course in Miracles* (1992). Material that was inadvertently omitted from the first edition of the Course was included in the second edition. This necessitated amending a few Course quotes included in the book. Footnotes have been added to help identify them; these passages may be found on pages 15, 69, 178, and 184. In addition, the notation for all references to *A Course in Miracles* has been revised to reflect the numbering system used in the second edition of *A Course in Miracles*. Thus, references to *A Course in Miracles* are now given in two ways: the first, unchanged from before, cites the pages from the first edition; the second cites the appropriate numbering from the second edition. An example of the new second-edition notation from each book in *A Course in Miracles* follows:

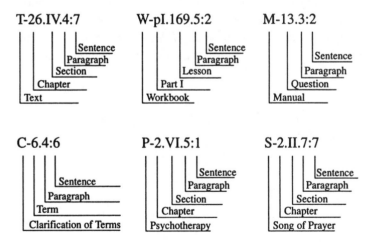

Finally, an index of *A Course in Miracles* references for both first and second editions has been included.

Preface to First Edition

A Vast Illusion began as a series of classes held at Crompond, New York, later released as a tape album called "Time According to *A Course in Miracles*." A transcription of this tape set formed the basis for this book. However, the transcript has been carefully reviewed, edited, and augmented, and so this book is an expansion of many of the ideas originally presented in the classes. We have held to the basic format of these classes nonetheless, so that the reader may have the feeling of participation in a classroom, exploring the depth of meaning found in the many passages on time contained in the Course.

I wish to express my gratitude to Rosemarie LoSasso, the Foundation's Publications Director, who did the initial edit of the transcription, and subsequently supervised the final editing and publication of this book with her usual conscientious and loving devotion; and to my wife Gloria, who together with me went through Rosemarie's edit, and painstakingly worked through the basic contours of the book until it flowed from beginning to end. It is our hope that this book will convey the essence of Jesus' teachings on time, which form the foundation for the Course's thought system.

INTRODUCTION

The question of time is clearly the most difficult area to understand in *A Course in Miracles*. This is so not only because of the subject matter, but because the Course says relatively little about it. As we study the three books, we will often see hints of the theory of time, occasionally a paragraph or two, and rarely, an entire section devoted to its metaphysics. And then the subject is dropped and the reader apparently left hanging in the air. Yet there is one passage in the manual for teachers, which we shall talk about shortly, that very specifically states that to understand the Atonement plan, one must understand the concept of time that the Course sets forth. In other places, however, Jesus says that time is an area that we really cannot understand.

In this book, in order to formulate a coherent presentation, I am going to pull together in three parts the various passages in *A Course in Miracles* that bear on time. The *first* part will be a discussion of the origin and metaphysics of time. The *second* will deal with time and the plan of the Atonement, centering on the role of the miracle and the time collapse it fosters. The *third* will discuss the end of time, and includes the Course's concepts of the real world, Second Coming, Last Judgment, and finally God's last step.

One final note, this book is not meant for a reader new to *A Course in Miracles*, as it assumes a certain familiarity with its basic concepts. Those readers interested in learning more about the Course and its scribing may consult *A Talk Given on "A Course in Miracles": An Introduction* and *Forgiveness and Jesus: The Meeting Place of "A Course in Miracles" and Christianity*. See Related Material at the end of this book for further information.

PART I

THE ORIGIN AND NATURE OF TIME

INTRODUCTION TO PART I

Part I introduces the key principles which comprise *A Course in Miracles'* view of the origin and nature of time. After a general discussion in Chapter 1, Chapter 2 begins with an analysis of the passages in the Course which pertain to the principles from which they are drawn. Part I concludes with a line-by-line analysis of two complete sections from the text that bear directly on time's metaphysics.

One quick note before we begin: as we proceed with our discussion it is important to keep in mind that the different symbols used to explain time are just that—symbols. There is, in fact, no actual carpet of time, or video tape library, or kaleidoscope. We are simply using symbols to help represent concepts of time and our experience of it. Ultimately, none of the symbols, metaphors, images, or analogies that we shall use is wholly satisfactory, but put together, they do help us to account for the phenomenon of time as we are able to experience it. This is similar to the problems encountered by physicists involved in the study of light. Sometimes light appears to be a wave, and that explains certain of its properties. Other times it appears to be a particle, and that explains certain properties as well. But in our experience it is never a wave and a particle simultaneously. So in a sense we shall be following the same procedure by presenting different models to explain different aspects of the phenomenon of time.

Chapter 1

THE METAPHYSICS OF TIME

I have elsewhere[1] discussed the two levels on which *A Course in Miracles* is written, but a brief discussion now would be in order as well. The first level deals with the metaphysics of the Course, treating the difference between the perfect reality of Heaven and the imperfect illusory physical world; the second level contrasts, within the illusory world, the ego's teachings of separation and attack with the Holy Spirit's visions of joining and forgiveness. These two levels are seen in chart 1,[2] and we shall refer back to them throughout the book. In Part I, our emphasis will be almost entirely on the metaphysics (Level One), while Part II will focus on our experience of the ego's world of time, and its undoing through the miracle (Level Two). Part III integrates both levels, as it treats the end product of forgiveness (Level Two), which culminates in the undoing of the world that never was (Level One).

We begin now with the state of Heaven, which *A Course in Miracles* describes as

an awareness of perfect oneness, and the knowledge that there is nothing else; nothing outside this oneness, and nothing else within (text, p. 359; T-18.VI.1:6).

Therefore, God and Christ are one, even though God is First Cause and we as His Son are His Effect. This seemingly dualistic description should not be taken literally, but rather as the

---

1. See, e.g., the section on theory in my *Glossary-Index for "A Course in Miracles,"* and *Forgiveness and Jesus: The Meeting Place of "A Course in Miracles" and Christianity,* Fourth Edition, pp. 19-23. See Related Material at the back of this book for additional information.
2. See Appendix for this and all other charts.

Course's means of describing something that cannot be understood by a human brain:

> It must be understood that the word "first" as applied to Him [God] is not a time concept. He is first in the sense that He is the First in the Holy Trinity Itself. He is the Prime Creator, because He created His co-creators. Because He did, time applies neither to Him nor to what He created (text, p. 105; T-7.I.7:4-7).

This state of Heaven therefore is eternal, for "Eternity is an idea of God" (text, p. 73; T-5.III.6:3).

In an extremely important passage, *A Course in Miracles* states that "Into eternity, where all is one, there crept a tiny, mad idea, at which the Son of God remembered not to laugh" (text, p. 544; T-27.VIII.6:2). This "tiny, mad idea" is the belief that the Son can be separated from his Father, usurp his Father's function as Prime Creator, and thus the effect can seem to become First Cause. Further, the Course teaches: "In his forgetting did the thought become a serious idea, and possible of both accomplishment and real effects" (text, p. 544; T-27.VIII.6:3).

Moreover, *A Course in Miracles* clearly states that time is non-existent, and that its seeming origin was when the tiny, mad idea of separation was taken seriously. The Course outlines the effects of this seriousness:

> A timelessness in which is time made real; a part of God that can attack itself; a separate brother as an enemy; a mind within a body...(text, p. 544; T-27.VIII.7:1).

And yet, despite this seeming seriousness, Jesus says to us:

> Together, we can laugh them both [accomplishment and real effects] away, and understand that time cannot intrude upon eternity. It is a joke to think that time can come to circumvent eternity, which *means* there is no time (text, p. 544; T-27.VIII.6:4-5).

The Course uses the metaphor of sleep to describe the separation, and its ensuing thought system as a dream: "You dwell not here, but in eternity. You travel but in dreams, while safe at home" (text, p. 240; T-13.VII.17:6-7). Yet, when the Son of God seemed to fall asleep and have a dream of separation, the entire world of time appeared to roll out like a long carpet (see chart 2). It seemed to happen in one instant, a tiny tick of time. And within that tiny tick was contained the entire world of time and space as we know it, the entire scope of evolution, which within this world of illusion spans billions of years. One of the difficulties in understanding this concept—to which we shall return over and over again in this book—is that our experience of time, as well as its intellectual understanding, is linear. Therefore, billions of years seem like an interminably long period of time. In the reality of the illusion, however, this entire scope of billions of years occurred in one instant. At one point Jesus comments: "What is a hundred or a thousand years to Them [God and Christ], or tens of thousands?" (text, p. 521; T-26.IX.4:1). Thus, one of the handicaps of using the analogy of the carpet is that it depicts time as linear. The advantage on the other hand, is that it corresponds to our experience of time.

A Course in Miracles explains that simultaneously with the birth of the ego's thought of time God "gave" the Correction, the Holy Spirit, Who undid all the mistakes that were made in that one instant. This is illustrated in chart 2. The top part of the carpet represents the ego script, which is already written. The bottom half, which in a sense runs concurrently with the top because the Correction occurred simultaneously, represents the undoing of all those errors. More specifically, if the basic core of the separation world is defined as special relationships, then concurrent with these thoughts in our minds are thoughts of holy relationships, which undo our special relationships through forgiveness. In a sense, therefore, the top half of the carpet is the ego's world, a world of separation, specialness, and attack. The bottom half is the same script, as it were, but now healed, so that the Holy Spirit's thought of forgiveness—the Atonement principle that the separation never truly occurred—has already replaced the ego's.

We are thus basically speaking of a "dual duality," comparable to the two levels mentioned at the beginning of the chapter. The first duality is between being awake in eternity, and asleep in a dream of time. The second is between the two scripts, the ego's and the Holy Spirit's. Within this second duality, the split or separated mind is divided into three parts: the part the Course describes as the wrong mind, which contains the thought of separation taken seriously; the right mind, the part which contains the memory of God—the Holy Spirit— which remembers to laugh at the separation thought; and the part that chooses between these two, which we shall refer to as the decision maker or observer.

The ego's script was written and chosen by us as decision makers—we are, so to speak, the writers, directors, producers, actors, and actresses. It is so difficult to conceive that both scripts have *already* occurred because this understanding is so dramatically opposed to our own individual experience. However, it is an essential element of *A Course in Miracles'* metaphysics of time, without which one cannot truly understand the Course's teachings on forgiveness. In summary, then, we can say that the instant the entire physical world seemed to occur, in that same instant the Correction for it occurred as well. The Course explains, in the context of a section on sickness:

> Yet separation is but empty space, enclosing nothing, doing nothing, and as unsubstantial as the empty place between the ripples that a ship has made in passing by. And covered just as fast, as water rushes in to close the gap, and as the waves in joining cover it. Where is the gap between the waves when they have joined, and covered up the space which seemed to keep them separate for a little while? (text, p. 554; T-28.III.5:2-4)

Therefore, a helpful metaphor is the decision maker (observer) as the part of our minds (see chart 3) that chooses to review the ego's movie (wrong mind) or the Holy Spirit's correction (right mind). Remember that the entire movie *including* the correction has already been filmed, and encompasses the world of evolution, spanning billions of years. Within this gigantic epic is an *almost* infinite number of segments or video tapes, each corresponding to the expression of a thought: "All thinking produces form at some level" (text, p. 27; T-2.VI.9:14). We have available to us in our minds a "switch" whereby we can instantaneously interchange these smaller tapes, either within the ego or the Holy Spirit scripts, or move from one to the other, "tuning in" to either the ego's or the Holy Spirit's thought. Both have occurred and are *already* present in our minds in what we call the world of time. Another way of conceptualizing this phenomenon is that as we sit in front of our movie or video screen, the decision maker part of our minds is viewing the script at a *very slow speed*, experiencing all the effects of its thought, which occurred in one instant and has, in fact, already disappeared.

Thus, we are as observers sitting in front of a screen watching what has already taken place, as if it were occurring for the first time. Our *experience*, however, is that we are actually part of what we are observing. So in the right-hand part of chart 3, which represents the television screen, what we are seeing also includes all the aspects of the script which involve us. The reality is that we are really *observing* this, choosing which part of the script we wish to observe via the decision maker part of our minds. This is the meaning of *A Course in Miracles'* statement (discussed below) that we are watching something from a point at which it has already been completed.

Now the trick in all this, and why the Course refers to time as a magic trick or "sleight of hand" (workbook, p. 291; W-pI.158.4:1), is that it appears as if we are actually living in this moment. In truth, however, we are merely *re*-experiencing something that has already happened. Thus there is no *real* connection between the "we" that sits observing, and the "we" that we are observing, except that *we* have made a connection. And thus what we have made becomes real to us, *as if* the connection were real. When we turn the set off, what we have been observing is gone. Our fear of this of course is enormous, as we believe that if the image on the screen disappears, so do we. Thus we delay this choice for a long, long time, and that is why the world, including most spiritualities, attempts to keep real certain aspects of the giant epic movie.

An example of this phenomenon of becoming what we observe occurs while watching a movie in a theater. Even though intellectually we understand that there is really nothing on the screen except the projection of a film from a projector that is behind us, our *experience* nonetheless is that we are actually observing something on the screen that is real, for we feel the same emotions as if something were actually happening to us. We experience horror, fear, guilt, happiness, joy, or sadness, and can begin weeping or laughing as if something were really occurring. Thus, for all intents and purposes from the psychological point of view, something *is* happening on the screen.

None of this would have an impact on us at all, if what were on the screen did not remind us of what we believe is within ourselves. Even more specifically, it affects us *because* the thoughts underlying the emotions are within us: the outer is nothing more than the reflection of what is within—no more, no less. And so even though we realize on one level that what we are observing in front of us is illusory, we still react as if it were real, and were, in effect, happening to us or to people with whom we identify. Thus, it seems to us as if we are actually going through our daily activities, making choices in the *present* that determine *future* situations, controlled by events of the *past*. In reality, to state it once again, we are merely *watching* ourselves going through these activities, making choices that determine what is to come, and being affected by what has preceded this moment. This makes no sense when understood this way by a mind that has chosen reason, but we must never forget that the ego is literally built on no-sense. Thus, it *makes* no sense for us to attempt to understand non-sense.

Another example of psychological identification is our responding to what we read in the newspaper or watch on the television news. If we respond in terms of happiness, joy, anger, or fear, it could only be because psychologically we are identifying with the event. Otherwise, the situation or person would have no effect on us. Hence, we are only seeing ourselves, or better, a projection of ourselves, in that particular situation: we are *watching*, not *being*. A parallel to this is what is usually referred to as an out-of-body experience. Here, the individual appears to be literally outside the physical experience observing the body perform. This helpful analogy, however, should not be extended too far, as even the experience of being outside the body is part of the video tape library, as we still experience ourselves as separate beings. Besides, the mind does not dwell in the body at all.

Thus, we are observing events that seem to be real and happening right now. In actuality we are only observing what has already happened—we are replaying a tape as it were, yet *forgetting* that we are doing so. When we remember that we have chosen what we are experiencing, the chains that seemingly bound us to the screen, and ultimately to the observing chair itself, disappear and we are free. Thus, it is our denial of what we have chosen that causes us to believe that we are *in* the dream, and so it becomes as real to us as our sleeping dreams do at night. We live in a technological age of instant replays and VCRs, where we can fast-forward, reverse, pause, and still-frame, and who knows what ingenuity the ego will devise in the future? What is so interesting about these technological breakthroughs is that our intangible mind, through its physical instrument the brain, is devising a mirror of the same mechanisms of the mind that not only made up the brain, but the entire physical universe as well. We are merely living out the thoughts of the mind, having produced the world of form by projection, a world that has never left its source in the mind.

It should really come as no surprise that this entire world, and all of our experiences here, are a grand deception. The original ego thought of separation from God was a lie; how then can what is projected from this thought be anything but a lie? Thus we should never underestimate the power of our ego-body to lie and deceive. It is also clear, to anticipate our discussion later in the book, that we can never awaken to reality from this dream of "reality" without help from outside the ego dream. This help is the Holy Spirit, or His manifestation Jesus. It was believing that we could exist on our own, without God, that led us into the dream in the first place, and so it is by choosing the Help of God that we awaken from it.

It is this kind of overall explanation which makes sensible some of the otherwise inexplicable passages that occur in *A Course in Miracles.* For example, one line, which I will discuss later, states: "The revelation that the Father and the Son are one will come in time to every mind" (workbook, p. 291; W-pI.158.2:8). Furthermore, the time when this recognition will come to us has already been set: the script of our acceptance is already written. What is *not* set is *when* we will choose to re-experience that part of the script. The significant implications of this idea will be discussed in Chapter 2.

Returning to our VCR analogy, let us assume that we all have remote controls and can press any number of different buttons. The decision maker (or observer) in our minds then chooses to press the button that activates the tape containing our awakening from the dream, which is the acceptance of the Atonement. At that point we are choosing to switch to the Holy Spirit's script, forgiving everyone in the world and calling forth the remembrance that we are one with God. Once again, that part of the script has already been filmed and thus has already "happened," but we are still free to choose *when* we will review it. This choice is the only notion of free will that the Course accepts as meaningful (text, intro.; workbook, pp. 291,316; T-in.1; W-pI.158.2:8-9; W-pI.169.8:1-2). And of course we cannot choose *not* to choose again; but we can delay this choice. As the Course explains:

> You can temporize and you are capable of enormous procrastination, but you cannot depart entirely from your Creator, Who set the limits on your ability to miscreate (text, p. 18; T-2.III.3:3).

This limit, the Holy Spirit's presence in our minds, ensures that at some point within the hologram of time, we shall choose to awaken from the dream.

A Course in Miracles teaches, however, that we do not abruptly awaken from the dream. Before we can fully awaken, we first have to switch from the ego's nightmares to the Holy Spirit's happy dreams. That progression—from nightmares to happy dreams—undoes the belief that God will punish us. Only then can we accept the Atonement for ourselves. This intermediate step, the attainment of which is the goal of the Course, is expressively described in this passage:

> Nothing more fearful than an idle dream has terrified God's Son, and made him think that he has lost his innocence, denied his Father, and made war upon himself. So fearful is the dream, so seeming real, he could not waken to reality without the sweat of terror and a scream of mortal fear, unless a gentler dream preceded his awaking, and allowed his calmer mind to welcome, not to fear, the Voice That calls with love to waken him; a gentler dream, in which his suffering was healed and where his brother was his friend.[3] God willed he waken gently and with joy, and gave him means to waken without fear (text, p. 542; T-27.VII.13:3-5).

There is an interesting parallel found in the teachings of Basilides, one of the great Gnostic teachers of the second century. He had a fascinating theory, which on first reading

---

3. The portion of this sentence following the semicolon was inadvertently omitted from the first edition of *A Course in Miracles*.

sounds totally preposterous. Basilides maintained that Jesus did not die on the cross. Rather, he changed his form and instead Simon of Cyrene hung crucified, while Jesus was off on a tree laughing. Basilides, who remained in opposition to Church teachings and its leaders, saw Jesus derisively laughing at all the people (primarily the Jews) who could not understand what was truly happening. The content of Basilides' inspiration was correct; namely, that Jesus "remembered" to laugh at the tiny, mad idea of the ego and not take it seriously. Thus, he knew that *he* was not being crucified, as he was not his body. Merely an observer, Jesus watched himself, knowing that what he was seeing was not real but only a dream. We may thus conclude that Basilides' mind could not fully encompass the magnitude of the thought of Jesus' *non-derisive* laughter. The inspiration thus filtered through his limited ego mind, manifesting itself in the form of attack.

Related to the concept of not taking the world's dream seriously is what psychologists term "lucid dreaming," referring to the phenomenon of people, who in the midst of a nocturnal dream, are aware that they are dreaming. In the dream itself they are aware that they are the dreamer *and* the dream. Thus, they may be in the midst of a terrifying nightmare, and suddenly can remember it is a dream. The dream continues, but the terror disappears. *A Course in Miracles'* counterpart to the lucid dreamer is the happy dreamer, who while living in this illusory world, suddenly realizes that he or she is not really here.

To continue with the analogy of the lucid dreamer, but now in the context of sitting in front of a VCR, it would be as if we as observers were watching a video tape, and suddenly realize that we are watching something that has already happened. We are observing ourselves as a figure in the dream, yet still within the dream, but now we are aware that it *is* nothing but a dream. This shift in awareness is represented in chart 3 by the two lines emanating from the observer, representing the ego and the Holy Spirit. It is as if there are two voices speaking to us as we view our screens. The ego is saying: "Keep tuned to my station and believe that the body's drama you are watching is really happening to you." The Holy Spirit's Voice reminds us that what we are observing is nothing but a dream. Before we can really hear the full clarity of His message, however, we first have to consider the idea that there is another way of looking at the dream. This other way, again, is the happy dream of forgiveness.

The VCR (or movie) analogy is a somewhat simplified way of presenting the concept, and has the drawback of being linear. A computer, with all its complexity, is in fact a better analogy to use, except that it is a more complicated way of making the point. Imagine ourselves sitting in front of a computer screen, with a myriad number of programs from which we can choose, and many different buttons we can press. This analogy better reflects the complexity of our individual lives and our interactions with the world. The computer also serves as a helpful analogy of the relationship between the mind (observer) and the brain (body), inasmuch as the mind has programmed the brain, just as the computer programmer tells the computer what to do. Without a program and a source of energy, the computer cannot function. Likewise, the brain (and therefore the body) is totally "lifeless" without "instructions" from the mind.

Another helpful analogy is a kaleidoscope, a small tube in which mirrors reflect light transmitted through bits of loose colored glass contained at one end, causing them to appear as symmetrical designs—and often beautiful ones at that—when viewed from the other end. Actually, the state of the split mind is better understood as a kaleidoscope within a kaleidoscope, a split within a split, the first one being the projection outward from the primordial split mind, which is the original piece of glass. The projection is the original thought of separation or fragmentation from God. Therefore, the world that is projected out is identical to the separation thought that has been projected, and so the glass continues to shatter. Each projected thought, as it were, becomes its own kaleidoscope. The actual process is mind-boggling, and defies any attempt at rational or logical apprehension, for the complexity is overwhelming to our very limited human thinking. The trick of time is that this seeming instant of fragmentation now appears to have happened over an immense span of time; time's linearity is but the veil that hides the simultaneous co-existence of every part of the shattered glass.

Transferring to the kaleidoscope the previously discussed idea of the observer and the observed, we can understand that the observer—the decision maker—is outside of what it observes. *Within* the kaleidoscope there is no difference between the observer and the observed. They are one: the part is in the whole; the whole is in each part. This is similar to a psychotherapist analyzing a dream, interpreting all its symbols as being part of the dreamer; i.e., the dream and dreamer are one. We who have dreamed the dreams of our lives, in truth stand outside of them, yet we still believe we are in them. Moreover, we believe that we are controlled by them.

Still another way of conceptualizing the "mind within a mind" model is to think of each fragment as a computer chip, filled with information (or thoughts), and each thought itself is a chip, and on and on. The process "begins," to the extent that one can speak of a temporal limit to what is beyond all time, with the single chip of the one Son's separation thought. From there the chip fragments continuously—chip within chip, kaleidoscope within kaleidoscope. As *A Course in Miracles* describes the process:

> You who believe that God is fear made but one substitution. It has taken many forms, because it was the substitution of illusion for truth; of fragmentation for wholeness. It has become so splintered and subdivided and divided again, over and over, that it is now almost impossible to perceive it once was one, and still is what it was....You do not realize the magnitude of that one error. It was so vast and so completely incredible that from it a world of total unreality *had* to

emerge. What else could come of it? Its fragmented aspects are fearful enough, as you begin to look at them. But nothing you have seen begins to show you the enormity of the original error, which seemed to cast you out of Heaven, to shatter knowledge into meaningless bits of disunited perceptions, and to force you to make further substitutions (text, pp. 347-48; T-18.I.4:1-3; 5:2-6).

This kaleidoscope image also incorporates one of the key ideas of a hologram: the whole is contained in every part. The holographic process consists of splitting a laser beam of light (a beam with a single wave length as opposed to the multiple waves of ordinary light) into two. One beam (called the reference beam) illuminates the object being photographed, while the other (called the working beam) interferes with the light that is reflected from the object. Both beams are then directed to a photographic plate, where their interaction is then recorded and forms the hologram. When, finally, a laser beam shines through this holographic image it is perceived by the viewer three-dimensionally. Even more to the point here, any part of the object perceived in the photograph contains within it the whole. In other words, the part defines the whole and recreates for the perceiver, as it were, the nature of the whole object.

In this respect, the statement in the Seth material (a series of books by Jane Roberts, channeled from an entity named Seth), that all incarnations are occurring simultaneously, is similar to the Course's teachings that all events have occurred in one instant, yet appear to be unfolding sequentially over time. Thus all incarnations, that in this world of time and space would span billions of years, are encapsulated in a time-space hologram of this one instant. If we think of the mind of the Sonship of God as being a unified, pristine pane of glass—the Christ as God created Him—then the separation is the seeming shattering of the glass into billions and billions of pieces. This is what is conveyed in the kaleidoscope image, where the little pieces of glass represent the shattered parts of the

Sonship. Thus, the observing part of our minds sits in front of the kaleidoscope, which in our earlier image was the VCR set, and can turn the tube and see whatever it has chosen to see and experience at any particular time.

Given these premises, we can begin to realize that at any given moment our minds can make a decision, for example, to be living in New York State at the end of the twentieth century, while in another part of our minds we experience ourselves in a totally different time and space, another period in history, past or future. Again, we can think of the chip within a chip image, or kaleidoscope within a kaleidoscope. We are unaware of this because we have limited our minds by making laws of time and space, which program our brains and limit the experience of ourselves. People who have past life regressions, or who can look into the future, are simply removing some of the limiting barriers that formerly prevented them from experiencing much more of what is actually within their own minds.

There is a very important adaptive purpose in these barriers. For example, consider the world of perception from a purely physiological point of view. Our brains are continually bombarded by thousands upon thousands of sensory stimuli—sights, sounds, smells, etc. We automatically—and it is so automatic that we are not aware of it—screen out everything that is not needed at the time. For example, when one gives a speech that is being taped, the attention is on the talking and interaction with the audience. When the tape is replayed, however, one hears sounds that were not in awareness during the taping: cars passing, birds chirping, rain falling, or refrigerator motors whirring, all of which were not heard at the time of the taping because the brain had selectively tuned them out. This obviously is a very important adaptive mechanism, because there is no way that we could function in this material world if we were paying equal attention to all stimuli simultaneously.

If we move from the physiological to the psychological dimension of the mind, we observe this same screening-out process at work. There would be no way that we could live in this world if, for example, at the same moment I am talking with you I am involved in talking with thousands of other people from previous or future incarnations, all of whom are included in the script that is already written. Thus, it is an adaptive part of living in the world of time, as we set it up, that we pay attention only to what is currently occurring in a particular dimension of time and space that we have chosen to experience. And yet, again, the whole of the mind's experience is found within every fragment of that experience.

In summary, then, the carpet, video tape, kaleidoscope, and hologram images all help in different ways to illustrate some key parts of *A Course in Miracles*' concept of time; namely, that we are observing what has already happened, and that what appear to us to be distinct events taking place in a linear progression of past, present, and future, are rather all present simultaneously in our minds because the whole of time occurred in one single instant. We focus directly only on segments of the total fragmentation at any given moment, and choose whether to view the ego's version of separation, attack, anger, and specialness, or the Holy Spirit's correction of all this through forgiveness and holy relationships. Thus our only true choice, always and ever, regardless of its form, is whether to choose the ego or the Holy Spirit, to remain asleep in the observer's chair or to awaken from the dream, leave the chair entirely, and reunite with our Source.

We will come back to these central ideas many times as we encounter them in various passages from the Course. We will then develop them more in depth and deal with some of the difficulties and paradoxes involved in these ideas.

Q: Before going on, would you say something about the frequent misunderstanding of what these principles imply? This idea that everything has already occurred seems to encourage a fatalistic attitude toward events in our lives, because it suggests that we have no choice in a particular situation. For instance, it could be interpreted to mean that if someone shoots his wife, that since the script was already written there was no possible way for him to decide otherwise than for him to shoot his wife. People are inclined to think that it does not really matter because the script is already written. Would it not be more accurate to think that not only do we have a choice of what video to focus in on, but we also have a choice of what aspect in that video we are going to focus on? Thus, not only has it occurred in time that this man has shot his wife, it has also occurred in the same instant that he has not shot his wife, and that he actually chose one of these to focus on. Is this what you are saying?

A: Yes. It is helpful in this case to go back to charts 2 and 3, and consider the ego version where you attack your wife, and the Holy Spirit's version where you forgive your wife. There could be other kinds of options as well. The aforementioned line in the Course "All thinking produces form at some level" (text, p. 27; T-2.VI.9:14) is enlightening in this regard. Applying it to your example, it means that the thoughts of shooting your wife, of putting the revolver down, or of doing something else entirely, have already happened. Thus you are not really having a new thought, but merely accessing different thoughts in your mind. Therefore, you are re-experiencing a thought that you once had. This is a mind-boggling idea, but it is the key to understanding what *A Course in Miracles* says about time. We are *re*-experiencing because we are observing again on the screen what has already happened. That is why a computer analogy is a little more helpful than that of the video tape. A computer expands the possibilities immensely, whereas as I have already said, the video tape is limited to a linear modality. The main idea is that it is all there, so it does make a difference what you are choosing to observe right now. If you continue to choose the ego script then you become more involved with your guilt, which means that your finger, as it were, becomes almost frozen on the ego button. You just keep playing the same script of guilt over and over again.

Many years ago the physiological psychologist Donald Hebb from McGill University proposed a theory that learning occurs when certain neural pathways in the brain become fixed. These pathways become like a canal: the more it is used through habit patterns, the deeper it becomes, and so the more difficult it is to break out of it. Analogous to this is the guilt-attack cycle, wherein the more we attack people the more guilt we feel, which makes us attack even more. So it does make a difference how often we choose to see dreams of vengeance, murder, jealousy, depression, and guilt, for such choices root us still further in the ego thought system, and so we are merely choosing to be more and more miserable. In the end, from a Level One perspective, it does not make any difference as we will see when we look at chart 4. But it does make a difference certainly in terms of what we are experiencing as we sit in the chair looking at all of it. This is evident in the question posed in the workbook, "Why wait for Heaven?" (workbook, p. 347; W-pI.188.1:1). Why would we delay when we could be at perfect peace, and why exchange that peace for anxiety and conflict? In other words, why remain asleep tortured by nightmares, when we can simply awaken to the peace of God?

Q: When Einstein's brain was studied it was discovered that it had more crevices and deeper pathways in it. It was not any heavier, or a different size from anybody else's brain. Is this an example of what you are saying?

A: Yes, and this implies that he used his brain more. I think that it would be possible to find a counterpart for that in terms of right-minded thinking; we are not talking about right brain and left brain, incidentally, but right-minded thinking, i.e., forgiveness as opposed to guilt and attack.

It is interesting to note the physiological expressions of the dynamics of the mind, as we have just been considering. Since these dynamics represent the thoughts that are in our minds, it makes sense that they will be projected out onto our bodies. Similarly, we find these mind dynamics expressed in current technology, such as in movies, video tapes, and computers: in all of these, we find the outward expression of what has already happened in our minds.

Returning to the original question, again let me caution against adopting a *laissez faire*, fatalistic, or passive approach to our experience here. In fact, such an approach is really an ego trap for keeping us here. *A Course in Miracles* teaches us that we *are* responsible for what we are experiencing (text, p. 418; T-21.II.2:3-5); however, *what* we are responsible for is choosing to review this experience in our minds, which has already happened. In other words, we are responsible for *what* we are viewing; i.e., which video tape or computer files we are going to access.

Still another point is relevant here. If one seeks to use these metaphysical principles as a justification for doing nothing, then one is misunderstanding the different levels. On the level that says that all has already happened, and in fact that nothing has happened—"all" being thought—then there is no body that can even do nothing, or even have such a thought. But once I believe I am here, puzzling over a question such as this, then I am already believing that time and space are real. Therefore, seeking to justify a behavior (or absence of a behavior) on grounds of it being an illusion is not being honest, since I have *already* chosen to believe that I am here. Thus we must remain faithful to the context of our underlying belief system if we are ultimately to change it.

Q: Would it be accurate to say that when our fingers are stuck on the ego remote control button, as we are making ego choices, and then we decide to change to the Holy Spirit's button, that that channel would still show the same action but it would be viewed differently? And isn't it also true that if we had listened to the Holy Spirit earlier, we would not have had to go through all this extra time, we would not have had to be stuck on the ego button?

A: That is quite right. This will be brought out when we talk about the miracle in Part Two. The lesson in all of this is that we do not have to sit and watch the same patterns or themes in our movies again for two hours, five hours, five years, or five lifetimes. This is one of the basic ideas in the Course: saving time. We do not have to sit through all these terrible reruns, which is what our experience in this world really is. *All* experiences are reruns. This means that even though we are experiencing ourselves talking about things for the first time and interacting with others for the first time, we are really, in terms of the analogy we have been using, sitting in front of a screen watching ourselves going through these experiences. However, we have so repressed the observer dimension that it seems as if we are sitting in a room talking, over a period of time, and our experience is that we are doing this for the first time. In reality, though, we are observing something that has already happened. That again is the mind-boggling aspect of this idea. Our freedom does not lie in choosing what is in the script, or on the video tape, computer program, or the kaleidoscopic pieces of glass; our freedom rather lies in choosing what we are going to see *when*, and how quickly we are going to let go of guilt by choosing the Holy Spirit's version.

Furthermore, as an added comment on your question, if we had only listened to the Holy Spirit at the beginning, there would have been no ego scripts to undo. *A Course in Miracles* emphasizes that the ego speaks first, is wrong, and that the Holy Spirit is the Answer (text, pp. 80,92; T-5.VI.3:5-4:3; T-6.IV.1:1-2). If there had been no mistake, there would have been no need for the Answer. In another context, the "Exultet," a liturgical hymn for the Easter Vigil ascribed to the fourth-century St. Ambrose, exclaims the blessing of Jesus' presence: "O happy fault, O necessary sin of Adam, which gained for us so great a Redeemer!" Thus, if there had been no original sin ("happy fault"), there would have been no Redeemer.

Q: To return to the Seth books, there was an interesting account of Jane Roberts and her husband sitting in a restaurant. As they looked across the table at each other they both recognized that what they were seeing were their "probable realities." In other words, they saw an aspect of what they could have been, which was understood to be a negative thing in their lives. They recognized that they could have made that one choice which would have led to these negative experiences. They were aware that they were seeing the other channel, so to speak, and were very grateful for being where they were. Does this correspond to the idea you are explaining?

A: Yes, that is a good example of how this phenomenon works. There are many other examples like that in esoteric literature which, if looked at from this point of view, make a lot of sense. When we discuss the notion of the miracle, we shall see that the real power of *A Course in Miracles* lies in its speaking to us very practically within this metaphysical context, i.e., how we learn to press the Holy Spirit's button, and ultimately switch the television set off and leave the observer's chair entirely.

Chapter 2

COMMENTARY ON VARIOUS TEXTS

We now begin our study of the passages in *A Course in Miracles* which pertain to the origin and nature of time. With very few exceptions we will be looking only at portions of sections. We start with the manual for teachers, the section called "Who Are Their Pupils?" (manual, p. 4; M-2) beginning with the second paragraph and on through to the fourth paragraph. This opens with an idea that I mentioned right at the beginning:

In order to understand the teaching-learning plan of salvation, it is necessary to grasp the concept of time that the course sets forth.

This is the only place in the material which states that it is necessary that we understand the idea of time that the Course is presenting. In many other places Jesus indicates that we could not understand it (e.g., text, p. 484; workbook, pp. 316, 360; T-25.I.7; W-pI.169.10; W-pI.194.4). Despite this, we are going to bite the bullet and try to understand what our ego-programmed brains prevent us from understanding: that time is illusory. However, we *are* able to understand time's *purpose* according to the ego and the Holy Spirit, and this will be the principal theme of Part II. Incidentally, we find a similar approach to "understanding" the ego thought system set forth in the introductory paragraph to the five laws of chaos. Jesus tells us there:

> The "laws" of chaos can be brought to light, though never understood. Chaotic laws are hardly meaningful, and therefore out of reason's sphere. Yet they appear to be an obstacle to reason and to truth. Let us, then, look upon them calmly, that we may look beyond them, understanding what they are, not what they would maintain. *It is essential it be understood*

27

what they are for, because it is their purpose to make mean-ingless, and to attack the truth (text, p. 455; T-23.II.1:1-5, my italics).

Atonement corrects illusions, not truth.

This is a standard idea with which we are all familiar by now. It means that Atonement has nothing to do with eternity or the truth of God; it has to do only with correcting the dream of separation, in time, not the *oneness* of reality. That is why "Atonement" should not be misread as "At-one-ment." The latter *would* be correct if the term had to do with Heaven, the state of unity for which correction is certainly not needed. In chart 2, the Atonement applies *only* to what is to the right of the vertical line that separates Heaven from the carpet of time. As Jesus instructs us in an important passage found in a sec-tion on special relationships:

> Your task is not to seek for love, but merely to seek and find all of the barriers within yourself that you have built against it. It is not necessary to seek for what is true, but it *is* necessary to seek for what is false (text, p. 315; T-16.IV.6:1-2).

The focus of the Atonement therefore is not on love, but on re-moving the obstacles to the awareness of love's presence. Love and truth simply *are*, and need not be sought; simply re-membered as the barriers of guilt are removed.

Therefore, it [Atonement] corrects what never was. Fur-ther, the plan for this correction was established and completed simultaneously, for the Will of God is entirely apart from time. So is all reality, being of Him. The instant the idea of separation entered the mind of God's Son, in that same instant was God's Answer given. In time this happened very long ago. In reality it never happened at all.

In the very instant that the idea of separation seemed to oc-cur, in that same instant God created the Holy Spirit, extended Himself into the dream, and thus at that same instant the entire script was corrected. While *A Course in Miracles* talks of the Holy Spirit as a person whom God created in response to the separation, in fact this cannot be taken literally. Jesus reminds us that we cannot even think of God without a body (text, p. 364; T-18.VIII.1:7), and so the Course speaks of God and the Holy Spirit *as if* they were in bodies, so that we would have a means of relating to them. Moreover, how could God give a response to a mistake the Course teaches He does not even recognize, since it never happened? Thus, *A Course in Miracles'* treatment of the Holy Spirit's creation should be taken metaphorically as a way of describing a process to which we, in our limited understanding, could relate. We shall return to this important point in Part II, when we discuss the Holy Spirit's "plan."

It would actually thus be better to speak of the Holy Spirit as a thought or memory of God's Love that we carried with us into the dream when we fell asleep. This memory, then—the Holy Spirit—undid all of the errors within the dream, since it reminds us that we never left God. And thus were all the thoughts which encompass the entire scope of evolution un-done in that single instant when we believed we had fallen asleep—the thought of perfect Love casting out the thought of fear. Referring back to chart 2, when the ego's script was writ-ten (the top part of the carpet) the Holy Spirit's script was written at the same time (the bottom part). Reality is entirely apart from time, and so there is no reconciling the world of time with the world of eternity, the world of illusion with the world of truth. Referring to chart 4, we may also speak of two holograms, the ego's hologram of hate, and the Holy Spirit's hologram of correction.

Therefore, within the world of illusion, the world of time, everything happened billions of years ago, right at the moment of the "big bang." In reality, of course, none of it happened at all; the world is just a dream of the impossible.

The world of time is the world of illusion. What happened long ago seems to be happening now. Choices made long since appear to be open; yet to be made.

We are really seeing something that has already happened. It seemed to occur long ago, and in that one instant the entire script was written, all video tapes were shot, and everything in the kaleidoscope seemed to appear within it. Yet, in our experience it seems to be happening right now. As we have been saying, our experience is of sitting in this room together, at a particular time and space in history, going through something that seems to be new and fresh. I am saying something, one of you may say something, and it seems to be happening right now; in reality, to state it again, it has already happened. Actually, the often-quoted statement from Ecclesiastes, "There is no new thing under the sun" (Ec 1:9),[4] is a wise statement indeed. I am not sure how the biblical author meant it, probably not quite like this, but the idea that there is literally nothing new under the sun is exactly what *A Course in Miracles* is saying.

What has been learned and understood and long ago passed by is looked upon as a new thought, a fresh idea, a different approach.

Everything that we have learned and understood throughout the whole span of evolution occurred within that one instant of time, within that one tiny tick. We do not experience events in this way, of course, yet we have already seen that our experiences—mediated through our sensory organs and mind-programmed brain—distort and conceal the truth. For example, I may suddenly have an ingenious idea: I am going to invent the wheel, work out a chemical equation that will revolutionize science, or split the atom. When these ideas occur,

4. Unless otherwise noted, all biblical quotations are from *The Jerusalem Bible* (NY: Bantam, Doubleday, Dell Publishing Group, Inc., 1966). The exceptions are the King James Version, noted as KJV.

they seem to be totally new. Yet, they remain mere replays of what has already occurred in the hologram of time.

Because your will is free you can accept what has already happened at any time you choose, and only then will you realize that it was always there. As the course emphasizes, you are not free to choose the curriculum, or even the form in which you will learn it. You are free, however, to decide when you want to learn it. And as you accept it, it is already learned.

When we accept the Atonement for ourselves, thereby un-doing the guilt that limited the awareness of who we truly are, we become lucid dreamers, i.e., realizing within the dream that we are dreaming. So I can accept at any time what is already there in the hologram of correction in chart 4.

Let me read the opening lines from the introduction to the text, to which the second part of this passage is a reference:

> This is a course in miracles. It is a required course. Only the time you take it is voluntary. Free will does not mean that you can establish the curriculum. It means only that you can elect what you want to take at a given time (text, intro.; T-in.1:1-5).

We cannot establish the curriculum now because it has already been established by us. We can choose, though, what station, film, video tape, or part of the kaleidoscope we are going to observe and re-experience at any given time. Yet what we are observing has already happened. The forms in which we are going to learn the curriculum have been chosen as well, as this passage indicates. This means that we chose all the mistakes, (special hate and special love relationships), and we can choose now to accept all their corrections (holy relationships). "And as you accept it, it is already learned" because it has been *already* learned. The mistake, having already been cor-rected, now waits for our choice to accept and re-experience its loving correction.

31

Time really, then, goes backward to an instant so ancient that it is beyond all memory, and past even the possibility of remembering. Yet because it is an instant that is relived again and again and still again, it seems to be now.

We experience what has already happened as happening now, precisely because we are continually choosing to see ourselves as separate. This "instant so ancient" is that split second when the entire thought system of the ego seemed to come into existence. Yet that instant has been so defended against that it can never be remembered. Nor must it be. However, our decision to be guilty now—the effects of this instant—can be remembered, and it is this we undo.

Q: Those are really such difficult lines to comprehend. An intellectual understanding is one thing; but it is quite another matter to get into the full implications of what it means on the level of experience.

A: It is certainly true that the entire thought system of *A Course in Miracles* is built on this idea, but as it says, and fortunately for us too, to practice the Course does not require understanding time's metaphysics. Yet, this is certainly the underlying foundation of the Course. That will become even clearer when we discuss the Atonement and the function of the miracle in Part II. When we discuss "The Little Hindrance" a bit later we shall find the same idea: our reliving over and over again that ancient instant. And it is that reliving that roots the observer or decision maker to the chair and to the ego button. It should be mentioned that despite my anthropomorphizing part of the split mind as the decision maker and/or observer, they are not to be equated with a human form or brain, since mind is immaterial, intangible, and invisible.

Q: There seem to be some similarities but also some differences between this particular teaching of the Course and what the law of karma implies. For example, the karmic tradition teaches that if you are a victimizer in one of your lives, you might come back as a victim. *A Course in Miracles* seems to imply something different, though, implying that you will come back in that same role because you are reliving the same thing. On the other hand, perhaps the law of karma could be understood to mean that at that instant of separation you chose to be a victim or a victimizer, and that you are going to keep playing out that role in a different form in each lifetime. This interpretation seems to fit in better with the Course's idea that "...even the form in which you will learn it [has been chosen already]."

A: A current and common interpretation of the law of karma is that you go back and forth in your roles—as a victim and as a victimizer, persecutor and "persecutee." *A Course in Miracles* could be understood as saying that you could choose a script in which you are a victim throughout the whole scope of time. However, I do not think this would preclude the possibility of interchanging roles at times, either. In other words, even though you may have scripted one main form in which you play out your ego drama, as for example that of being a victim, it is also possible that you could alternate; your role could be that of a victimizer also. This is based on the psychological dynamic that you could not really see yourself as a victimizer unless you also experienced yourself as a victim. If one is in your mind, then the other must be as well: *all* victimizers feel justified in their thoughts or actions because in their perception they have been victims themselves.

A common clinical example is that of a battered child who is seen by the world as a victim, and then grows up and becomes a battering parent. Similarly, a person could have been a victimizer in a Nazi concentration camp, and yet at home have been a victim. It is interesting to note that Jesus has been seen by some people in esoteric traditions as always being a victim in his previous incarnations. He was thought to be the biblical Joseph, Socrates, and other "victimized" people, each of whose roles always was to be the teacher of truth who is persecuted to the ultimate extent. The problem with this line of thought is that it is impossible to understand how it all works, since it is always understood within a linear framework, which is illusory to begin with. The essence of *A Course in Miracles'* teaching is that we are constantly reliving the initial separation. This principle must not be lost sight of in seeking to understand and apply its teachings.

And thus it is that pupil and teacher seem to come together in the present, finding each other as if they had not met before.

This does not mean simply that they had met before in a previous lifetime, but that they had met before in the instant that the whole carpet spun out. It is therefore not the usual *deja vu* experience such as remembering when we spent time together in the Middle Ages, or in the time of Jesus, Atlantis, or whenever. This would imply a linear view of time, which would miss the whole point here. Rather, *A Course in Miracles* is speaking of that one original instant when all relationships occurred, and which we now recall to our minds.

Q: That really seems to be the only satisfactory explanation of *deja vu*: i.e., this meeting, situation, or circumstance is very familiar to me. Isn't that right?

A: That is exactly right. And what *"deja vu"* means is "already seen." Not only has it been already seen; it has already been lived through at the mind level, and we are merely experiencing it again. It is that re-living that is the crucial idea here.

Q: Does this approach help to explain why psychics will predict that something is going to happen—for example, that in 1986 California is going to break off from the continent—and then it does not happen? Isn't it accurate to say that on one level this event has occurred and that is what the psychic has tuned into?

A: Yes. It is important to keep this in mind, as we have been saying, that even though all events have already occurred, we do not know which of these events people will choose to re-experience, which video tape they are going to choose. The choices are myriad. In addition, it is helpful to consider why we do not bump into buildings that have yet to be built in the future, while we certainly can walk into structures that were built in the past. A proposed building still in the architect's mind does not exist for us, while the pyramids of ancient Egypt are quite real in our experience. If all has happened simultaneously in one instant, one could well ask why this phenomenon occurs.

The answer lies in recognizing that our brains have been programmed by our minds to think and experience *only* in linear time. And thus because we *believe* it is impossible to hit up against something that is not there yet, we do not do so. We cannot violate what we have already made real for ourselves. But change our belief system and our experience must change accordingly. Of course it is almost impossible for us here, bound by our minds to linearity, to conceive of how life could possibly continue that way. Imagine viewing a movie in which the time sequence was all wrong: what pleasure or understanding could we derive from a movie if the final frames appeared sandwiched between the beginning and the middle; if the movie were upside down in spots, sideways in others? Clearly it would all make no sense to us, the experience being thoroughly discombobulated in our minds and violating all notions of reality. That is what it would be like if figures and events from the past or future suddenly appeared in front of us.

The pupil comes at the right time to the right place. This is inevitable, because he made the right choice in that ancient instant which he now relives. So has the teacher, too, made an inevitable choice out of an ancient past. God's Will in

everything but seems to take time in the working-out. What could delay the power of eternity?

The "right choice" refers to the bottom half of the carpet in chart 2—the Holy Spirit's script, the right-minded view. Thus, in terms of my special relationship with another, the decision to go about it differently is also built into the system: its file is already programmed into the computer, simply waiting to be called up to the screen, as it were.

This right choice but seems to take time because we have made linear time real for ourselves. And so it seems as if we have to play out this whole script—the carpet of time—from beginning to end. The "power of eternity" in this world is manifest through the Holy Spirit's Atonement plan; and, again, this plan has already been accomplished. In the instant the separation seemed to happen, in that same instant it was corrected and undone—"What could delay the power of eternity?"

Q: Could the teacher-student relationship refer to a relationship with anyone whom we choose to see as our teacher, for example the people we are with who are calling out for love or helping us to realize that love is our nature, or does it refer more to the formal teacher-student setting?

A: No, it does not mean just the formal setting of teacher and student. A teacher would be anyone who teaches you that you are forgiven. There may be times when that happens within the formal teacher-pupil context, but the prevailing meaning is that a teacher is anyone who provides you with a classroom of forgiveness. This means in turn that that teacher is also a pupil, because he or she is learning the same lesson from you. For example, since we experience ourselves as separate from God and from each other, this being the cause of all of our guilt and suffering, joining with one perceived as other than ourselves—teacher *and* pupil—heals this ego thought.

Let us move to the workbook and look at portions of four lessons. We will start with Lesson 7, "I see only the past," the second paragraph:

Old ideas about time are very difficult to change, because everything you believe is rooted in time; and depends on your not learning these new ideas about it.

This lesson, as well as other early lessons, do not directly talk about the ideas that we have been discussing just now, but they do bear on them. The workbook begins on a practical and seemingly unsophisticated level, and deals with our everyday experience, a primary element of which is that we interpret everything in terms of the past. This means that we see everything in terms of a linear view of time. Because we are so rooted in this linearity, our brains having been so programmed, it is very difficult to accept the different view of time we have been discussing. The lesson then states, "Yet that is precisely why you need new ideas about time." The process through which the workbook teaches us these "new ideas" is different from that of the textbook. The workbook gives us very specific exercises to do; it directs us to consider ordinary things, a cup for example, and recognize that what we know about it is based entirely on past learning. As we practice these exercises, our minds become more open to viewing time differently.

The logical extension of these early ideas can be seen in the important passages we are about to consider. The first one is in Lesson 158, paragraph two (workbook, p. 291; W-pI.158.2:8):

The revelation that the Father and the Son are one will come in time to every mind.

This statement reflects a linear view. And we will see later that there are many passages in *A Course in Miracles* that speak of our experiences *as if* they were occurring in a linear framework. These passages could be misunderstood because of this, but such misunderstandings can be avoided by keeping in mind that since we believe we are in time, and we believe time is linear, then the language has to be in accord with these beliefs. But the Course will sometimes suddenly shift its focus to the other view as it does in the next two lines:

Yet is that time determined by the mind itself, not taught. The time is set already.

Here we find the same idea: what is already set is the time (meaning the video tape) we choose to accept the Atonement for ourselves, expressed here as the recognition that the Father and the Son are one. That fragment is already built into the script, in terms of the carpet in chart 2, the different pieces of the kaleidoscope in chart 3, or the correction hologram in chart 4. The undoing has already occurred. And that part of the script was already determined by the mind, or, better, by the decision maker in the mind. This acceptance of the Atonement therefore is not determined by something that we are going through now in the world of time and space, since our "presence" in the world of time and space is merely the effect of the mind's decision: we are not really here at all.

It appears to be quite arbitrary. Yet there is no step along the road that anyone takes but by chance. It has already been taken by him, although he has not yet embarked on it.

This is the kind of thinking in the Course that many of its students find to be the most difficult to comprehend. The Atonement road has already been taken; we have already walked through this journey. Our experience, though, is that we have not yet started on it, and *A Course in Miracles* teaches that it is as if we will make the journey for the first time. Yet, this journey is already completed. One of my favorite lines from this material that bears on our having not yet embarked on our journey comes from the Course's companion pamphlet, "Psychotherapy: Purpose, Process and Practice." I usually read this to the therapists attending my workshops on psychotherapy and *A Course in Miracles* as a way of encouraging humility: "Most professional therapists are still at the *very start* of the *beginning* stage of the *first* journey" ("Psychotherapy,"[5] p. 20; P-3.II.8:5, my italics).

The above statement that nothing is arbitrary clearly means that nothing in our lives is accidental. It *seems* as if I have a choice whether to lift my right arm or my left, but I have already done both. The reason is, as we mentioned earlier, that if all thinking produces form on some level, then simply having the thought of lifting either arm has already produced a behavioral response (a video tape) somewhere in the hologram of my mind. I do have a choice, however, as to whether I re-experience the lifting of my right arm or my left.

For time but seems to go in one direction. We but undertake a journey that is over. Yet it seems to have a future still unknown to us.

We certainly do experience ourselves as being on a linear journey through time, and there are many, many passages in the Course that talk about the *process* of our learning. There are six stages mentioned in the manual in discussing the development of trust (manual, pp. 8-10; M-4.I.3-8), e.g., and in one of the sections in the text on special and holy relationships Jesus says that the only difficult time is at the beginning (text, p. 337; T-17.V.2:5), and then things get better, clearly implying a process occurring over time. Elsewhere we are told that we are on a "journey without distance" (text, p. 139; T-8.VI.9:7). And here in the workbook Jesus tells us that the journey is already over, we have already accepted the Atonement, and all illusions have been undone. The final line takes us back to the linear view of time, acknowledging our experience that we do not know the future, which seems not to have happened yet.

---

5. Foundation for Inner Peace, Glen Ellen, CA, 1976.

We come now to a very important line that explains how time seems to happen:

Time is a trick, a sleight of hand, a vast illusion in which figures come and go as if by magic.

This is a crucial statement in terms of why we have such trouble with these concepts, why the old ideas of time are so deeply rooted in us. It is all a trick; a magic show. Magicians by definition are people who produce illusions, who make it appear as if they are actually sawing a boxed woman in half, or pulling a rabbit out of a hat. But, as we know, it is all a trick done by sleight of hand: "The hand is quicker than the eye." This is the analogy here. The ego's magic is so skillful that we are convinced, just as we are in the presence of an expert magician, that what we have perceived is really here and has occurred. In truth, however, the woman is whole, the rabbit was not pulled out of a hat, and we are not really here in a body and in the world.

Yet there is a plan behind appearances that does not change. The script is written. When experience will come to end your doubting has been set.

Both scripts are written: the wrong-minded script of the ego and the right-minded script of the Holy Spirit. These scripts do not change. All events and experiences are already built into the system, which in a sense is closed. The images of the hologram, video tape libraries, and kaleidoscope reflect this closed system. There is therefore nothing we can see there that is new, no choice we can make that has not already been made. And this of course includes the time when we will accept the revelation that the Father and Son are one.

It seems within our experiences that we could choose. It appears as if we could choose to forgive or condemn each other, and that *we* are in control of this choice. *A Course in Miracles* teaches us, however, that this is not the case at all. The moment of decision and of choice is really something quite different. Let us go back to the image of ourselves as observers: we sit here (in our minds) in front of the screen, and our only choice is which buttons we will push. That is our *only* choice. And the buttons we push show us what has already happened, what part of the script we choose to re-experience. It is no different from being in the mood for a sad movie, and then deciding to play that video tape on the VCR. We thus cry for two hours because that was the decision already made *before* viewing the movie. Likewise, being in the mood for a good laugh, we select a comedy. All that we believe we are experiencing here in the world but reflects a decision made from that point outside time when the decision maker in our minds made the choice we have forgotten, believing it is being made here and now, where we believe we are.

For we but see the journey from the point at which it ended, looking back on it, imagining we make it once again; reviewing mentally what has gone by.

Our experience to the contrary, all that we are doing is reviewing mentally what has already happened. And we are looking at the journey from the point at which it ended. We are already outside it; it is already finished. Yet, for the insane reason of guilt we all share, we are still choosing to punish ourselves by reviewing mentally the nightmare illusions of the ego. And thus we continue to see a movie that makes us upset and brings us pain. We do this because of our identification with the ego thought system that teaches us that we have indeed established for ourselves a will and self that is separate from God. And once believing we have accomplished the impossible, we must believe that God has become the enemy who demands our punishment through pain and death. Thus it is the ego voice that demands that we continue to re-experience pain, which serves the purpose of making our guilt and sin real (since it is they that demand our punishment). And this in turn ensures the survival of the ego. As *A Course in Miracles* explains:

> Hallucinations disappear when they are recognized for what they are....[they] serve a purpose, and when that purpose is no longer held they disappear (text, p. 413; T-20.VIII.8:1,6).

And:

> Healing is accomplished the instant the sufferer no longer sees any value in pain. Who would choose suffering unless he thought it brought him something, and something of value to him?...Sickness is a method, conceived in madness, for placing God's Son on his Father's throne (manual, p. 16; M-5.I.1:1-2,7).

Q: Would you mind going over this once again using a concrete example? It is still not entirely clear to me. Here I am in Crompond, New York, in 1985, sitting at this table. Are you saying that I as the observer have to make the choice right now, whether to focus on forgiving or condemning acts, both of which I have already done with respect to the same situation?

A: It seems as if the "you" who are making the choice is the "you" who are sitting here at this table, right now. But this is not the case. To quote the question from the text: "Who is the 'you' who are living in this world?" (text, p. 54; T-4.II.11:8). The "you" who are the observer is outside of time and space, and therefore is outside of Crompond, New York, 1985. In other words, the "you" who are the observer in the mind is not identical with the "you" who are sitting here at this table. This is a crucial distinction. The "you" sitting here could also be thought of as a puppet who is re-experiencing what has been chosen by the puppeteer, the observer-you (again, in the mind). It does not seem to us to be occurring this way, though. Rather, it seems that the "you" at this table are the real "you" who are making the decisions. We experience it in that way because we believe we actually are in this world as a physical and psychological self. *A Course in Miracles* appeals to us on

42

this level precisely because we think that is our real self. When this distinction is clearly seen, we can understand more fully why the Course describes time as "a trick" and "a sleight of hand." It truly is a magic show.

To state it another way, the observer in the mind is the *cause*, while the "you" in the world are the *effect*. Even though cause and effect are in truth simultaneous and therefore remain together, they are nonetheless not the same, just as God as Cause is not identical with Christ, the Effect, though they are one. This is similar to understanding that the figures perceived on a movie screen are the *effect* of the film running through the projector, which is their *cause*. We shall return to a consideration of cause and effect in Chapter 4.

Let us move on now to Lesson 167, the ninth paragraph (workbook, p. 312; W-pI.167.9).

What seems to be the opposite of life is merely sleeping. When the mind elects to be what it is not, and to assume an alien power which it does not have, a foreign state it cannot enter, or a false condition not within its Source, it merely seems to go to sleep a while.

This is a clear statement that the ego and its world is a dream, and that we have merely fallen asleep. In the dream we believed that we had the power to oppose and defeat God, usurping His authority, making up a body we call our self to inhabit a material world of duality and fragmentation. And yet all this is nothing but a dream. This is elucidated further in the text in an important passage that describes what seemed to occur in the separation:

First, you believe that what God created can be changed by your own mind.

Second, you believe that what is perfect can be rendered imperfect or lacking.

Third, you believe that you can distort the creations of God, including yourself.

Fourth, you believe that you can create yourself, and that the direction of your own creation is up to you.

These related distortions represent a picture of what actually occurred in the separation, or the "detour into fear" (text, p. 14; T-2.I.2:1).

Further on in the text, a powerful passage also describes the insane content of the ego dream that could never happen in reality.

> This is the anti-Christ; the strange idea there is a power past omnipotence, a place beyond the infinite, a time transcending the eternal. Here the world of idols has been set by the idea this power and place and time are given form, and shape the world where the impossible has happened. Here the deathless come to die, the all-encompassing to suffer loss, the timeless to be made the slaves of time. Here does the changeless change; the peace of God, forever given to all living things, give way to chaos. And the Son of God, as perfect, sinless and as loving as his Father, come to hate a little while; to suffer pain and finally to die (text, p. 576; T-29.VIII.6:2-6).

Back now to Lesson 167, paragraph nine, in the workbook:

It [the mind] dreams of time; an interval in which what seems to happen never has occurred, the changes wrought are substanceless, and all events are nowhere. When the mind awakes, it but continues as it always was.

These ideas are shown in chart 5, where, as you recall, the straight line labeled "eternity" represents Heaven, where we really are, and the little dip labeled "time" represents the dream. When we awaken, that dream disappears and we are still on the line which we never left. As the Course says elsewhere: "You are at home in God, dreaming of exile..." (text, p. 169; T-10.I.2:1).

Helen Schucman, scribe of the Course, once had an experience that reflected this teaching. One morning while brushing her hair she saw herself on this single line of eternity. In this unbroken line there was a tiny, tiny dip, which in the text is referred to as a "tiny tick of time" (text, p. 511; T-26.V.3:5). Joel Goldsmith entitled one of his books *A Parenthesis in Eternity*, a wonderful phrase which depicts the seeming expanse of time in much the same way. The dip is a tiny little nothing. When compared with the vastness and infinity of eternity, it seems laughable to conceive that it has any significance. To quote this important passage again:

> Together, we [Jesus and ourselves] can laugh them both [the accomplishment and real effects of the tiny, mad idea] away, and understand that time cannot intrude upon eternity (text, p. 544; T-27.VIII.6:4).

Earlier, the text employs the images of the smallest sunbeam believing it is the sun, or the faintest, almost imperceptible ripple hailing itself as the ocean (text, p. 364; T-18.VIII.3:3-4). Within this "tiny, mad idea" the world seemed to occur, which in reality is nothing more than the dream of a sleeping mind which will one day awaken to the eternity that has continued as it always is.

Let us move now to Lesson 169, which contains another very clear statement of *A Course in Miracles'* view of time. We begin with paragraph four, which refers back to what was said in Lesson 158 about the time being already set when we shall accept the revelation that the Father and Son are one.

We have perhaps appeared to contradict our statement that the revelation of the Father and the Son as one has been already set. But we have also said the mind determines when that time will be, and has determined it. And yet we urge you to bear witness to the Word of God to hasten the experience of truth, and speed its advent into every mind that recognizes truth's effects on you.

The different levels which we discussed earlier are evident in these passages. The Level One idea expressed here is that the Atonement has already been accepted. Level Two statements reflect our beliefs that we actually are here, and therefore what is really being appealed to is the part of our minds that can choose to press buttons (the video or computer analogy), that is, choose to seek forgiveness instead of condemnation. That is the basis of Jesus urging us "to bear witness to the Word of God" and press the right button and awaken from the dream, even though on the other level it has already happened. That is the kind of paradox that we find here. Thus, on the one level, our experience is that we have yet to choose this time. On the other, we have *already* chosen it and there is "no new thing under the sun": the time has already happened.

Oneness is simply the idea God is. And in His Being, He encompasses all things. No mind holds anything but Him.

Of course, we think we hold all kinds of other things. This is the belief conveyed in the kaleidoscope image in chart 3. In reality the kaleidoscope (the split mind) is nothing because it is outside God, and so too are all of its contents, representing *all* of our experiences as individualized selves. They are all equally unreal and thus not truly there.

We say "God is," and then we cease to speak, for in that knowledge words are meaningless. There are no lips to speak them, and no part of mind sufficiently distinct to feel that it is now aware of something not itself. It has united with its Source. And like its Source Itself, it merely is.

We cannot speak nor write nor even think of this at all. It comes to every mind when total recognition that its will is God's has been completely given and received completely.

Oneness is the state that is beyond everything of this world. In fact, the body was specifically made to keep the awareness of this simple truth hidden from us. That is why Jesus says that it cannot be spoken of nor understood by us at all, who still believe we are in our bodies. This is also why there are relatively few passages in *A Course in Miracles* that speak of this state of oneness, for how can you speak of what is beyond all words? Besides, the manual says, in the context of a discussion of the role of words in healing:

God does not understand words, for they were made by separated minds to keep them in the illusion of separation (manual, p. 51; M-21.1:7).

Without seeing that there are different levels on which *A Course in Miracles* expresses itself, the implication of the final sentence in the above passage from the workbook—the recognition will occur some time in the future—can be confusing and even seem to contradict other passages which speak of the unreality of time. The Course itself, we must remember, comes within a world of illusion; and since we believe we live in a world of linear time, the Course addresses itself to us within that context. Similarly, *A Course in Miracles* comes in a Christian context because it is attempting to correct the errors of Christianity which have had such a major effect on Western history. Thus, it is really working within the forms that we believe we are in. This important point will be discussed again in passages we shall consider in Chapter 3.

It [total recognition of our oneness] returns the mind into the endless present, where the past and future cannot be conceived. It lies beyond salvation; past all thought of time, forgiveness and the holy face of Christ. The Son of God has merely disappeared into His Father, as His Father has in him. The world has never been at all. Eternity remains a constant state.

This is the moment of the total acceptance of the Atonement, meaning that the self and will are no longer experienced as separate from our Creator and Source. In that revelation, which transcends all of time, we find ourselves in eternity where individuality and personality have disappeared. This experience is the moment when we totally awaken from the dream of time and are back in eternity. All that we believed was real is now gone, and we are back in the home we never left.

This is beyond experience we try to hasten.

The idea of *A Course in Miracles* is to save or collapse time, or to hasten us to that moment that is "beyond experience"; yet what we are hastening *to* is beyond anything we could understand. The experience the Course does try to have us reach is that of living in the happy dream. This will eventually lead us beyond the world entirely, and that cannot be explained with words. Lesson 107 states it this way:

> Can you imagine what a state of mind without illusions is? How it would feel? Try to remember when there was a time,—perhaps a minute, maybe even less—when nothing came to interrupt your peace; when you were certain you were loved and safe. Then try to picture what it would be like to have that moment be extended to the end of time and to eternity. Then let the sense of quiet that you felt be multiplied a hundred times, and then be multiplied another hundred more.
>
> And now you have a hint, not more than just the faintest intimation of the state your mind will rest in when the truth has come (workbook, p. 189; W-pI.107.2:1-3:1).

And then we read this beautiful passage which closes Lesson 157:

> Into Christ's Presence will we enter now, serenely unaware of everything except His shining face and perfect Love. The vision of His face will stay with you, but there will be an instant which transcends all vision, even this, the holiest. This you will never teach, for you attained it not through learning. Yet the vision speaks of your rememberance [sic] of what you knew that instant, and will surely know again (workbook, p. 290; W-pI.157.9).

Yet forgiveness, taught and learned, brings with it the experiences which bear witness that the time the mind itself determined to abandon all but this is now at hand.

The two levels we have been speaking about are present here again, in one sentence. The video tapes in which the mind has determined to abandon the world of time and the ego (Level One) are already present, and yet the experience is still something that we have to choose through our learning of forgiveness (Level Two).

Q: In terms of the VCR analogy, are you saying that when we, from the perspective of the observer, begin to choose to forgive, to focus on that particular video tape, we eventually focus on that exact time and space framework where we already have decided to open up to the revelation that the Father and the Son are one? And that choice is completely outside of time, which is why we can seemingly dawdle forever? We can keep looking at these other videos, and keep looking at ourselves doing everything else except to be enlightened in 1985 in Crompond, New York?

A: That is right. The ego has taught us that "that exact time and space framework"—the acceptance of the Atonement—means certain death. It does, of course, but this "death" is simply the disappearance of the ego, back into "the nothingness from which it came" (manual, p. 32; M-13.1:2). But as long as we continue to identify with the ego, we shall fear the Love of God which does dispel the ego's darkness of fear. And this then becomes the attraction of the ego's video tapes of fear. This is analogous to the attraction of guilt, pain, and death that is described in the discussion of the obstacles to peace in Chapter 19 in the text.

We do not hasten it, in that what you will offer was concealed from Him Who teaches what forgiveness means.

All learning was already in His Mind, accomplished and complete.

When you speak of hastening something you are implying that you do not have it now, and so it has to be attained in the future. Despite the fact that part of us is trying to delay the gift that the Holy Spirit is giving us—and what we "offer" to Him would be our willingness to accept His gift—none of this makes any difference because it has already happened. This is explained in the following paragraph in this lesson.

Before we go on to that paragraph, however, I want to make a few more comments about these lines. First, they are a bit tricky because they are in verse, and so a couple of words have been left out which would have made the meaning clearer. It also is difficult to understand because the paragraphing was done incorrectly. When Helen originally took this down she had not broken off the paragraph as it is here. Later, for some reason, probably having to do with some stylistic concern, she did. When we went over this lesson in our editing we kept it that way; but it would make more sense if the next sentence— "All learning was already in His Mind"—were actually a continuation of that preceding paragraph. With words added or changed, therefore, the passage could be read like this:

> We do not hasten it [which means the time in which we will accept what forgiveness is and recognize that we are one with God], as if it were necessary that we do so, as if what you will offer *were* concealed from Him Who teaches what forgiveness means.

In other words, this really is a subjunctive statement, which is why I changed "was concealed" to "were concealed"; it is what grammarians call a "contrary to fact" situation. We do not hasten that time as if what we will offer were concealed (what we will offer to the Holy Spirit is the acceptance of forgiveness).

And finally, the Atonement does not have to be accomplished because it was already done. All the wrong-minded mistakes as well as all the right-minded corrections have already occurred. Thus, our learning is accomplished in the Holy Spirit's Mind, which is now in our mind. Not only is the ego's script written, but the Holy Spirit's Atonement script is written as well.

He [the Holy Spirit] recognized all that time holds, and gave it to all minds that each one might determine, from a point where time was ended, when it is released to revelation and eternity. We have repeated several times before that you but make a journey that is done.

That "point where time was ended" is where the observer is in chart 3. Putting these passages together we can see the important emphasis placed in *A Course in Miracles* on the journey being already over. The journey is given to us from the point of view of the observer sitting in front of a screen, where we will choose to tune into that part of the script. This then is the point when we have already accepted the ending.

For oneness must be here.

In other words, oneness is not in the past nor in the future. It need not be hastened because oneness is a constant state of being. It is not in the future, but here, *now.* The error that oneness does not exist has already been corrected. This is difficult to comprehend because it "is beyond experience we try to hasten" (two paragraphs above in this lesson). So on one level *A Course in Miracles* is trying to save us time, and on the other level it tells us that time is an illusion. Therefore nothing has to be saved, because nothing was ever lost. Oneness is always here; oneness *is.* One of Helen's poems expresses this idea very nicely. It is called "Heaven's Gift." Let me read it now:

> No one can rob infinity. For when
> Something is taken, angels join their wings
> And close the space so rapidly it seems
> To be illusion; unoccurred, undone.

No one can take away from everything.
Its very wholeness is a guarantee
It is complete forever. There can be
No loss left unrestored before it comes.

No one can lessen love. It is itself
The Great Restorer. It can but return
All that is taken to itself. It knows
No loss, no limit and no lessening.

Heaven can only give. This is the sign
That losing is impossible. It seemed
That it was gone. Yet angels quickly came
And promised they would bring it back to you.
                    (*The Gifts of God*, p. 80)

Whatever time the mind has set for revelation is entirely irrelevant to what must be a constant state, forever as it always was; forever to remain as it is now. We merely take the part assigned long since, and fully recognized as perfectly fulfilled by Him Who wrote salvation's script in His Creator's Name, and in the Name of His Creator's Son.

Referring to chart 5, within the tiny tick of time we have already chosen when that revelation will occur, which is the acceptance of the Atonement. But all of that is still irrelevant with respect to the solid line which represents eternity, "a constant state." The part that has been "assigned" to us is the undoing of the ego script. That is the path of the Atonement, and it has already been "perfectly fulfilled" because that is the Holy Spirit's function, and what He wills is already done.

Now comes that wonderfully infuriating passage:

There is no need to further clarify what no one in the world can understand. When revelation of your oneness comes, it will be known and fully understood. Now we have work to do, for those in time can speak of things beyond [which is what we are trying to do in this book], and listen to words which explain what is to come is past already

[what we have been discussing]. Yet what meaning can the words convey to those who count the hours still, and rise and work and go to sleep by them?

Jesus is telling us that we are so rooted in the belief of the linearity of time that it is impossible for us to conceive of a state that is beyond that experience. That is why we all find these passages so frustrating and difficult to understand. Yet they are clearly not here to confound or tease us. Despite our inability to comprehend the state of timelessness, we *can* comprehend that our experience of time is illusory, and that we cling to it as a means of keeping the Holy Spirit's Love—the reflection of eternity—away from us. Similarly, the Course explains that while the ego does not understand God, it does understand that there is a power greater than itself (text, p. 53; T-4.II.8:8). Breaking down our investment in the truth of our belief system is one of the major goals of the Course: "To learn this course requires willingness to question every value that you hold" (text, p. 464; T-24.in.2:1). And so these mind-boggling passages on time help serve that purpose.

Lesson 169 continues to say—even though we are not going to review it here—that we do have to do our part, which is to forgive. Forgiveness has nothing to do with eternity, but rather is rooted in the world of time and space, being the means through which we begin to change our minds and eventually recognize that we are the dreamer of the dream. Those sections in the text that deal with the dreamer and the dream, and cause and effect (text, pp. 539-46, 550-53; T-27.VII-VIII; T-28.II), refer back to these metaphysical principles that we are not in the body at all, but are rather *observing* this dream, "reviewing mentally what has already gone by" (workbook, p. 291; W-pI.158.4:5). Forgiveness, practiced in the present moment, enables us to begin to accept and experience that truth. The guilt we have made real in our minds makes time real—past, present, and future—and that illusion is ultimately what interferes with our acceptance of time as holographic and not linear.

Q: There seems to be a contradiction of terms in this lesson because at the very beginning grace is made synonymous with revelation. Grace is something that is beyond all learning; it would seem to be that moment when we choose to recognize that the Father and the Son are one. Then at the end of the lesson grace is spoken of as a step before that. It says that "we ask for grace, and for experience that comes from grace. We welcome the release it offers everyone. We do not ask for the unaskable." Then it talks about it as though it is a step beyond grace.

A: At the beginning of the lesson, grace is not really equated with revelation, or at least not with Heaven. In a sense, grace is treated as the final aspect of the real world, where Jesus is. It is not quite eternity. The lesson begins with the lines:

> Grace is an aspect of the Love of God which is most like the state prevailing in the unity of truth. It is the world's most lofty aspiration, for it leads beyond the world entirely (workbook, p. 315; W-pI.169.1:1-2).

Grace is thus like a borderland between this world and Heaven. It is right at the finish line, so to speak, beyond this world of illusion and guilt, sin and attack, but it is not the unity of Heaven. In that sense, then, we would say that someone like Jesus is in a state of grace.

Q: It seems as if that would be the goal to which the Course aspires; yet it says grace is not the goal.

A: The goal of the Course is forgiveness and peace in this world. Grace really is not discussed very much, since it refers to the ultimate end of the real world, the inevitable result of the peace that precedes it. Thus when we learn to forgive truly, grace comes automatically, as it were, having always been there. When every last remaining Son attains the state of grace, then we enter into the Second Coming, the Last Judgment, and God's last step. It does not really happen like this, of course, for as we shall see in Part III, these so-called stages are but metaphorical ways of describing a non-linear process.

We turn now to two sections from the text, "The Little Hindrance" (text, p. 511; T-26.V), and "The Present Memory" (text, p. 547; T-28.I). These are the only two sections in the text which are devoted in their entirety to a discussion of time. The study of these two sections will complete Part I.

Chapter 3

COMMENTARY ON "THE LITTLE HINDRANCE"

In this first part of the book, which deals with the origin and nature of time, we are concerned mostly with passages which present *A Course in Miracles'* basic metaphysics of time. The two sections we are about to study do that as well, but they also serve as a bridge into Part II, which will deal more with the Course's view of time in relation to the plan of the Atonement, and its direct relevance to the central teaching on the miracle's collapse of time through forgiveness.

As we continue this discussion of time's metaphysics, it is important to keep in mind our previous statement that *A Course in Miracles* is written on two different levels (see chart 1). To state it briefly again, Level One reflects the basic metaphysics of the Course and is essentially what we have discussed so far. The Level One treatment of time incorporates the ideas that everything has already happened, having all occurred in a split second, and that we really are not experiencing anything for the first time. We are, in effect, sitting in front of a TV screen, kaleidoscope, or a computer, and merely by choice "reviewing mentally what has gone by." This is intelligible only when time is regarded as non-linear, as the experience of past, present, future is merely part of the ego's trickery.

The point I want to emphasize now, however, is that *A Course in Miracles* frequently speaks about time as if it were linear. For example, Lesson 194 is entitled, "I place the future in the Hands of God." This clearly views time in a linear context. However, the fourth paragraph in this lesson begins with what we would call a Level One statement. It indicates that time is not sequential, that past and present are the same:

> God holds your future as He holds your past and present.
> They are one to Him, and so they should be one to you (work-
> book, p. 360; W-pI.194.4:1-2).

But then there is a shift to Level Two:

> Yet in this world, the temporal progression still seems real.
> And so you are not asked to understand the lack of sequence
> really found in time. You are but asked to let the future go,
> and place it in God's Hands (workbook, p. 360;
> W-pI.194.4:3-5).

Thus, Jesus is saying that even though time is an illusion and
there is no past, present, and future, he will talk about time *as
if* it were linear, because that is what we believe. An even more
explicit statement of this is found in the text, coming in the
context of a discussion of the oneness of Christ that is within
our split minds as the Holy Spirit. This oneness teaches us the
truth, even though we believe we are in a place where we are
not.

> All this takes note of time and place as if they were dis-
> crete, for while you think that part of you is separate, the
> concept of a oneness joined as one is meaningless....[And so
> must this Oneness] use the language that this mind can under-
> stand, in the condition in which it thinks it is. And It must use
> all learning to transfer illusions to the truth, taking all false
> ideas of what you are, and leading you beyond them to the
> truth that *is* beyond them (text, p. 484; T-25.I.7:1,4-5).

In a reference I unfortunately cannot locate, the Indian holy
man Sai Baba mentioned how the masterpiece of Eastern spir-
ituality, the *Bhagavad Gita*, is written on different levels. He
explained this in terms of the *Gita*'s ability to appeal to many,
many people who are at different stages of their own spiritual
development. The same is true of *A Course in Miracles*: as we
remove our guilt through forgiveness, we shall understand the
Course on deeper and deeper levels. One of the levels of understanding which will deepen will involve time. Many
phrases are strewn through the material which would catapult

us into an entirely different dimension of understanding if we really paid attention to them. Yet the major thrust of the Course is *not* that understanding, but rather to help us with the very practical problems we believe we have, all of which involve our experience of time's linearity. As *A Course in Miracles* says of itself:

> This is not a course in philosophical speculation, nor is it concerned with precise terminology. It is concerned only with Atonement, or the correction of perception (manual, p. 73; C-in.1:1-2).

Finally, the Course says elsewhere of the ego's use of time that it takes the guilt of the past, projects it into the fear of the future, and thus overlooks the present entirely (text, p. 229; T-13.IV.4:2-5).

Therefore, since this is how we live, being what we believe, *A Course in Miracles'* manner of speaking will match that level of understanding (Level Two). Every once in a while, however, Jesus does slip back into this other realm (Level One), stating that the world of time has already happened, and that time is unreal. We can see in this the Course's integration of its very practical approach to where we believe we are, with the larger metaphysical framework which views the world entirely differently.

We now turn to the beginning of "The Little Hindrance" in Chapter 26 in the text (p. 511; T-26.V), after which we turn to "The Present Memory." Both sections will be studied in their entirety.

A little hindrance can seem large indeed to those who do not understand that miracles are all the same. Yet teaching that is what this course is for. This is its only purpose, for only that is all there is to learn. And you can learn it many different ways.

The "little hindrance" was referred to in the text's preceding section, "Where Sin Has Left," which spoke of it as the "tiny spot of sin" that still keeps us from Heaven (text, p. 510; T-26.IV.6:1). The little hindrance seems large indeed as long as we believe the sin of separation is real, for our guilt has us believe that we actually destroyed the Love of God and fragmented the unity of Heaven. Thus is the world of separation made real, along with the seemingly infinite range of problems to be solved. Hence, the first principle of miracles—there is no order of difficulty among them—seems impossible and beyond our attainment. It is the purpose of *A Course in Miracles* to teach us that it is not only possible, but perfectly natural: "Miracles are natural. When they do not occur something has gone wrong" (text, p. 1; T-1.I.6). This statement reflects the very practical thrust of the Course. It is not teaching us simply the intellectual concept that time is an illusion; it is teaching us to recognize that all of our problems are the same. The ultimate understanding of why that is so rests on the idea that time is an illusion; but the full understanding of that concept is not necessary in order to practice the forgiveness that is the Course's goal.

Therefore, we do not have to comprehend thoroughly the metaphysical view of time. Rather, we learn the necessity of recognizing that all of our problems are but different forms of unforgiveness, and so if we bring these problems to the Holy Spirit, which is what the miracle entails, then the problem of guilt, our *only* problem, will disappear. The form in which we had previously identified our problem may not necessarily disappear, but what *will* disappear is the problem that we have made within ourselves. This principle can be learned in many different ways, for the Holy Spirit uses the different forms that we have made real in our minds to teach us that they are all fundamentally illusory.

All learning is a help or hindrance to the gate of Heaven. Nothing in between is possible. There are two teachers

only, who point in different ways. And you will go along the way your chosen teacher leads. There are but two directions you can take, while time remains and choice is meaningful.

This reflects one of the prevalent themes in *A Course in Miracles*, that everything boils down to one of two basic choices. Using the analogy of our sitting in front of the television set, there are only two buttons we can choose to press: the ego's and the Holy Spirit's. As the text says earlier, which will be reiterated shortly:

> Each day, each hour and minute, even each second, you are deciding between the crucifixion and the resurrection; between the ego and the Holy Spirit. The ego is the choice for guilt; the Holy Spirit the choice for guiltlessness. The power of decision is all that is yours. What you can decide between is fixed, because there are no alternatives except truth and illusion. And there is no overlap between them, because they are opposites which cannot be reconciled and cannot both be true. You are guilty or guiltless, bound or free, unhappy or happy (text, p. 255; T-14.III.4).

For never will another road be made except the way to Heaven. You but choose whether to go toward Heaven, or away to nowhere. There is nothing else to choose.

Near the end of the text, the same theme is presented:

> Real choice is no illusion. But the world has none to offer. All its roads but lead to disappointment, nothingness and death. There is no choice in its alternatives. Seek not escape from problems here. The world was made that problems could not *be* escaped. Be not deceived by all the different names its roads are given. They have but one end. And each is but the means to gain that end, for it is here that all its roads will lead, however differently they seem to start; however differently they seem to go. Their end is certain, for there is no choice among them. All of them will lead to death....No pathway in the world can lead to Him [God], nor any worldly

goal be one with His.... [Yet] There is no road that leads away from Him. A journey from yourself does not exist.... You can not escape from what you are. For God is merciful, and did not let His Son abandon Him.... Nowhere but where He is can you be found. There *is* no path that does not lead to Him (text, pp. 607-10; T-31.IV.2:1-11; 9:3; 10:4-5; 11:3-4,6-7).

This choice between Heaven and the world is an illusion as well, because, of the two choices, only one is true. And so there is really no choice at all. But within our experience in this world it does appear as if we have two choices. We choose whether we will be angry or forgiving, whether we will separate from others or join with them. The passage continues:

All choices in the world depend on this; you choose between your brother and yourself, and you will gain as much as he will lose, and what you lose is what is given him. How utterly opposed to truth is this, when all the lesson's purpose is to teach that what your brother loses *you* have lost, and what he gains is what is given *you* (text, p. 609; T-31.IV.8:4-5).

Nothing is ever lost but time, which in the end is meaningless.

Thus, our egos to the contrary, we cannot lose Heaven. We cannot lose the innocence with which God created us. This is the central teaching of the Course's metaphysics, and is the principle of the Atonement. In the Course's companion pamphlet, "Psychotherapy: Purpose, Process and Practice," Jesus states: "And who could weep but for his innocence?" ("Psychotherapy," p. 8; P-2.IV.1:7), meaning that all of our sorrow stems from the belief that we have thrown away the innocence of Christ, our true Identity, and which now, we are told by the ego, we shall never regain. The Holy Spirit, on the other hand, reminds us that although we can block this innocence from our awareness, by choosing to remain asleep and dream of time, this has no effect upon the reality that we are awake in God. All that we seem to lose is time, the time in which we choose to remain asleep and dream the ego's nightmare illusions. All the while, however, we remain safely within our Father's house, awake in Love. The time at which we choose to awaken from this dream is our choice, but we have no choice as to where we truly are.

For it [time] is but a little hindrance to eternity, quite meaningless to the real Teacher of the world. Yet since you do believe in it, why should you waste it going nowhere, when it can be used to reach a goal as high as learning can achieve? Think not the way to Heaven's gate is difficult at all. Nothing you undertake with certain purpose and high resolve and happy confidence, holding your brother's hand and keeping step to Heaven's song, is difficult to do. But it is hard indeed to wander off, alone and miserable, down a road that leads to nothing and that has no purpose.

Since we do believe in time, the Holy Spirit will help us use it as a way of ultimately learning that there is no time. There is an oft-quoted saying, "It is much more difficult to frown than to smile," meaning that we have to use many more muscles in frowning. *A Course in Miracles* thus teaches us that it is much more difficult to go against the Holy Spirit and choose the ego, than it is to follow the Holy Spirit. Our experience, however, is quite the opposite. It would seem to us that holding on to our anger is easy, and in fact is what we really want, and that the most difficult thing would be to let it go. This is just another example of how the ego turns everything upside down.

God gave His Teacher [the Holy Spirit] to replace the one you made, not to conflict with it.

Some people's conscious experience is that the Holy Spirit is threatening them in some way. Unconsciously, anyone who identifies with the ego's thought system, and this would include most everyone who walks this earth, *must* feel this conflict the outcome of which can only be the destruction of the sinning self: "Its ending is inevitable, for its outcome must be death" (manual, p. 43; M-17.6:2). A classic Christian poem, "The Hound of Heaven" by Francis Thompson, expresses this notion that Jesus is out to get us, hounding us until we return to him. In reality, of course, he does nothing except gently call to us to return to the home we never truly left.

And what He would replace has been replaced. Time lasted but an instant in your mind, with no effect upon eternity.

And back we are into the metaphysical framework. "What He would replace"—the ego's guilt and fear replaced by the Love of God—has already happened; i.e., the ego's hologram of hate has been replaced by the Holy Spirit's hologram of correction. Chart 5 illustrates this in terms of that tiny dip in the line of eternity. That was how Helen had seen time, recognizing that time lasted no longer than the infinitesimal instant that never really happened in the first place.

And so is all time past, and everything exactly as it was before the way to nothingness was made.

"Everything exactly as it was" refers to the state of unity in Heaven, and the "way to nothingness" represents the world, which despite its sound and fury still symbolizes nothing. Moreover, the world, and the ego thought system that spawned it, had no power to change the perfection of Heaven. A bad dream, in the end, remains what it always was: a bad dream.

The tiny tick of time in which the first mistake was made, and all of them within that one mistake, held also the Correction for that one, and all of them that came within the first. And in that tiny instant time was gone, for that was all it ever was. What God gave answer to is answered and is gone.

It is not only the initial mistake of our having believed we could separate from God that occurred in that single instant, but everything that followed from that mistake as well. The projection of error outward that made the world, and all the subsequent fragmenting that came from that projection, occurred—over and over again—within that tiny tick of time. However, that "tiny tick of time" also held the Correction for that one mistake, and thus all the expressions of forgiveness that came within that first instant. This is represented in chart 2: the ego script and the Holy Spirit's correction; the projections of our guilt as well as their undoing through forgiveness. And in chart 3, the kaleidoscope, the little tick marks in the time and memory circles all refer to the ego mistakes as well as their correction. Everything occurred within that one instant.

The problem remains that as we sit in front of the screen, reviewing mentally what is in our minds, we believe and experience that things have happened, things are actually happening now, and things will continue to happen in the future. We have all fallen into the ego's trap by buying into its magic trick of time.

To you who still believe you live in time and know not it is gone, the Holy Spirit still guides you through the infinitely small and senseless maze you still perceive in time, though it has long since gone.

The Holy Spirit will lead us through not only what we believe has happened, but what we believe is happening now. This is the whole thrust of *A Course in Miracles*. Even though time is an illusion and the world has never happened, the Holy Spirit's loving presence in our separated minds guides us as if we were hearing Him for the first time, as if we were experiencing forgiveness for the first time, as if we were really here. In other words, He joins the illusions of our minds so He can teach us what reality is. Thus again we can see that even though time is illusory, Jesus speaks to us as if it were real. I call attention to this point again, to caution against taking as literally true many of the statements in the Course, when they are actually meant metaphorically.

You think you live in what is past. Each thing you look upon you saw but for an instant, long ago, before its unreality gave way to truth.

We experience living in this body and temporal world because we *believe* we are truly here. It is our thought that gives reality to the illusion. The second sentence echoes the idea we discussed earlier from the teacher's manual and workbook: It seems as if we are looking at things and experiencing them for the first time, but in reality we are simply, again, "reviewing mentally what has already gone by." Recall that it is not *we*, our physical and psychological selves, that are perceiving and experiencing the world. As *A Course in Miracles* tells us, our eyes are sightless and our ears do not hear: perception is a lie. It is the split mind that exists outside time that projects its dualistic thoughts of separation onto the body, which following orders, sees and hears accordingly. We read in the text:

> Let not your eyes behold a dream; your ears bear witness to illusion. They were made to look upon a world that is not there; to hear the voices that can make no sound....For eyes and ears are senses without sense, and what they see and hear they but report. It is not they that hear and see, but you, who put together every jagged piece, each senseless scrap and shred of evidence, and make a witness to the world you want....It is indeed a senseless point of view to hold responsible for sight a thing that cannot see, and blame it for the sounds you do not like, although it cannot hear (text, pp. 558-60; T-28.V.5:3-4,6-7; T-28.VI.2:1).

Not one illusion still remains unanswered in your mind. Uncertainty was brought to certainty so long ago that it is hard indeed to hold it to your heart, as if it were before you still.

Although this is not our experience, it *is* hard work indeed to keep "real" the illusory nature of time, because in reality it has already been corrected. And it is this ongoing strain of attempting to deny reality and make the unreal real that is the true source of the strain and fatigue that is our experience of living in this body.

The tiny instant you would keep and make eternal, passed away in Heaven too soon for anything to notice it had come. What disappeared too quickly to affect the simple knowledge of the Son of God can hardly still be there, for you to choose to be your teacher. Only in the past,—an ancient past, too short to make a world in answer to creation,—did this world appear to rise. So very long ago, for such a tiny interval of time, that not one note in Heaven's song was missed.

Even though the actual words would suggest that the tiny instant of separation actually occurred, Jesus certainly does not mean it that way. Otherwise, his words would contradict the Holy Spirit's Atonement principle. The meaning of the statement, rather, is that although we believe this world is a monumental reality and magnificent creation, in truth Heaven does not even know it exists. Using the analogy of the sun and ocean (God) and the smallest sunbeam and almost imperceptible ripple (the ego), the Course states in a passage alluded to earlier:

> Yet neither sun nor ocean is even aware of all this strange and meaningless activity. They merely continue, unaware that they are feared and hated by a tiny segment of themselves (text, p. 364; T-18.VIII.4:1-2).

And in a particularly poetic passage:

> Nothing that God knows not exists. And what He knows exists forever, changelessly....And in the Mind of God there is no ending, nor a time in which His Thoughts were absent or could suffer change....Beyond all idols is the Thought [our

true Self] God holds of you. Completely unaffected by the turmoil and the terror of the world, the dreams of birth and death that here are dreamed, the myriad of forms that fear can take; quite undisturbed, the Thought God holds of you remains exactly as it always was (text, pp. 587-88; T-30.III.6:1-2,4; 10:1-2).

This is why the image of a tick of time or slight dip is so helpful. It is particularly helpful to keep this perspective in mind when we find ourselves becoming upset about anything, whether judged as trivial or major. *A Course in Miracles* is not saying that we should ignore or deny what we are feeling; but rather that there is another way of looking at these things. As we have seen, the idea of the Course is not to awaken us suddenly from this nightmare, but to have us first change the nightmare into happy dreams.

Yet in each unforgiving act or thought, in every judgment and in all belief in sin, is that one instant still called back, as if it could be made again in time.

Whenever we feel any lack of forgiveness in ourselves, all that we are doing is calling forth that ancient instant, which has already been undone. It appears as if our upset is due to what another has done, here and now, but in reality it is the result of our decision, *here and now*, to continue to make real for ourselves that ancient instant of seeming separation, the original judgment against ourselves and against our Creator.

You keep an ancient memory before your eyes. And he who lives in memories alone is unaware of where he is.
Forgiveness is the great release from time. It is the key to learning that the past is over. Madness speaks no more. There *is* no other teacher and no other way. For what has been undone no longer is. And who can stand upon a distant shore, and dream himself across an ocean, to a place and time that have long since gone by? How real a hindrance can this dream be to where he really is? For this is

fact, and does not change whatever dreams he has. Yet can he still imagine he is elsewhere, and in another time. In the extreme, he can delude himself that this is true, and pass from mere imagining into belief and into madness, quite convinced that where he would prefer to be, he *is*.[6]

Is this a hindrance to the place whereon he stands? Is any echo from the past that he may hear a fact in what is there to hear where he is now?

Helen received a message as a way of helping her understand this idea, which discussed our having fallen asleep, dreaming that we were across the ocean on a very, very distant shore. We believed that that is where we really were—just as the Course says, quoted earlier, that we "are at home in God dreaming of exile" (text, p. 169; T-10.I.2:1). Our true reality, however, remains in Heaven, dreaming that we are thousands of miles across the ocean on a distant shore and have forgotten where we really are. In "The Present Memory," which we will discuss next, there is a reference to that distant shore analogy.

Thus, the fact that we are dreaming that we are on a distant shore is not a hindrance to the reality that we are really on this present shore—"at home in God"—having this bad dream that we are in exile; the fact that we believe that we are in this tiny dip of time does not change the fact that we are really one with God in eternity. All that we believe has happened, is happening now, or yet will happen—all this has no reality at all outside of our dreaming mind, and thus has no effect. The shadows of the past, which in our personal experience reflect some aspect of specialness, have no effect on where we really are.

And how much can his own illusions about time and place effect a change in where he really is?

6. This paragraph was inadvertently omitted from the first edition of *A Course in Miracles*. In my presentation, which was prior to the publication of the second edition, I commented on this paragraph by attributing it to an unpublished message Helen had received from Jesus.

The unforgiven is a voice that calls from out a past forevermore gone by. And everything that points to it as real is but a wish that what is gone could be made real again and seen as here and now, in place of what is *really* now and here.

That lovely section in the text, "The Forgotten Song" (pp. 415-17; T-21.I), speaks about an ancient melody that we hear, reminding us of our real home. Yet we dream of a distant place and hear a different song, the ego's raucous shrieking. But none of these illusions about where we are can have any effect on the "now and here" of our home with God. What we see as "here and now" is the world we believe we are in. Once again, it is as if we are sitting in front of a television screen believing that what we are observing is actually happening, forgetting the fact that we are simply watching it in our minds. Thus, the "now and here" is the holy instant in our minds in which we experience God's Love; the "here and now" is the illusion that we are in a world of time and space, into which the thoughts from that seeming instant of separation are being projected.

Is this a hindrance to the truth the past is gone, and cannot be returned to you? And do you want that fearful instant kept, when Heaven seemed to disappear and God was feared and made a symbol of your hate?

From here to the end of this section Jesus is speaking of that one ancient instant when we believed we had attacked God and separated from Him, and then believed in fear that God was attacking us in return. This instant of terror houses our sin, guilt, and fear, underlying *all* our experiences. Every fearful and hateful thought has its origin here, while every forgiving and healing thought has its origin in this instant as well.

Q: What is the relationship between the observer in chart 3 and that which chooses within a lifetime what we wish to focus on? According to the text, this choosing element apparently is neither right-minded nor wrong-minded.

A: The observer or decision maker (in the split mind) is not the you who are here, but rather it exists outside of time. It is not in Heaven, is not Christ, but rather is outside of the experiences that are recorded on the television screen, so to speak. Remember that the mind is not in the body. In other words, when we experience ourselves as making a choice whether to live in one place or another, take one job or another, to attack or to forgive, what is really happening is that the observer has chosen that that is the tape that will be played.

Q: So it is this observer of whom I am not aware who has chosen that I be in this place, in this time. Is that correct?

A: Yes. Your observer, so to speak, has chosen to play a specific tape in which you have this particular body and personality, living in the twentieth century. But there could be another part of your observer's mind which may be tuning into another lifetime that you have had or will have.

Q: What about the individual choices that I make within this lifetime, what is that aspect of choosing?

A: The point is that you are not really choosing now at all. In truth, what appears to be a choice here is simply a video tape that reflects a choice made on the level of the mind, which is outside of time and space. The problem we have in understanding these concepts is that this is not our experience. That is why *A Course in Miracles* is really aimed at the *we* that we believe we are, the particular body/personality structure which is in this world and which makes choices. Earlier I mentioned Basilides' story about Jesus laughing during the crucifixion, knowing that he was not that crucified body on the cross. He knew that what appeared to people's eyes was a dream; that knowledge or awakening is what the Course means by resurrection.

Q: Is the observer, then, a mind that has been healed?

A: No, not at all. When the observer's mind is healed and right-mindedness has corrected wrong-mindedness—the Holy Spirit's videos have corrected the ego's—then there is nothing more to observe or to choose. That is the attainment of the real world, in which there are no more videos. In other words, to use our television set analogy, as we sit in front of the screen we can choose to hear the ego's voice, and then go through everything above the dotted line in chart 2 which represents the myriad forms in which we see ourselves as victims or victimizers; or we can choose the corrections for these, which are below the dotted line of chart 2.

Therefore, the observer is neither right- nor wrong-minded, but chooses to identify with either the right (the Holy Spirit) or wrong (the ego) mind. What is healed is the observer's faulty choice, correcting the original identification with the ego's thought system of separation.

Q: Could we be the director at the same time and change something we do not like in the movie we originally made?

A: We cannot do anything new because everything has already happened. You cannot change the script but you can choose what part of the script you are going to re-experience. And basically, which is over-simplifying it somewhat, you could choose to go through a situation with forgiveness or go through a situation with anger and resentment. There is no concept of choice within the kaleidoscope on the right-hand side of chart 3; the choice rests only with the observer in the mind. In the context of your question, therefore, the change in a movie we did not like would actually be another movie, which also occurred in that original instant.

The first paragraph in this section, "The Little Hindrance," says that there are only two choices that we could ever make. It appears as if we have choices in this world because that is where we are stuck, but the truth of it is that the choice is on a totally different level. Practicing *A Course in Miracles* and its specific thrust of undoing the ego will eventually lead us back to that point of realizing it is all a dream; but our world is nowhere near that realization, which is why the message had to come through this way.

In view of this, it is a somewhat tragic mistake when people who read the Course fall into the trap of denying this world saying "the whole world is an illusion; therefore it does not matter what I do." The thrust of *A Course in Miracles* is just the opposite. Even though it does say that the world is an illusion and everything has already happened, what we choose does make a difference here because it reflects a choice made by the observer. It is these choices which will get us unstuck from where we are right now, or else root us more deeply in the world.

At other times I have said that *A Course in Miracles* is not Jesus' final word, but that it is the perfect message for the world as it is now: a message written on a level we can understand, which nonetheless leads us to deeper and deeper levels of understanding, ultimately even beyond the message itself. The world is strongly ego-based as we all know, and that is why the Course is pitched on this level. When the world learns the Course's lesson, which will probably take many, many centuries, we will not need it anymore. Then I think Jesus' love will provide a message that would be on "higher levels" in the sense that we would no longer require a course that discusses the ego thought system in such depth. That is why it would be a terrible mistake for people to treat *A Course in Miracles* the way the Bible has been treated, as God's final word. If we shift from a linear context of events unfolding one after the other to the holographic context, we can say that there already exists a higher message anyone can tune into. The

Love of the Holy Spirit in our minds is perfect. As the veils of our fear and guilt fall away, we are able to hear His Voice with increasing clarity. The famous quotation from the Bible is relevant here: "If anyone has ears to hear, let him listen!" (Mt 11:1). At this point the world is not ready to hear that higher level of truth.

Returning to the text, the important point here is that everything we do on an ego basis is a remembrance of that one mistake, that ancient instant when we believed we attacked God and became convinced that He would attack us in return.

Forget the time of terror that has been so long ago corrected and undone. Can sin withstand the Will of God? Can it be up to you to see the past and put it in the present? You can *not* go back.

Yet that is what we always try to do: "go back." This theme is poignantly and powerfully expressed in Lesson 182, "I will be still an instant and go home." Here we find described the futile search for an earthly home we believed we once had, defending against the true home that is within our minds in the present:

> We speak today for everyone who walks this world, for he is not at home. He goes uncertainly about in endless search, seeking in darkness what he cannot find; not recognizing what it is he seeks. A thousand homes he makes, yet none contents his restless mind. He does not understand he builds in vain. The home he seeks can not be made by him. There is no substitute for Heaven. All he ever made was hell.
>
> Perhaps you think it is your childhood home that you would find again. The childhood of your body, and its place of shelter, are a memory now so distorted that you merely hold a picture of a past that never happened. Yet there is a Child in you Who seeks His Father's house, and knows that He is alien here. This childhood is eternal, with an innocence that will endure forever. Where this Child shall go is holy

ground. It is His holiness that lights up Heaven, and that brings to earth the pure reflection of the light above, wherein are earth and Heaven joined as one (workbook, p. 331; W-pI.182.3-4).

This theme of not being able to return home is also reminiscent of Thomas Wolfe's famous novel, *You Can't Go Home Again.* In this sense, we cannot return to the ego's home again. We believe we can, but we lived in that home only for one seeming instant, and that mistake was corrected. What we try to do in this world, however, is choose to re-experience all those ego dimensions of our minds, reflecting the ego's original statement that I am *not* as God created me. All the time, of course, we believe that we *are* in dimensions outside of Heaven.

And everything that points the way in the direction of the past but sets you on a mission whose accomplishment can only be unreal. Such is the justice your All-Loving Father has ensured must come to you. And from your own unfairness to yourself has He protected you. You cannot lose your way because there is no way but His, and nowhere can you go except to Him.

Would God allow His Son to lose his way along a road long since a memory of time gone by?

This statement reminds us that our experience as separate individuals in this world only seems to be real; but the belief in the world is simply a mistake which has already been corrected and undone. Only in illusions does it seem that we can will in opposition to the Will of God. God's protection of us, therefore, does not come from a magical white knight who watches over us. Rather our protection is simply His Being, and by extension His Son's Being (Christ), which ensures that our unfairness to ourselves has had no effect, since it never happened. Nothing exists outside of His Being; there *can* be no other way but God, as we have already seen. Thus, it is impossible that a part of God can leave its Source and "lose his way." The presence of the Holy Spirit in the observer's mind, which is the memory of God's Being, is truth's protection that does not "allow" the Son to make the unreal real, nor have happen what could never happen.

A dreadful instant in a distant past, now perfectly corrected, is of no concern nor value. Let the dead and gone be peacefully forgotten. Resurrection has come to take its place. And now you are a part of resurrection, not of death.

This reflects the well-known statement of Jesus in the gospel, "Let the dead bury their dead" (Mt 8:22, KJV). Paying attention to what never happened and therefore does not exist—i.e., what is dead—simply makes the error real, preventing us from recognizing its illusory nature and awakening from the dream. "Resurrection," again, is the Course's term for awakening from the dream of death. It therefore has nothing to do with the resurrection of the body. On the level of the mind, we simply realize that the world is all a dream and that what we are watching has already happened. As the Holy Spirit is already present in our minds as the Atonement thought that reflects the Love of God, and as we are also a thought, then we must be a part of that Atonement or resurrection thought as well. Similarly, the Course tells us that we were with Jesus when he arose:

> He [the Holy Spirit] offers thanks to you as well as him [Jesus] for you arose with him when he began to save the world (manual, p. 86; C-6.5:5).

Thus, the resurrection has *already* happened within us; it simply awaits our acceptance of this fact.

No past illusions have the power to keep you in a place of death, a vault God's Son entered an instant, to be instantly restored unto His Father's perfect Love. And how can he be kept in chains long since removed and gone forever from his mind?

The Son whom God created is as free as God created him. He [the Son] was reborn the instant that he chose to die instead of live. And will you not forgive him now, because he made an error in the past that God remembers not, and is not there?

Belief in the separation is the "place of death," the "vault." In that same instant in which we entered this vault, God restored us to Himself. That is one of the key themes that recurs over and over again in *A Course in Miracles*: we are still with God, as He created us. Each and every time we find ourselves attacking someone else or ourselves, it is because we are still holding on to that ancient memory that we had attacked God, and therefore do not deserve to be forgiven.

The Course's use of the phrase "born again," incidentally, should not be confused with the fundamentalist's meaning. Because there is no linear time, each and every seeming instant within the observer's mind offers the opportunity of being free from the prison of the past. In truth there is no past; we have no history—personal or collective. And so in each instant we are choosing the ego's tale of a sinful and unforgiving past, or the Holy Spirit's truth of a forgiving present in which no sin ever occurred.

Now you are shifting back and forth between the past and present. Sometimes the past seems real, as if it *were* the present. Voices [ego] from the past are heard and then are doubted.

This sounds like a description from a clinical psychiatry textbook of a psychotic person who is hearing voices. The Course uses this parallel very often, and it does so in the lines which follow. It *is* true that we are insane, not clinically insane as usually defined, but insane because we are still listening to a voice from the past that is already gone. A psychotic person in many cases can hear voices from the past. That person could be in a situation, and suddenly hear a cruel voice of a parent, teacher, or friend from forty or fifty years ago, and actually experience that happening right now. But on another level we all do this, because we are still hearing that voice from the ancient instant that says we have attacked God, and that God will attack us in return.

Q: So is the point here that we hear these voices and we believe in them, and then we begin to doubt them because we are learning there is another Voice to hear?

A: That is right. Jesus is saying here that we are going back and forth. Earlier in the text he repeatedly tells us that we are not totally insane (text, pp. 322,338,344; T-16.VI.8:8; T-17.V.7:9; T-17.VII.10:2), which means that we hear these voices of the past and we do begin to doubt them, but at times they can sound very real and convincing, as we all know.

You are like to one who still hallucinates, but lacks conviction in what he perceives.

A good friend of mine from graduate school had a paranoid break many years ago, and is still in the hospital. His psychosis is unusual as he is always aware that he is hallucinating, that he is having paranoid ideation, and yet he cannot change what he is doing. Actually, that is even more painful than being oblivious to it. He knows exactly what is going on and how insane his thoughts are, but he feels impotent to change them. This is the same kind of situation in which we find ourselves, except that now we are not talking about clinical paranoia. Our position is different in that we would know that the voice is that of the ego, and that we ultimately have control over it.

These passages in the text are telling us that we can make another choice. We are in a position to begin to understand *A Course in Miracles'* teachings, and realize that what seems to be real is not. As this realization develops we begin to have a sense that things are not the way that they appear to be. So, for example, even if we get really angry, there is a part of us that is not quite as convinced as it had been in the past that our anger is justified.

This is the borderland between the worlds, the bridge between the past and present. Here the shadow of the past remains, but still a present light is dimly recognized. Once it is seen, this light can never be forgotten. It must draw you from the past into the present, where you really are.

At "the borderland between the worlds" we still hear the voice of the ego and have ego reactions to events, but are also aware that there is something else in our minds, the loving presence of the Holy Spirit. We may even be ready to understand this present teaching, not just on a conceptual level but experientially as well—understanding from within ourselves that the whole world is a dream, that we are literally watching ourselves going through what we do each day: waking up in the morning, getting dressed, eating meals, having fights, feeling happy, peaceful, or conflicted, and doing daily chores. As we begin to experience the illusory nature of this world, we can never totally lose that sense again. We can try as hard as we can to deny it, but there is a part of us which, once it has seen through the ego's shadows, will never be the same again. Once the light of this truth is seen, it serves as an anchor on the stormy ego seas, keeping us from drifting off totally; or, to use another analogy of the sea, the truth beams in our minds like a lighthouse, calling us back from the ego's darkness of guilt and fear to the forgiveness and Love of the Holy Spirit.

The shadow voices do not change the laws of time nor of eternity. They come from what is past and gone, and hinder not the true existence of the here and now. The real world is the second part of the hallucination time and death are real, and have existence that can be perceived. This terrible illusion was denied in but the time it took for God to give His Answer to illusion for all time and every

circumstance. And then it was no more to be experienced as there.

This is the central idea we have seen several times already. Referring to chart 5, that tiny tick of time, the tiny instant has had no effect at all on the solid line of eternity, whose song is totally unaffected by the seeming interference of the ego's dissonant chords. The real world is also part of the illusory world, but it is free from all of the *pain* of the illusion: how can something that is not there cause pain, and to what? The real world is free from all the projections of guilt of the illusion. Therefore, the first part of the hallucination is the thought system of the ego, which is the mistaken belief that time and death are real. The second part, also within the framework of the illusion, undoes the belief in the reality of time and death. This is similar to the Course's discussion of forgiveness as the only illusion that does not breed more illusions. As the manual states:

> Forgiveness, then, is an illusion, but because of its purpose, which is the Holy Spirit's, it has one difference. Unlike all other illusions it leads away from error and not towards it (manual, p. 79; C-3.1:3-4).

And so, even though we continue in the dream to experience ourselves as real, living in a world we believe is really out there, the dream is not reality. There yet remains within our mind the happy thought of awakening that is God's Answer, and which has already undone the ego's entire thought system. We shall return in Part III to the real world, the attainment of which is the goal of the Course.

Each day, and every minute in each day, and every instant that each minute holds, you but relive the single instant when the time of terror took the place of love. And so you die each day to live again, until you cross the gap between the past and present, which is not a gap at all. [And the following seems to be a very clear statement of

reincarnation:] **Such is each life; a seeming interval from birth to death and on to life again, a repetition of an instant gone by long ago that cannot be relived. [Yet, we believe we can relive it.] And all of time is but the mad belief that what is over is still here and now.**

This expresses the same idea just mentioned; namely, that each instant that we experience to be our lives, perceiving ourselves as separated beings, we but relive that ancient instant. The first sentence of the paragraph just quoted, incidentally, was phrased incorrectly in the original printing of the Course. Its closing phrase was originally printed as "terror was replaced by love." The corrected version, in later printings, is: "terror took the place of love." The mistaken version is actually also correct, except that that is not the precise point that is being made here. There did seem to be a single instant when terror took the place of love and the ego substituted for Heaven, yet in that same seeming instant terror was replaced by love through the Holy Spirit's presence in our minds.

This passage also contains a reference to the earlier quoted idea that each moment we are choosing between crucifixion and resurrection (text, p. 255; T-14.III.4:1). This "dying" does not refer to physical death, of course, but rather to death as a symbol of the ego. In that sense, then, each time we choose to identify with any aspect of the ego thought system—be it anger, guilt, specialness, or pain—we are in effect dying, for we believe that in that choice we have once again killed God and Christ, and therefore deserve to be killed in return. And yet in each instant we also have the power to choose to live, by choosing to identify with the Voice for Life.

Forgive the past and let it go, for it *is* gone. You stand no longer on the ground that lies between the worlds. You have gone on, and reached the world that lies at Heaven's gate.

Jesus is being very optimistic here, but remember that within the holy instant—outside of time and space—the Answer has already been given and so we do stand at Heaven's gate. This is usually not the experience that we have, but Jesus is reminding us that there is another part of us, another video tape we could choose, that would actually have us at Heaven's gate. We already have completed this journey.

Q: How does that fit in with the statement that the time is set when each mind will accept the revelation that the Father and the Son are one?

A: There is already a video tape we can choose which would have us re-experience that moment when we wake up to the fact that we never separated; we have already experienced that awakening. But the observer still has the power to choose when he is going to play that tape.

Q: What is the ultimate purpose of being on a spiritual path now if the time is already set, if I chose at that instant when I was going to accept that revelation?

A: The point of the spiritual path is that it provides the means of getting us to the moment when we will choose to review mentally what has already gone by, to re-experience that total state of right-mindedness. That is what the spiritual path is about. It seems as if it is a linear journey, but our path trains us to take our fingers off the wrong-minded button, and to put them on the right-minded button instead. But also recall that we are really *not* on a spiritual path at all, since we are not here. What we experience as being on a path is simply the reflection of a decision made in the observer's mind.

Earlier I alluded to the work of Donald Hebb, a physiological psychologist from McGill University, who taught that learning occurred as people made synaptic connections in their brains. As people repeated the same action, a furrow was produced in their brains that would become deeper and deeper.

Thus, if you do something such as tying your shoes over and over again, you become good at it and a habit is formed; so even if it is a bad habit, e.g., tying your shoes wrong, over and over again, there is what Hebb called a cell assembly that gets built in, and which is very difficult to break out of. This is a helpful analogy in the following way: if we keep on choosing to attack and separate, which is what our current experiences can be, then the hand on the wrong-minded button becomes stronger and stronger, more attached to that button, which makes it more difficult to let go of it. In other words, it has become more difficult to actually awaken from the dream. Therefore, we need experiences that will enable us to break the habit pattern of the hand which is always on the wrong-minded button, so that we can begin to reinforce the right-minded choice. This means that we increasingly choose to replay tapes which involve forgiving and joining rather than separation.

Q: In other words, does this ultimately mean that there is a part of me that has chosen to fully accept revelation in a certain time-space sequence, and as I choose forgiveness, the other time-space sequences that I am walking through ultimately will dissolve, and then there will be only that moment of my acceptance of revelation?

A: Yes, that is exactly what this is saying. It is a way of practicing forgiveness, which is really *un*learning—a way of unlearning what we have taught ourselves. We have made very deep furrows in terms of our experience, furrows of separation, anxiety, guilt, and anger. And so we need to change these, which really means learning how to choose better tapes, happy dream tapes, tapes of forgiveness rather than those of attack.

There is no hindrance to the Will of God, nor any need that you repeat again a journey that was over long ago.

We believe that we have to repeat the journey, but in reality we do not. This is what *A Course in Miracles* means in the earlier section, "I Need Do Nothing" (text, p. 362; T-18.VII). Salvation does not need to be accomplished or achieved, but merely accepted. That is also what the Course means by describing forgiveness not as a "doing," but an "undoing." And, as we have seen, there is the statement in the text: "It is a journey without distance to a goal that has never changed" (text, p. 139; T-8.VI.9:7).

Look gently on your brother, and behold the world in which perception of your hate has been transformed into a world of love.

This is one of those wonderful moments in the Course when it suddenly shifts to our individual experience. The focus here is the same as in "The Obstacles to Peace," when the discussion of the final obstacle focused on forgiveness of our one special love/hate partner (text, pp. 393-95; T-19.IV-D.8-21). Here, too, we see that what heals this terrible instant that we relive over and over again, is looking gently on this one particular person whom we have to forgive. This is the very powerful, practical emphasis of the Course: we do not have to become preoccupied with metaphysical concepts such as the illusory nature of time. All we really need do is forgive. At that moment our world will be transformed from hate into a world of love; that is the holiest spot on earth spoken of later in the text (p. 522; T-26.IX.6:1). When we actually totally forgive one person, the whole Sonship is healed. Again, this is the meaning of the statement that we were with Jesus when he arose (manual, p. 86; C-6.5:5). Since minds are joined, a healing thought within any part of the Sonship heals the whole. This is also the meaning of the workbook lesson, "When I am healed I am not healed alone" (workbook, pp. 254-56; W-pI.137).

Chapter 4

COMMENTARY ON "THE PRESENT MEMORY"

This section opens Chapter 28, and thus falls between the two final sections of Chapter 27, "The Dreamer of the Dream" and "The Hero of the Dream," and the section immediately following it, "Reversing Effect and Cause." These aforementioned sections form a unity of discussion of cause and effect, how the ego reverses them so that the cause (the mind of the dreamer) becomes the effect, and the effect (the dream of the world) becomes the cause. Thus, the function of the miracle (which we will discuss in depth in Part II) is to give "back to cause the function of causation, not effect" (text, p. 552; T-28.II.9:3). This involves the realization that everything is in our mind, that reality is not out there in the world. Because of the importance of the theme of cause and effect for our discussion of this section, I shall begin with a brief explanation of it.[7]

In Heaven, Cause (God the Creator-Father) is totally unified with His Effect (Christ the created Son). As we have already seen, there is no place where the Father ends and the Son begins. Though there is a distinction between Cause and Effect, Creator and created, Father and Son, there is no duality consciousness in Heaven to perceive this. God's and Christ's undivided unity is beyond the capacity of a separated mind (and therefore brain) to understand or know.

In the separation it appeared as if Effect had been split off from Cause, so that now the effect, the Son of God, was independent of his Cause, God. This was the beginning of the

---

7. For a fuller discussion of this important principle, the interested reader may consult my tape set "Cause and Effect" (see listing in Related Material in the back of this book) which draws upon the relevant sections and passages from *A Course in Miracles*. Pages 63-78 in *Forgiveness and Jesus*, Fourth Edition, also summarize this teaching.

ego's dream of death, of sin, guilt, and punishment. The Holy Spirit's Atonement principle undoes this dream by expressing that Cause and Effect could never be separate—a part of God could never become separate from Him—and therefore the impossible never happened. But of course, by identifying with the ego thought system we believed the separation did happen, thus setting into motion the ego's cosmic plot of sustaining its own illusory existence.

In succinct form, this is how the ego accomplished its design: the ego tells the Son that not only has he separated himself from God, but that he has committed a heinous sin for which he should feel guilty, a guilt that inevitably deserves punishment at the hands of an avenging Father. Thus the ego has first established sin and guilt as real, and then instructs the foolish Son to believe that he requires a defense against the inevitable punishment. This defense is the projection of the thought of separation from the mind, resulting in a separated physical world (the birth of the universe!). In this world the Son believes he can hide from God:

> The world was made as an attack on God. It symbolizes fear. And what is fear except love's absence? Thus the world was meant to be a place where God could enter not, and where His Son could be apart from Him (workbook, p. 403; W-pII.3.2:1-4).

Finally, in order for the ruse to work, the Son must forget he made the world, so that the world appears objectively real, outside and independent of his mind. Thus the ego's dynamic of miscreation (or making) is "forgotten," denied in a masterful stroke of tactical strategy. It now appears, within the Son's experience, that the outer world (including one's own body) is the cause of his own suffering and pain, rather than his pain (i.e., his guilt) being the cause of the world.

Restating this now in terms of cause and effect, we observe that the separated mind is the cause, and the physical world is the effect. Because cause and effect remain unified, on earth as well as in Heaven, the thought of the separated world has never left its source within the separated mind: the outer and inner are one and the same, as are the observer and observed. However, the ego has first split off effect from cause—the world from the mind—and then reverses them so that the world now appears to be the cause of the pain we experience within. As we shall see presently, the miracle is the device whereby cause and effect are restored to their proper positions. Thus, the cause of my distress is not external to me, but is rather a decision made in my mind: my mind is the *cause* of my body's pain; my distress is the inevitable *effect* of my faulty choice.

To further develop this principle, we see that a cause could not be what it is unless it were causing an effect, and an effect could not be what it is unless it were being caused by something. Moreover, as linear time is illusory, cause and effect are simultaneous, as we discussed in Part I. Thus, since cause and effect are inextricably intertwined, if one exists the other must as well, and conversely, if one does not exist, the other does not either. The effects of sin are not only the body itself, but specifically the pain, suffering, and death we experience in the body. Belief in the cause (sin) demands belief in its effect (the reality of the body, either through pleasure or pain), as does the belief in the effect demand belief in the cause. Therefore, not making the cause (sin) real by remembering our Identity as Christ removes the experience of bodily pleasure or pain as real. It also follows that not making the effect real (pleasure or pain of the body) removes the belief in the cause (the sin of separation).

We turn now to "The Present Memory," and recall to mind that time is not linear. Events are not happening now nor are they yet to happen. Everything has already happened, and time is seen within a holographic rather than a linear model. The Holy Spirit's use of memory, the "present memory," refers to our remembering right here and now, with the help of the Holy

Spirit, that we have never left our Father's House. The ego's use of memory, on the other hand, is to remind us of our past sins to reinforce our guilt, causing us to be afraid of the future. But the faculty of remembering is used by the Holy Spirit to undo our belief in the past, so that we can recall that ancient memory, "the forgotten song" referred to in the section of the same name (see above, p. 70), and remember that we never left God. Now we begin with "The Present Memory" (text, p. 547; T-28.I).

The miracle does nothing. All it does is to undo. And thus it cancels out the interference to what has been done. It does not add, but merely takes away. And what it takes away is long since gone, but being kept in memory appears to have immediate effects. This world was over long ago. The thoughts that made it are no longer in the mind that thought of them and loved them for a little while. The miracle but shows the past is gone, and what has truly gone has no effects. Remembering a cause can but produce illusions of its presence, not effects.

As *A Course in Miracles* frequently emphasizes, the miracle (as well as the Atonement, forgiveness, or salvation) does not do anything, since there is nothing that needs to be done. Rather, it corrects (or undoes) the ego's belief that there is a problem (i.e., our guilt) that needs defense (i.e., the world and the body) and atonement (i.e., sacrifice and suffering). The ego holds on to that ancient memory of our belief in having separated from God, and it was that separation thought that became the cause of the world of the body, suffering, and death. In our experience of individual lives, whenever we feel pain, or accuse someone else of victimizing us, we are actually reliving that ancient moment, saying, "Look at the misery of my life; my sin against God has had very real effects." And the ego tells us, even if we are not conscious of it, that this pain ultimately is our punishment because of what we did against God.

"What it takes away is long since gone": the miracle takes away the cause and effect connection. It helps us realize that these terrible effects we believe are real, are not so, and if they are not real—if they are not effects—they cannot have a cause. If something is not a cause it does not exist, which is the Holy Spirit's way of teaching us that sin is an illusion: it never really happened. That is why it is imperative when working with *A Course in Miracles* to recognize that it teaches that the world is an illusion. If we acknowledge the world, and therefore the body, as real, we are saying sin has had effects. If we believe the body is eternal, or resurrects and therefore has died (which of course means that it once lived), we are saying the body has a reality, and therefore that sin has had an effect and must be real as well.

A Course in Miracles is teaching us that the body is not real because the world is not real. They are illusory because they came from the illusory belief that we have sinned against God. "The thoughts that made it are no longer in the mind that thought of them and loved them for a little while": the Holy Spirit has already undone the illusory thought that made the world; the mistakes have already been corrected.

All the effects of guilt are here no more. For guilt is over. In its passing went its consequences, left without a cause.

This is another way of saying what was discussed above. Guilt is over because sin has been undone. The seeming separation from God which led to our guilt was corrected in that same instant, which meant it did not have any effects. And so the world, which is the effect of guilt, is over as well, with all the seeming consequences of pain, suffering, and death. And yet we still sit in front of the screen replaying the ancient scripts, as if it all were happening today, as if our sin and guilt were real and had real effects.

Why would you cling to it in memory if you did not desire its effects?

The thought expressed here has important implications for psychological theory and psychotherapy. The past does have an effect on us, if we choose in the present to hold on to it. Strictly speaking, if I continue to believe that my parents abused me and did not love me, then I will see my adult sufferings as a direct effect of that abuse. And I will be able to say: "Yes, the reason I am like this is because I was mistreated when I was a child." All of this is true within the illusory nature of the ego's world, a belief upheld by many personality theorists. The real truth, however, is that I am choosing in the *present* to hold on to that memory. If I change my mind in the present, then no matter what my parents did or did not do, it would have no effect. And I choose to hold on to the bitter memory because I desire its effects of pain now, but wish to deny my responsibility for choosing it. Instead, the responsibility is projected onto the past and specific figures in it, and so I put on the "face of innocence" (text, p. 610; T-31.V.2:6).

The same is true of the larger picture. We believe our suffering in this world is a direct result of our sin against God, and so we cling to the past as if it were still here. And that is only because we are choosing *now* to hold on to the past; the pain belonging to it is what sustains the ego's existence. We are choosing, as the observer, to hear the ego's voice. So we play the ego's tapes, which are tapes of separation, misery, suffering, anxiety, guilt, depression, sickness, and death. Furthermore, we are choosing to play those tapes because that relives for us the seeming reality of the time of separation. We are not aware at all that the problem is not what we believe we are experiencing or observing; the problem is that we are choosing, from the point of view of the observer, to make it real for us now, even though that "now" no longer exists, being a defense against the true now of the holy instant. As the text states:

> Once you were unaware of what the cause of everything the world appeared to thrust upon you, uninvited and unasked,

must really be. Of one thing you were sure: of all the many causes you perceived as bringing pain and suffering to you, your guilt was not among them (text, p. 541; T-27.VII.7:3-4).

Remembering is as selective as perception, being its past tense. It is perception of the past as if it were occurring now, and still were there to see.

Perception, as the Course teaches us over and over again, is a choice. A section called "Perception and Choice" (text, pp. 487-89; T-25.III) teaches that what we see comes from our desire to see a specific thing, a desire which is then projected out. Consequently we see something, not because it is truly there, but because we *wish* to see it there. Remembering works in the exact same way; the only difference is that perception, as we experience it, occurs in the present. I am perceiving you right now. If I remember something you did yesterday, then obviously that is in the past. But the past and the present in the split mind are different forms of the same illusion.

Q: What about the type of situation in which you have not been loving and then have contrition or what is called "healthy guilt"? If you then think that you have somehow to make up for what you have done, is that not also a way of holding on to the past?

A: Yes, in fact it is an example of atoning for our past sins, and that of course makes the past real.

Q: So is the idea then that healing does not ask that you do anything, but rather simply to recognize that a mistake was made, ask the Holy Spirit for a corrected perception, and then let it go, trusting that by letting it go the "wrongs" that took place would be healed?

A: That is exactly the idea. If we then feel guided by the Holy Spirit to go and talk to the person, this would have to be done from a corrected perception which would lead to a different attitude if the healing were to occur. But what most of us do is feel guilty for something, and then feel we have to make up for it to the person, or we deny the guilt altogether, and continue going on as if nothing happened, but the guilt of the past remains deep within us. So either way, the ego's atoning or denying serve the ego's purpose of making the past real.

Memory, like perception, is a skill made up by you to take the place of what God gave in your creation. And like all the things you made, it can be used to serve another purpose [the Holy Spirit's], and to be the means for something else. It can be used to heal and not to hurt, if you so wish it be.

We made up memory because memory obviously implies a linear view of time, past and present, and so time becomes a substitute for the eternal present, which is the closest we can come to the state of reality. And yet, despite its ego purpose of attack, time can be used by the Holy Spirit to help us. In a lovely statement, *A Course in Miracles* teaches:

> The body was not made by love. Yet love does not condemn it and can use it lovingly, respecting what the Son of God has made and using it to save him from illusions (text, p. 359; T-18.VI.4:7-8).

This teaching is one of the important ones in the Course, and is the basis for our examples of the Holy Spirit's video tapes or the hologram of correction: the Holy Spirit's use of what we made for the purpose of separation or attack, as a means to join and heal.

Q: How would you apply this idea in the text to the case of someone who has memories of being a battered child, for example? How can memory be used in a right-minded sense?

A: One way might be, as the Course says in a couple of places, to think of the positive things that this person did for you, rather than focus only on the negative. For example, this statement from the text:

> Have you consistently appreciated the good efforts, and over-looked mistakes? Or has your appreciation flickered and grown dim in what seemed to be the light of the mistakes? (text, p. 339; T-17.V.11:7-8)

That is a beginning step. It is like saying, "My parents were not all bad." This is not going to be the ultimate healing, but if all we are doing is focusing on the negative, it can be helpful to see that our parents did some good things as well. In terms of therapy, it could be helpful to have the person see that he or she is focusing only on the bad things, but that there were good things, too. This would be the beginning of a shift in the person's attitude toward the past.

A more sophisticated way, however, would be to "remember" the past hurts but give them a different interpretation, saying, for example "but this was my parents' call for help, as well as mine." These steps would lead us to the ultimate stage—the memory of God—which is what this section, "The Present Memory," is really talking about.

It should be mentioned, however, that in a situation involving a battered child, there is a real danger of skipping over those steps that are almost always necessary in learning the lessons of this particular classroom. These steps usually include recalling to mind the memory of the abuse, and allowing oneself to feel the hurt, shame, and anger *before* one can then shift to a truly forgiving perception of the battering adult. As one workbook lesson ends, speaking in the context of God's last step:

> God will take this final step Himself. Do not deny the little steps He asks you take to Him (workbook, p. 359; W-pI.193.13:6-7).

All too often people may deny the pain of these memories they have made real, but feel they have let them go as part of their spiritual process of forgiveness. But all they have really done is place a spiritual cover over the pain, believing in ostrich-like fashion that because they do not see (or feel) the problem it is not there. In the words that Helen Schucman, scribe of the Course, heard herself say as she awoke one morning: "Never underestimate the power of denial." In circumstances involving painful events such as child abuse, a good rule of thumb to apply is that a person would not have chosen this particular video tape were there not lessons to be learned in terms of forgiving victimization (in oneself as "victim" and the adult as "victimizer"). And if so, such a painful lesson would almost always call forth painful memories and therefore a painful process of forgiveness. Within our dream-world, such a process inevitably requires some time. If the "letting-go" occurs too quickly, the chances are likely that the guilt and anger—already made real—have not truly been let go, but simply re-pressed. Thus they will surface again in other forms. As the text says regarding sin:

> Sometimes a sin can be repeated over and over, with obvi-ously distressing results, but without the loss of its appeal. And suddenly, you change its status from a sin to a mistake. Now you will not repeat it; you will merely stop and let it go, unless the guilt remains. For then you will but change the form of sin, granting that it was an error, but keeping it uncor-rectable. This is not really a change in your perception, for it is sin that calls for punishment, not error (text, p. 377; T-19.III.3:3-7).

Nothing employed for healing represents an effort to do anything at all.

In other words, in our right mind (which is the only place healing can occur) we do not do anything, for nothing *has* to be done; a miracle does not do anything, it simply undoes—that is how the section began. Whenever we experience our-selves as expending effort—which is different from our *bodies* behaving in certain ways—we know that our egos have gotten in the way. When Lesson 155 tells us to "step back and let Him lead the way" (workbook, p. 284; W-pI.155), it is making the same point as when the Course elsewhere tells us to undo the interferences that prevent the Holy Spirit's Love and healing from extending through us. Love simply *is*; it does nothing at all.

It is a recognition that you have no needs which mean that something must be done.

If I believe I have a need, then obviously I have to do something about it; the idea behind the miracle (or healing) is that nothing has to be done. This of course does not mean that our bodies do not do things in this world, but simply that we recognize that it is the Holy Spirit's Love that is "doing" it through us. Our only need, therefore, is to remember that we have no needs. The Course states that

> the only meaningful prayer is for forgiveness, because those who have been forgiven have everything....The prayer for forgiveness is nothing more than a request that you may be able to recognize what you already have (text, p. 40; T-3.V.6:3,5).

And so, to state it once again, the miracle simply undoes our faulty belief system, which then inevitably leads to the memory of our one need—the Love of God.

It is an unselective memory, that is not used to interfere with truth.

I can have memories of the past, but I do not need to judge them. I do not think "this is a good thing, or a bad thing; this is a good person, or a bad person." As an early workbook lesson says, in the context of choosing thoughts to which we would apply the day's idea of our thoughts not meaning anything:

> If you are already aware of unhappy thoughts, use them as subjects for the idea. Do not, however, select only the

thoughts you think are "bad." You will find, if you train yourself to look at your thoughts, that they represent such a
mixture that, in a sense, none of them can be called "good" or
"bad." This is why they do not mean anything....None of
them represents your real thoughts, which are being covered
up by them. The "good" ones are but shadows of what lies beyond, and shadows make sight difficult. The "bad" ones are
blocks to sight, and make seeing impossible. You do not want
either (workbook, p. 6; W-pI.4.1:4-7; 2:3-6).

Therefore, instead of judging what my memory holds, I am to
realize that these were learning lessons *I* chose to re-
experience, so that I could learn the ultimate lesson of accepting the Atonement.

**All things the Holy Spirit can employ for healing have
been given Him, without the content and the purposes for
which they have been made. They are but skills without an
application. They await their use. They have no dedication
and no aim.**

Now we are back to our dual script—everything the Holy
Spirit will use has already happened. Specifically, if there is a
relationship that has really been a terrible one, it is given to the
Holy Spirit, but without the ego purpose of specialness it was
made to serve. Thus, the relationship becomes an instrument
of salvation. This theme is restated later in the text in a powerful passage that expresses the Holy Spirit's reinterpretation
of our specialness:

> Such is the Holy Spirit's kind perception of specialness;
> His use of what you made, to heal instead of harm....The spe-
> cialness he [the Son] chose to hurt himself did God appoint to
> be the means for his salvation, from the very instant that the
> choice was made (text, p. 493; T-25.VI.4:1; 6:6).

The form remains the same—the relationship itself—but the
content has been shifted from the special one of guilt, murder,
and separation, to the holy one of forgiveness, love, and

joining. All things in the world are neutral—"My body is a wholly neutral thing" (workbook, p. 435; W-pII.294)— awaiting a purpose to be assigned to them. As the Course says: "The test of everything on earth is simply this; 'What is it *for*?'" (text, p. 479; T-24.VII.6:1). Things either serve the ego's or the Holy Spirit's purpose, as the mind elects.

The Holy Spirit can indeed make use of memory, for God Himself is there. Yet this is not a memory of past events, but only of a present state. You are so long accustomed to believe that memory holds only what is past, that it is hard for you to realize it is a skill that can remember *now.*

This is a totally different view of memory, and basically points to that very important notion of the observer which we have been referring to in chart 3. There can be no memory of past events, for there *are* no past events. There is only a decision made in the present by the observer to hold on to the memory of the thought of separation that is no longer there. Memory is a skill that will help us to remember ultimately that our true reality is the one we never left. Thus the ability to remember that the ego made to imprison us in the memory of our sin of separation, can now be used by the Holy Spirit to remember our present state with God, in which the sin of separation never occurred.

The limitations on remembering the world imposes on it are as vast as those you let the world impose on you. There is no link of memory to the past. If you would have it there, then there it is. But only your desire made the link, and only you have held it to a part of time where guilt appears to linger still.

We are so totally identified with the world's view of linear time, that it seems impossible for us to believe that time can be anything else. In truth, of course, the illusory world is powerless to impose anything on us, for, in fact, it is simply the power of our own minds that places such limitations upon us. The statement that there is no memory link to the past refers to what was mentioned earlier about holding on to painful memories of the past. What we remember in the present has nothing to do with the past. It really is but a choice in the present to hold on to our guilt and the belief that the separation is real. Remembering the bad things my parents did to me thirty or forty years ago is just an excuse that the ego uses to achieve its aim of hiding its foundation thought of separation from awareness.

The Holy Spirit's use of memory is quite apart from time. He does not seek to use it as a means to keep the past, but rather as a way to let it go. Memory holds the message it receives, and does what it is given it to do. It does not write the message, nor appoint what it is for. Like to the body, it is purposeless within itself.

This is an important idea in *A Course in Miracles*, and it appears quite a few times. The body does not do anything; it merely carries out the messages the mind has given it. This theme of messages and messengers is found also in "The Attraction of Guilt" in Chapter 19, which emphasizes that the problem is the *messengers* we send out, not the *messages* that are brought back. The messengers simply do what we told them to do. Similarly, regarding the world, the Course states:

> The world you see is but the idle witness that you were right. This witness is insane. You trained it in its testimony, and as it gave it back to you, you listened and convinced yourself that what it saw was true. You did this to yourself. See only this, and you will also see how circular the reasoning on which your "seeing" rests (text, p. 418; T-21.II.5:1-5).

The same principle works with memory. We can either use memory to hold on to the guilt and sin of the past, of that ancient past that we are reliving, or we can use memory to let the past go and have the memory of God dawn on us.

Similarly, early in the text Jesus discusses the two uses of denial: the ego's need to deny the guilt it has first made real, as opposed to the Holy Spirit's denial of the ego's denial of truth. The Holy Spirit denies the reality of the ego's story of sin, guilt, and fear, and denies that the ego has indeed changed our reality as God's Son:

> [Peace] denies the ability of anything not of God to affect you. This is the proper use of denial. It is not used to hide anything, but to correct error....True denial is a powerful protective device. You can and should deny any belief that error can hurt you. This kind of denial is not a concealment but a correction....Denial of error is a strong defense of truth, but denial of truth results in miscreation, the projections of the ego (text, p. 16; T-2.II.1:11-13; 2:1-3,5).

And if it [memory] seems to serve to cherish ancient hate, and gives you pictures of injustices and hurts that you were saving, this is what you asked its message be and that it is.

The problem is not the specific form of past hurts we are recalling to mind, but rather that we have chosen *in the present* to look only upon those past hurts, those ancient hates. Thus, it is not the specific event or person that is the cause of our distress, but rather the split mind (or more properly, the decision maker) that chose to be upset in the first place. Once that choice to be upset is made, the mind then uses the "pictures of injustices" to justify a feeling for which it does not want to accept responsibility. It is an insidious and particularly vicious form of relating to others, though never recognized as such because our guilt prevents us from ever looking at what the ego tells us is the horrible truth about ourselves. Indeed, as we have seen, when we finally are able to look, we see that the ego's emperor has no clothes on, that its "truth" is simply nonexistent. There are no words the ego hates to hear more than this simple statement of truth that follows a description in the

Course of the ego's war on God: "And God thinks otherwise" (text, p. 452; T-23.I.2:7).

Committed to its vaults [the ego's vault of its memory], the history of all the body's past is hidden there. All of the strange associations made to keep the past alive, the present dead, are stored within it, waiting your command that they be brought to you, and lived again.

If we take this within a larger context, the ego's memory vault is represented by the kaleidoscope on the right-hand side of chart 3. The body's past is hidden, not in the body or its brain, but in the *mind* of the decision maker. Recalling our image of the observer sitting in front of the television screen with the remote control, we press a button and that is what we see, what we have recalled from our video library, our "memory banks." The ego lives only in the past, because that is where it believes sin is, while the Holy Spirit's Love, containing the memory of God, lives only in the present, untouched by the sin, guilt, and fear that is the ego's "life." Thus, this present cannot be experienced by a body (brain), but only by the mind that has chosen to remember God, in what *A Course in Miracles* refers to as the holy instant.

And thus do their effects appear to be increased by time, which took away their cause.

In this sentence, "effects" refers to the body, whose number certainly appears to increase as time goes on. And the world of time and space, with which we so identify, has effectively done its job of concealing from us the world's cause, which is the thought of separation now buried in the vaults of our mind.

This non-linear conceptual scheme is totally and radically different from what we usually hear presented. The model of the world used by scientists has been a linear one for the most part. The quantum physicists are increasingly moving away from this, although they would most probably not accept the kinds of statements the Course is making. Einstein's relativity theory of course was a major shift in terms of how we look at time. However, I do not think these physicists apprehend *A Course in Miracles'* level of understanding that the thought in back of the universe of time and space, that was its seeming cause, is also illusory, being a thought of guilt.

Yet time is but another phase of what does nothing. It works hand in hand with all the other attributes with which you seek to keep concealed the truth about yourself.

This refers to the ego, the thought of separation which contains the ancient cause of sin. Yet, this thought does nothing; it has had no effect. Therefore, since the thought of separation is nothing, all that results from it, such as time, is also nothing: "Ideas leave not their source." Time, thus, is just another device the ego uses—obviously, a very powerful one, as is its use of death, space, and the body—to keep concealed the truth about ourselves. This truth of course is that we are eternal spirit. The ego would have us believe that our identity is our body bound by time and space. Thus, this body serves as a most effective smokescreen, distracting our attention from the mind, where we truly are.

Time neither takes away nor can restore. And yet you make strange use of it, as if the past had caused the present, which is but a consequence in which no change can be made possible because its cause has gone.

This of course is the traditional psychological point of view. For example, take again someone who believes he is having trouble as an adult because he was abandoned as a child. In effect, the basic premise here closes off all possibility of change because the cause is gone. No hope of healing can exist because the deed is done and the past cannot be changed. Within the dream, the abandonment did in fact happen. And so since the past cannot be undone, the man is stuck: the innocent and hopeless victim as an adult of what went wrong in his childhood. And so there is actually nothing that he can do about his situation. Psychoanalytic theory is inherently pessimistic, because it teaches that there is no way out: the past cannot be changed. The best one can do is try to become "free" of some of the blocks (hurtful and painful memories). However, we still remain within a closed system in which the past does have real effects.

That same model also holds on an unconscious cosmic level, where we say that our sins against God are real, and there is nothing we can do about it. That is the central stone in the ego's foundation: there is nothing we can do about our sinfulness. We cannot change what the ego has made to be reality; we cannot change our individual bodies, the laws of nature, the laws of the world. We are, for all intents and purposes, totally powerless.

This hopelessness is the context of the manual's references to the dreariness of the world and the weary march of time (manual, p. 3; M-1.4:4-5). We feel as if we are stuck in a prison house, the cause of which is now gone, and so cannot be changed. Listening to the ego's voice, we believe that the past has caused the present, and that the present now is the effect of the past. So in this larger metaphysical view, the ancient past of our sin of separation against God has caused all the problems of the present. It caused this world, the body, and all the attendant problems. And so this world is the consequence or effect, and no change is ever possible because the cause is gone: it has already happened in the past.

Finally, when *A Course in Miracles* says that the cause or the past is gone, it means something quite different from what the ego means. The past is gone because it never happened; it was never there in the first place. This is the major difference between these two approaches, and within it lies the difference between Heaven and hell.

Yet change must have a cause that will endure, or else it will not last. No change can be made in the present if its

cause is past. Only the past is held in memory as you make use of it, and so it is a way to hold the past against the now.

If there is going to be change, and ultimately the mind is the only place where we can have true change, it must be on the level of the cause. The ego tells us that the cause is already finished. You cannot change the cause that has already happened, so therefore you are stuck with the consequences or the effect. On the other hand, Jesus is teaching us that the only way we can change something is by changing the cause, the belief that we have separated from God. That change can occur only within the mind, because that is where the belief "resides," and it is this *belief* that is the problem. *A Course in Miracles* helps us make another choice by returning us to that ancient moment when we chose to believe we could be separate from God. We do that in the context of our relationships with each other, precisely because it is within this context that we relive that ancient moment over and over again.

Remember nothing that you taught yourself, for you were badly taught. And who would keep a senseless lesson in his mind, when he can learn and can preserve a better one?

This is another way of looking at the Course's fundamental purpose of teaching us that we have learned senseless lessons that make us suffer, and that our suffering comes about, not because it simply has happened to us, but because we have *chosen* to suffer, to learn these senseless lessons. But there is another Teacher in our minds who will teach us different ones. Ultimately this means that there is a Teacher in our minds who will remind us that we should choose His tapes. This theme of choosing another Teacher appears frequently in *A Course in Miracles*. I like to combine a phrase from this passage with an earlier statement in the text (p. 211; T-12.V.8:3), so that it reads thus: "Resign now as your own teacher, for you were badly taught."

When ancient memories of hate appear, remember that their cause is gone. And so you cannot understand what they are for.

Jesus is now telling us that whenever we feel ourselves getting angry at someone, the anger and the hatred are really coming from this ancient hatred that we are just re-experiencing over and over again. All we have to remember is that the cause is gone. The cause was the sin of being separate and that thought has already been undone. In terms of our experience, this translates into my no longer seeing you as an enemy who is separate from me; I see you as my brother and friend, joined with me. As the text says earlier:

> In separation from your brother was the first attack upon yourself begun. And it is this the world bears witness to (text, p. 540; T-27.VII.6:4-5).

Therefore, it is when we share the common interest of salvation and join with our brothers, originally perceived as separate from us, that we undo the cause of separation.

Let not the cause that you would give them now be what it was that made them what they were, or seemed to be. Be glad that it is gone, for this is what you would be pardoned from.

The "cause" is the reliving of that ancient instant of being separate, and "them" refers back to the ancient memories. In other words, Jesus is asking us not to make the error of separation real. We would be pardoned from, or forgiven for, our sin of being separate. Whenever we are upset we are really bringing to mind this ancient memory which is inherently causeless; its cause was undone in that very instant when it seemed to happen.

And see, instead, the new effects of cause accepted _now_, with consequences _here_. They will surprise you with their loveliness. The ancient new ideas they bring will be the

happy consequences of a Cause so ancient that it far exceeds the span of memory which your perception sees.

This passage was written in 1967, about the time that the Gestalt psychology emphasis on living in the "here and now" began to become popular. The "cause accepted *now*" would be the Holy Spirit's Atonement principle, with consequences of joy and peace experienced now. It is what *A Course in Miracles* refers to as the forgiven or real world, which contains such loveliness in it:

> Can you imagine how beautiful those you forgive will look to you? In no fantasy have you ever seen anything so lovely. Nothing you see here, sleeping or waking, comes near to such loveliness....For you will see the Son of God. You will behold the beauty the Holy Spirit loves to look upon, and which He thanks the Father for.... This loveliness is not a fantasy. It is the real world, bright and clean and new, with everything sparkling under the open sun (text, p. 328; T-17.II.1:1-3,6-7; 2:1-2).

Or in Miranda's words from Shakespeare's "The Tempest":

> O wonder
> How many goodly creatures are there here!
> How beauteous mankind is! O brave new world,
> That has such people in't. (V,i)

This loveliness, of course, is not anything external, but rather comes from the *inner* experience of the loveliness of Christ, our Identity and all our brothers' as well. The "new" ideas, such as peace, joy, and love, are ancient because they reflect the Atonement principle, which occurred in that one instant. Thus they reflect the eternal nature of Heaven. They are new only because they *seem* to be such in our experience; new to our remembering, although in truth they were always there.

This is the Cause [the capitalization tells us that this is God] the Holy Spirit has remembered for you, when you would forget.

When we forget God and find ourselves becoming upset, for example, we can remember to ask the Holy Spirit to be *present* to us. At once—in whatever form the experience would speak to us—we feel His gentle hand tapping us on the shoulder, saying: "My brother, choose again. There is no need to continue to see yourself as separate, and attack someone else; you no longer have to protect your guilt by projecting it onto another. There is no cause of guilt within you, as the thought of sin has already been undone." Thus do we let the Holy Spirit awaken us from the dream, as we welcome God's Love back into our forgetful mind. The *cause* of our upset—the separation from God—has been undone through our joining with His Love through the Holy Spirit, and through that joining are all the effects undone as well.

It [the Cause] is not past because He let It not be unremembered. It has never changed, because there never was a time in which He did not keep It safely in your mind. Its consequences will indeed seem new, because you thought that you remembered not their Cause.

The state of being with God is always present because the Holy Spirit has never let it leave our memory, as He is in truth this memory of God's Love. The memory is within our minds, and because it is, there is a part of us that does remember that we have never really left our Father's House. Even though our split minds may continue to dissociate this Love and play only the ego tapes, still are the Holy Spirit's within our minds as well. His Love patiently awaits the time when we accept what He has already accepted for us. When we suddenly have an experience of God's Love, it will seem to be totally new. Yet all that has happened is that we were suddenly able to release our fingers from the ego's wrong-minded button, and finally play a tape in which God's Love would appear. That tape was always held for us by the Holy Spirit. This thought parallels an earlier one in the text, where Jesus says that he has saved all our loving thoughts and kindnesses and kept them for us in their perfect radiance (text, p. 76; T-5.IV.8:1-4). The experience will thus appear new to us even though it really is not. *Nothing* is new.

Yet was It never absent from your mind, for it was not your Father's Will that He be unremembered by His Son.

The Father's Will is manifested in our mind through the Holy Spirit, and that is the link back to Him. Thus, there is always a part of our minds—the decision maker—that can choose to remember what the Holy Spirit is holding for us. God's Will is simply the expression of the truth of His Being, and Christ's Being joined with His: Father and Son, God and Christ, can never be separated, nor forgotten one by the other.

What *you* remember never was. It came from causelessness which you confused with cause. It can deserve but laughter, when you learn you have remembered consequences that were causeless and could never be effects.

The "you" here is the decision maker or observer in our minds, which has chosen to identify with the ego. The ego would have us remember all the sins of the past, which never were to begin with. Thus, what we remember—pain, sorrow, and misery—are the effects of their cause, sin. We are now being taught, however, that sin has had no effects, being without a cause. Sin merely came from a silly thought—"a tiny, mad idea"—in our minds that was undone the instant that it seemed to occur.

The cause-effect idea, simply stated again, is that if something is not an effect it cannot have a cause, and if there is no cause it cannot exist. Our experiences in this world consist of our continual attempts to teach ourselves that sin is real, a cause with the very real effect of misery that proves that sin is so. But we could just as easily play a different tape in which happiness instead of misery is the effect, showing us that sin had no effects at all. Another way of stating this is that the world is causeless. The seeming cause of sin was undone and corrected in the same instant in which it seemed to come into existence. Thus, the idea that we could actually sin against our Source is so preposterous, that we could only laugh at the silliness of it all. To quote this important passage a third time:

> Together, we [Jesus and ourselves] can laugh them [the separation thought and its seeming effects] both away, and understand that time cannot intrude upon eternity. It is a joke to think that time can come to circumvent eternity, which *means* there is no time (text, p. 544; T-27.VIII.6:4-5).

Thus, at last, with Jesus' love beside us we do remember to laugh.

The miracle reminds you of a Cause [God] forever present, perfectly untouched by time and interference. Never changed from what It is. And you are Its effect, as changeless and as perfect as Itself. Its memory does not lie in the past, nor waits the future. It is not revealed in miracles. They but remind you that It has not gone. When you forgive It for your sins, It will no longer be denied.

Once again, the miracle does nothing. It does not bring to us the Love of God, because His Love is already in us. The miracle simply reminds us that, in truth, there is no real interference—i.e., sin—to the Love of God, and so we, as extensions of that Love, have never changed from our reality as Christ. In a wonderful early passage, Jesus makes the same point speaking of the Holy Spirit's role:

> The Voice of the Holy Spirit does not command, because it is incapable of arrogance. It does not demand, because it does not seek control. It does not overcome, because it does not attack. It merely reminds. It is compelling only because of what it reminds you *of* (text, p. 70; T-5.II.7:1-5).

You who have sought to lay a judgment on your own Creator cannot understand it is not He Who laid a judgment on His Son.

This is another way of saying that because we are so guilty we cannot begin to understand that it is not God's Will that we suffer. This is succinctly expressed in this statement closing a section on specialness: "Forgive your Father it was not His Will that you be crucified" (text, p. 471; T-24.III.8:13). It is impossible for our ego selves to conceive that God does not choose to crucify or punish us, and of course this is what our egos hold against our loving Father. Our belief that we have sinned against Him leads us, due to the dynamic of projection, to believe He must attack us in return. It thus becomes impossible for us to believe that our sin, guilt, and fear of punishment is just a bad dream that we have made up. Since we have judged against Him in the dream, we must believe He will judge us too.

You would deny Him His Effects, yet have They never been denied.

A Course in Miracles states that God is First Cause and all of us, as Christ, are the Effects of this First Cause. Moreover, as we have already seen, there is nowhere where God ends and we begin. However, the intent of that tiny, mad idea of separation was to deny that God was First Cause, and that we ourselves were His Effects. Thus the Son of God has become the self split off from its Source, his own origin as it were, with cause and effect now the same:

> The ego believes it is completely on its own, which is merely another way of describing how it thinks it originated....The ego is the mind's belief that it is completely on its own (text, p. 53; T-4.II.8:1,4).

There was no time in which His Son could be condemned for what was causeless and against His [God's] Will. What your remembering would witness to is but the fear of God.

109

He has not done the thing you fear. No more have you. And so your innocence has not been lost.

How can God condemn us for the thought of separation, which the Atonement principle states clearly has never happened? The truth remains that we are still as God created us, and that His Will and ours are one. It was our split mind that made up the drama of the separation and the emotion of fear. The ego would have us believe that we have really accomplished the impossible by separating from our Source. This is what the ego thought system witnesses to, and if we identify with the ego we will fear God's retaliation. What Jesus reminds us of here is that we are innocent, the drama is make-believe, and therefore we have nothing to fear.

You need no healing to be healed. In quietness, see in the miracle a lesson in allowing Cause to have Its Own Effects, and doing nothing that would interfere.

That most important teaching with which this section opened, and which appears many other times in the material, is restated here: the miracle does not do anything; healing does not do anything; neither does forgiveness nor salvation. They merely correct the mistaken *belief* in separation, restoring to our minds the awareness of what always was and is. Thus, we do not have to be healed because we *are* healed. There has never *been* anything in us that needed healing. Our belief in sin was nothing more than a bad dream. Thus, "allowing Cause to have Its Own Effects" and not interfering, means acknowledging that the ego in all its grandiosity has never, and *can* never usurp God as First Cause. Therefore we still remain as God created us—His Effect forever and forever. In the quietness of our minds we remember our Cause—"The memory of God comes to the quiet mind" (text, p. 452; T-23.I.1:1). The ego's raucous shrieking is finally chosen against, and the interference to remembering our Creator is gone, as we now see:

The miracle comes quietly into the mind that stops an instant and is still.

We can see how the whole tone of the section changes, mirroring the peace that comes when we choose to forgive instead of condemn, when we choose the gentle quiet of the Holy Spirit's peace over the cacophonous sounds of the ego's war. All we need do is to stop an instant and be still, to stop replaying the ego tapes and replay instead the Holy Spirit's gentle tapes of correction. Let me just mention, again, that in talking about tapes, kaleidoscopes, and holograms, I am merely using symbols. In reality of course there are no tapes, etc., but these symbols are the closest we can come, in terms of our current experience, to reflecting what seems to be happening in our minds. Thus we are talking about symbols as if they were real; it is always helpful in this regard to recall the statement from the manual "that words are but symbols of symbols. They are thus twice removed from reality" (manual, p. 51; M-21.1:9-10).

It [the miracle] reaches gently from that quiet time, and from the mind it healed in quiet then, to other minds to share its quietness. And they will join in doing nothing to prevent its radiant extension back into the Mind Which caused all minds to be.

This refers to the extension of the miracle which is not our responsibility. Our responsibility is simply to choose the quietness of the miracle in our minds, and then the Holy Spirit or Jesus takes that quiet and extends it to all minds, since minds are joined. As the text states:

> The only way to heal is to be healed. The miracle extends without your help, but you are needed that it can begin. Accept the miracle of healing, and it will go forth because of what it is. It is its nature to extend itself the instant it is born. And it is born the instant it is offered and received. No one can ask another to be healed. But he can let *himself* be healed,

and thus offer the other what he has received....Leave, then, the transfer of your learning [to heal] to the One Who really understands its laws, and Who will guarantee that they remain unviolated and unlimited. Your part is merely to apply what He has taught you to yourself, and He will do the rest (text, pp. 535, 537; T-27.V.1:1-7; 10:1-2).

The minds of the entire Sonship, which will accept the extension of the healing of an individual mind, will then extend back into the Mind of God—Creator and Cause of all minds. This is reminiscent of the workbook lesson referred to earlier, "When I am healed I am not healed alone" (workbook, pp. 254-56; W-pI.137), and the Course's image of the circle of Atonement (text, pp. 262-64; T-14.V).

Born out of sharing [joining with others in forgiveness], there can be no pause in time to cause the miracle delay in hastening to all unquiet minds, and bringing them an instant's stillness, when the memory of God returns to them. Their own remembering is quiet now, and what has come to take its place will not be wholly unremembered afterwards.

Elsewhere the text talks about *our belief* that an enormous amount of time is necessary between the time we choose forgiveness and when our minds are finally healed (text, pp. 280,519; T-15.I.2:1; T-26.VIII.1:1; 3:1-2). Thus, Jesus is reiterating that the miracle occurs in an instant. It does not take any time because there is no time, but it appears to do so because we are still trapped in the illusion. In reality, however, in the instant that we forgive, all minds are joined and healed with us. Because our minds are already joined, all that we have done is remove the barrier to the awareness of that reality. That is why it occurs in an instant, when the decision maker makes another choice.

Once we have experienced what it feels like to join truly with someone, rather than continually to attack, we can never totally lose that experience. No matter how we may try to fight it, the fact that we have had the experience of true peace that comes from forgiveness means that we can nevermore choose the ego one hundred percent of the time, despite our fear of identifying with God's Love: His Love will nevermore be "wholly unremembered."

He to Whom [the Holy Spirit] time is given offers thanks for every quiet instant given Him. For in that instant is God's memory allowed to offer all its treasures to the Son of God, for whom they have been kept. How gladly does He offer them unto the one for whom He has been given them! And His Creator [God] shares His thanks, because He would not be deprived of His Effects.

The Holy Spirit is holding all those treasures (e.g., peace, joy, love, totality, eternity) for us, awaiting the instant when we (the observer) would choose them. To see the face of Christ in each other is the Course's symbol of forgiveness, and it is through forgiveness that all the barriers of guilt in our minds are removed. What then remains is the memory of God that has been held in place by the Holy Spirit. This could be seen as the closest the Course comes to an actual formula, succinctly describing the process of forgiveness: we see the face of Christ in our brother, and then the memory of God dawns upon our minds.

The passage refers to the Holy Spirit's gladness in offering us all that has been given Him by God, Who in turn shares His gratitude. Jesus of course is speaking metaphorically about God offering His thanks to us for accepting the truth that we are forever His Effect: God has no dualistic mind that could offer thanks to another. Rather, the passage refers to the gratitude *our* split minds experience in learning that God is not angry because of what we believe we have done to Him. His "gratitude" is the expression of His Love that remains the unity it was and always will be, and which we now accept.

The instant's silence that His Son accepts gives welcome to eternity and Him [God], and lets Them enter where They would abide. For in that instant does the Son of God do nothing that would make himself afraid.

"They" and "Them" refer to Christ (the Son of God) and God, which is why the words are capitalized. This is the same usage found in the section in Chapter 26, "For They Have Come" (text, pp. 521-22; T-26.IX). Therefore, in the presence of God's Love all fear automatically disappears. Recall the text's earlier citation of the biblical statement "Perfect love casts out fear" (text, p. 12; T-1.VI.5:4).

The "instant" mentioned here is the holy instant, but not just the holy instant when we choose a miracle instead of a grievance. We find here a more cosmic sense to its meaning, referring to the one great holy instant when we totally forgive, and then the memory of God dawns upon our minds. This is equivalent to the attainment of the real world, which comes when we cease choosing those thoughts that have kept us afraid.

How instantly the memory of God arises in the mind that has no fear to keep the memory away! Its own remembering has gone.

Here, time is spoken about differently from its more common usage in the text. The main point in this passage is that the entire ego world can disappear in one instant. When we totally forgive, all illusions—our veils of guilt—will disappear at the same time. At that point the memory of God's Love dawns upon our minds. The purpose of all fear, of course, is to prevent this memory from returning to us. Without fear, everything that constitutes ego thinking in the mind has vanished. Once the observer in our split minds chooses to identify with the Holy Spirit, there is no longer any purpose in remembering the ego's thought of separation, which we now know never was. Thus the thought disappears, as *A Course in Miracles* says in another context, previously quoted, back into "the nothingness from which it came" (manual, p. 32; M-13.1:2).

There is no past to keep its [remembering] fearful image in the way of glad awakening to present peace. The trumpets of eternity resound throughout the stillness, yet disturb it not. And what is now remembered is not fear, but rather is the Cause that fear was made to render unremembered and undone. The stillness speaks in gentle sounds of love the Son of God remembers from before his own remembering came in between the present and the past, to shut them out.

With fear gone, all that remains in our minds is the memory of God, held there for us by the Holy Spirit, and at this point we begin to hear the "trumpets of eternity resound." It is really the heralding of our return home, now that our fear has been undone and we have let go of all bitter memories. What is left, again, is the memory of God. As we have seen, the purpose of fear and guilt is to be a defense, smokescreen, or distraction that keeps from us the memory of our real Cause, God. The ego tells us that our real cause is the ego itself, and what keeps us believing its lies is the idea that God is to be feared. This is how the ego uses memory, reminding us of our sins and justifying the guilt and fear that keeps the Love of God away from us. In the midst of that painful memory, the Holy Spirit was "placed" to retain for us the memory of our true thoughts of the Love of God: "In crucifixion is redemption laid" (text, p. 518; T-26.VII.17:1). Now that fear is gone, all that remains is the Love that the Holy Spirit has held for us.

Now is the Son of God at last aware of present Cause and Its benign effects.

This contrasts the Holy Spirit's use of memory, which focuses only in the present, with the ego's use of memory, which is focused only on the past. The Cause, *our Cause*, is in the present. As the Course says in several other places:

The only aspect of time that is eternal is *now* (text, p. 73; T-5.III.6:5).

His [the Holy Spirit] emphasis is therefore on the only aspect of time that can extend to the infinite, for *now* is the closest approximation of eternity that this world offers (text, p. 230; T-13.IV.7:5).

The present now remains the only time. Here in the present is the world set free (workbook, p. 236; W-pI.132.3:1-2).

LESSON 308
"This instant is the only time there is."

I have conceived of time in such a way that I defeat my aim. If I elect to reach past time to timelessness, I must change my perception of what time is for. Time's purpose cannot be to keep the past and future one. The only interval in which I can be saved from time is now. For in this instant has forgiveness come to set me free. The birth of Christ is now, without a past or future. He has come to give His present blessing to the world, restoring it to timelessness and love. And love is ever-present, here and now.

"Thanks for this instant, Father. It is now I am redeemed. This instant is the time You have appointed for Your Son's release, and for salvation of the world in him" (workbook, p. 443; W-pII.308.2).

The substitute for, and the defense against that present instant are our past memories, whose effects are certainly not benign: guilt, fear, punishment, suffering, sacrifice, and death. The effects of God as Cause are truly benign: peace, joy, happiness, and eternal life.

Now does he understand what he has made is causeless, having no effects at all. He has done nothing. And in seeing this, he understands he never had a need for doing anything, and never did.

This assertion is based on the cause-effect principle mentioned earlier. If what I believe I did has had no effect, then that shows that I could not have done it in the first place. If sin has no effect, i.e., if there is no punishment, no fear of death, then their seeming cause must be non-existent as well. Thus, what the ego has made is truly nothing because the effects, i.e., fear and hatred, have been undone for us by the Holy Spirit. Since there no longer are effects, their cause must be gone as well, since a cause cannot be a cause unless it produced effects.

Once this principle is accepted, we understand that we do not have to solve problems on our own. God, symbolically speaking, has already solved the problem by showing us through His Holy Spirit that there is nothing that has to be resolved. The ego tells us there *is* a problem, which ultimately is one of scarcity or guilt. This problem, we are warned by the ego, must be resolved. And so we are first impelled to make up a world, and then to do things in the world with our bodies or to other people's bodies. The basis of this ego approach is the belief that sin, as cause, is real, and therefore has to be atoned for and undone. Jesus is pointing out to us that nothing needs to be done, because there is no problem that has to be solved. There is no sin as cause, and therefore no effects that need to be defended against.

His Cause *is* Its Effects. There never was a cause beside It that could generate a different past or future. Its Effects are changelessly eternal, beyond fear, and past the world of sin entirely.

The Son of God's Cause is God, Whose Effects are His Son. We can also say that if our Cause (God) is Love, then the effect of Love would be the Love of the Son of God, which is his true Identity. If we say that our Cause is Truth, then the effect of Truth would be our own Truth, our Identity as Christ. In other words, there can be nothing in the Effect which is not in the Cause. Therefore, the Son cannot be different from his

Father in attributes, except that God is First Cause, and we as Christ are His Effect. That is the meaning of the biblical phrase Jesus quotes in the text: "I and my Father are one" (text, p. 5; T-1.II.4:7).

Listening to our egos, however, we believe, that there *was* a cause besides God, and that cause was the ego itself, which predicates its existence on the belief in sin, which in turn leads to guilt. Guilt engenders both concern over the past and fear of the future. This is generated by a single cause: the belief in separation or sin. These passages are teaching us, however, that everything of the ego has disappeared because there could never be a Cause other than God. This is how we know that God did not create this world. Nothing here is changeless, nor eternal; and, as we all know, there are elements of fear associated with everything in this world of separation and sin.

What has been lost, to see the causeless not? And where is sacrifice, when memory of God has come to take the place of loss? What better way to close the little gap between illusions and reality than to allow the memory of God to flow across it, making it a bridge an instant will suffice to reach beyond? For God has closed it with Himself.

From the ego's point of view, something indeed has been lost—a belief which is the origin of the scarcity principle—and we shall never retrieve it. In truth, all we have lost is the *awareness* of the innocence of Christ, to which our sinfulness testifies, we believe. We then believe that we must atone through sacrifice for that loss, brought about by our sin. Thus, sacrifice becomes a special bargain with God to win back His Love. When the memory of God dawns upon our minds, which is now washed clean by forgiveness, all pain and loss disappear and we perceive the causeless no longer.

The image of a bridge is a prominent symbol in the Course, and sometimes refers to the bridge between this world and the real world. Here, however, it refers to the bridge between perception and reality, and it is the Holy Spirit Who carries us across that bridge. The memory of God's Love—the Holy Spirit—present in that seeming instant of separation, closed the illusory gap between God and His Son. This is discussed again in "The Closing of the Gap" (text, pp. 563-65; T-29.I).

His memory has not gone by, and left a stranded Son forever on a shore where he can glimpse another shore that he can never reach. His Father wills that he be lifted up and gently carried over. He has built the bridge [the Holy Spirit], and it is He Who will transport His Son across it. Have no fear that He will fail in what He wills. Nor that you be excluded from the Will that is for you.

Earlier I talked about the image Helen had of the shore that is our home—Heaven—but that we dream we are on a distant shore. This metaphor made it clear that our dreaming of exile has no effect on the truth of where we really are. Here in this passage the same image of a shore is used, but now the other way around: God would never leave us stranded on a shore with no way of returning home. Yet our belief is that we are hopelessly caught up in this world with no way of getting back. As *A Course in Miracles* states earlier:

Everyone is free to refuse to accept his inheritance, but he is not free to establish what his inheritance is (text, p. 44; T-3.VI.10:2).

What carries us across the bridge are the forgiveness lessons that the Holy Spirit teaches us through the miracle, the principal subject of Part II. At that point, having totally forgiven everyone, God takes the last step and carries us home. We will return to "God's last step" in Part III.

PART II

THE PLAN OF THE ATONEMENT: THE MIRACLE

INTRODUCTION TO PART II

Most of our discussion in this part will reflect the second level on which *A Course in Miracles* is written, and on this level, as we have seen, the Course gives us a view of time quite different from the metaphysical statements belonging to the first level. On Level Two, time is viewed as linear and we shall see this especially when we consider some of the passages on the miracle. This is not, as we have already discussed, because time *is* linear, but rather because we experience it that way. Because we do, we experience the Holy Spirit's working through us linearly as well. We will see this theme running through most of the passages we will be examining, namely that the Holy Spirit meets us where we are so that He can teach us what truth is. It is in seeking to understand these passages apart from the Level Two context that students often become confused about what *A Course in Miracles* is truly saying.

Thus, in many places the implication seems to be that time is linear—past, present, and future—and that saving time is a major concern. The Course says, for example, in the context of other spiritual paths:

> Many have spent a lifetime in preparation, and have indeed achieved their instants of success. This course does not attempt to teach more than they learned in time, but it does aim at saving time....Your way will be different, not in purpose but in means. A holy relationship is a means of saving time....Time has been saved for you because you and your brother are together. This is the special means this course is using to save you time....Save time for me [Jesus] by only this one preparation, and practice doing nothing else. "I need do nothing" [the theme of the section] is a statement of allegiance, a truly undivided loyalty. Believe it for just one instant, and you will accomplish more than is given to a century

of contemplation, or of struggle against temptation (text, pp. 362-63; T-18.VII.4:4-5; 5:1-2; 6:3-4,6-8).

This emphasis on saving time seems to contradict the view that time is illusory and non-linear that we have already stressed in Part I. As we shall see, however, it is not that *A Course in Miracles* is contradicting itself; rather, Jesus is meeting us where we are, within the illusion of time and its attendant pain. I shall return to this passage shortly.

In Part II, I have drawn together several different places in the Course which reflect its view of time in relation to the miracle and the Atonement. We will study selected passages rather than whole sections.

Chapter 5

THE PLAN OF *A COURSE IN MIRACLES*

We begin with paragraphs two and four of the section "Who Are God's Teachers?" in the manual for teachers (p. 3; M-1.2,4). These paragraphs, and another passage I shall read from the text, constitute an introduction to Part II, insofar as they talk about the overall plan.

They come from all over the world. They come from all religions and from no religion.

"They" refers to the teachers of God. Actually, it is only in the manual that the phrase "teachers of God" appears, although the term is implicit in the text and workbook, referring to students of *A Course in Miracles*. "A teacher of God is anyone who chooses to be one" (manual, p. 3; M-1.1:1), and as the Course often explains, we are both teachers and pupils at the same time. As a point of clarification, Jesus certainly does not mean by "teacher" someone who is teaching a class, leading a workshop, or writing a book. A "teacher" can be any of us, once we choose to teach the forgiveness lessons of the Holy Spirit that we would learn.

It is quite obvious here, as in other places, that while *A Course in Miracles* most definitely contains a religious thought system, it is not a religion, i.e., a formalized religious institution. A person could be truly religious as the Course means it, and not be a member of an organized religion, nor even believe in God in a conceptual sense. As the "Psychotherapy" pamphlet states in a section entitled "The Role of Religion in Psychotherapy": "Nor is belief in God a really meaningful concept..." ("Psychotherapy," p. 5; P-2.II.4:4). Theists and atheists, let alone agnostics, simply reflect belief systems, or forms, which may or may not share the love which alone is the content of true religion. In this world, love is reflected by forgiveness which, again, is defined in the Course as sharing with another the common interest of salvation:

> His [a teacher of God's] qualifications consist solely in this; somehow, somewhere he has made a deliberate choice in which he did not see his interests as apart from someone else's (manual, p. 3; M-1.1:1-2).

They are the ones who have answered. The Call is universal. It goes on all the time everywhere. It calls for teachers to speak for It and redeem the world.

If we think about our image in chart 3 of the observer sitting in front of a TV screen observing what has already gone by, the Holy Spirit represents this Call (that is why it is capitalized here). He is continually speaking to us in our minds, where He is present as we experience ourselves within the linear dimension of time and space. This Call is an appeal to us to learn and teach the world that there is no sin, the separation from God never truly happened, and that what we believe is reality is nothing more than a dream. This teaching, clearly, has nothing to do with form, but with the sharing of its content through our daily and ongoing practice of forgiveness.

Many hear It, but few will answer.

This of course is taken from the gospel statement, "Many are called, but few are chosen" (Mt 22:14). Jesus corrects this in the text when he says: "All are called but few choose to listen" (text, p. 39; T-3.IV.7:12). This is important: "few will answer." It is a common misconception among people who work with *A Course in Miracles*, or other spiritual paths for that matter, that simply because they consciously wish to practice spiritual principles that they have already done so. Lesson 185, "I want the peace of God," begins with the line, "To say these words is nothing. But to mean these words is everything" (workbook, p. 339; W-pI.185.1:1-2). Similarly, people could believe they are choosing to hear the Call and answering It, but they are really not doing that at all. As I have said many other times, this is not an easy path. It is humbling for a student of *A Course in Miracles* to reread the statement from the manual for teachers: "Only very few can hear God's Voice at all…" (manual, p. 30; M-12.3:3).

Yet it is all a matter of time. Everyone will answer in the end, but the end can be a long, long way off. It is because of this that the plan of the teachers was established. Their function is to save time.

In the end everyone will answer, because as we have seen everyone has already answered; in the moment that the separation occurred, in that same moment it was undone. But the end, in terms of our experience, can be a "long, long way off" and that refers to the time when everyone who is observing the screen of ego projections finally recognizes that it is nothing more than a dream. The ego drama is like a Cecil B. DeMille epic, which in our experience here goes on and on and on. This idea, that the end can be a long way off, will be reiterated in a passage dealing with the Last Judgment, which we shall discuss in Part III.

We have already seen that one of the claims *A Course in Miracles* makes for itself is that it will save us time. "The plan of the teachers" is to have more and more people hear the Holy Spirit's Call, and respond to it by joining with each other. That is what undoes the belief in separation. As people teach this lesson of forgiveness, it is reinforced within themselves.

Each one begins as a single light, but with the Call at its center it is a light that cannot be limited. And each one saves a thousand years of time as the world judges it. To the Call Itself time has no meaning.

This is another example of how *A Course in Miracles* is presented on two levels. A thousand years is saved, within our experience of time as linear. We shall see a little later, when we talk about the miracle, how that same idea is repeated. Thus, we are speaking of time as the world judges it. In reality, of course, there is no time that has to be saved, which is what the last line says. To the Holy Spirit, who is outside of time, its saving has no meaning. Yet He speaks to us about time—past, present, and future—as we experience it, because that is how our split mind works. The preceding line acknowledges that it seems as if we are working on our own, individually; but the passage continues by pointing out that since our minds are joined, the light that I let shine into my mind shines out to the entire Sonship. Since it is the Holy Spirit who extends that light through me, it has no limit. Let us skip now to paragraph four.

This is a manual for a special curriculum, intended for teachers of a special form of the universal course. There are many thousands of other forms, all with the same outcome.

The instruction given here is very important, for it can help prevent students of *A Course in Miracles* from making the common mistake of spiritual specialness. It is very clear that the Course is only one form among *many thousands* of other spiritual paths, all of which are part of the universal course: the Holy Spirit's basic course that teaches that we are all one, and that the separation from God has never happened. This is taught in many different ways, and *A Course in Miracles* is presenting one of these ways. If we resonate to its teaching, it becomes our path; if not, we can find another.

They merely save time. Yet it is time alone that winds on wearily, and the world is very tired now. It is old and worn and without hope.

The purpose of any path is to save time. In the present context this means to save the time in which we, as the observer, sit in front of the screen, "reviewing mentally what has gone by" (workbook, p. 291; W-pI.158.4:5). Thus, the thousand years *A Course in Miracles* frequently refers to as our time-saving, is really the time we save in *re*viewing these ancient videos we once believed were real.

Within the dimension of linear time, however, our time does wind on wearily, despite our attempts to disguise this pain through special relationships. Thus, this is a very clear statement of what most people in the world feel, if they opened themselves to it. Situations in the world seem to get worse and worse, problems become more complicated and seemingly insoluble. This is certainly true of political, social, economic, and environmental situations, let alone individual ones. The world seems to go on and on, without any hope of a way out of the pain. In the context of chart 3, we understand this as our continuing to replay old tapes, with one being worse than the other. We persist in this *re*viewing because there is a part of us that does not want to awaken from the dream, and so we use the "reality" of the dream as a defense against God's Love, which the ego has counseled would destroy us if we ever returned to it.

There was never a question of outcome, for what can change the Will of God? But time, with its illusions of change and death, wears out the world and all things in it. Yet time has an ending, and it is this that the teachers of God are appointed to bring about. For time is in their hands. Such was their choice, and it is given them.

In reality, there is no real hopelessness or despair here because the world has already ended. But that obviously is not our experience. And so Jesus reminds us in the text: "Be patient a while and remember that the outcome is as certain as God" (text, p. 52; T-4.II.5:8). That statement clearly implies a future event, as does the passage here in the manual. In reality, though, all that will be brought about is our awakening from the dream of the past, into the eternal present of God. The "choice" that is referred to is *when* people will choose to awaken from the dream. In other words, they can choose when they will press the right-minded button instead of the wrong-minded one, and choose finally to view and experience only happy dreams. Quoting again from the introduction to the text, we recall that free will "means only that you can elect what you want to take at a given time" (text, intro.; T-in.1:5).

Now let us turn to the text, the section "I Need Do Nothing" (text, p. 362; T-18.VII). The context of the segment we will look at is the Course's representation of itself as only one spiritual path. In its form, it is distinctive in comparison to other paths that emphasize long periods of contemplation and meditation. Such is not *its* path, however. While no judgment of others is intended, Jesus does claim that the Course will work more quickly than others.

Our basic problem is understood by *A Course in Miracles* as unconscious guilt, the hidden belief in sin, and nothing brings this to the surface more quickly than another person. It is in our relationships, as we all know, that our buttons get pushed the most strongly, and our sleeping guilt, now aroused, is inevitably projected onto others. Thus are we provided with the opportunity of forgiving it. If we see our guilt in another person, we can then deal with what has been unconscious in ourselves. This is the basis for the claim that *A Course in Miracles* saves time. We will discuss other aspects of this as we go along.

Before proceeding, let me say a couple of words about the Course's view of meditation, since that topic does come up in this section of the text. *A Course in Miracles* is certainly not against meditation; in fact, the workbook can be seen as a mind-training program to help students meditate as they set out on the first year's journey with the Course, "a beginning, not an end" (workbook, p. 477; W-ep.1:1). But meditation is certainly not the Course's basic thrust. Rather, its process is to have us become aware and attuned to the presence of the Holy Spirit so that we experience Him throughout the day, most especially when we are tempted to become upset by what someone else does or fails to do, or by some problematic situation in which we find ourselves.

Certainly, beginning each day by meditating or praying, and ending each day in similar fashion, thinking of God as often as we can in between—all of which the Course suggests we do—can help us quiet our minds. But simply doing that alone, without bringing the presence of the Holy Spirit or Jesus with us into our day, will not awaken us from the dream in which we have cloaked ourselves. The difference between these two approaches therefore can be seen in terms of understanding what meditation is.

Though not necessarily, meditation can reinforce a separation of the inner and the outer, since traditional meditation separates us from the everyday world, leading us to retreat, as it were, into our minds. The world is thus experienced as sinful at worst and distracting at best, as we seek to enter into a quiet space to be alone with God, or whoever the Ultimate is conceived as being. And thus is the world of sin made real, as is implied midway through the fourth paragraph in this section (text, p. 363; T-18.VII.4:6-11).

The purpose of the Course, however, is to help us realize that the inner and the outer are not truly separate, and one does not have to physically withdraw from the world in order to be close to God or to practice His message. The basic goal of *A Course in Miracles*, therefore, is to have us feel the Holy Spirit's presence and to remember His message throughout the day. That does not mean, of course, that if we find long periods of meditation personally helpful that we should stop; that would be foolish. Meditation is not the Course process, but neither is it antithetical to the Course as long as it does not foster separation of the world from our thoughts. Anything that brings us closer to the Holy Spirit, enabling us to live a more loving and peaceful life in the world, cannot be deleterious. But if meditation is not our particular form, there is nothing in *A Course in Miracles* that would argue for our meditating regularly, once the workbook's one-year training program is

complete. As with everything else, the "highly individualized" (manual, p. 67; M-29.2:6) curriculum of our lives is
guided by the Holy Spirit, and decisions should be left to His
Love.

Now let us look at the sixth paragraph in the section, "I
Need Do Nothing" (text, p. 363; T-18.VII.6), already cited in
the Introduction to this Part. The preceding line talks about the
happy realization that "I need do nothing," and this is the reference of the first sentence here:

**Here is the ultimate release which everyone will one day
find in his own way, at his own time. You do not need this
time. Time has been saved for you because you and your
brother are together. This is the special means this course
is using to save you time.**

Here the Course identifies the specific way in which it sees
itself as fitting into the plan of the Atonement. This way,
moreover, is the healing of relationships through forgiveness.
Focusing on relationships as our spiritual classroom saves
time, because as we have already briefly commented, and
shall discuss again with the miracle, other people seem to
bring to our awareness much of the guilt that otherwise would
take a considerably longer period of time to work through.

**You are not making use of the course if you insist on using
means which have served others well, neglecting what was
made for *you*.**

This parallels a statement of Jesus to Helen in the midst of
an angry judgment she was once making against someone
else: "Don't take another's path as your own, but neither
should you judge it."[8] In other words, simply because the

---

8. See my *Absence from Felicity: The Story of Helen Schucman and Her
Scribing of "A Course in Miracles,"* p. 450. Consult Related Material at the
end of this book for additional information.

Course works for you does not mean that you are better than another, or that the Course is better than that person's path. Your preference is simply a statement that this is the path with which you resonate. Another's path may be every bit as valid as yours.

Jesus is also cautioning us here about attempting to follow two spiritual paths simultaneously. While in principle it may be possible for a person to practice *A Course in Miracles* and pursue another path as well, it would usually be very difficult to do this without conflict. There are different spiritual paths because there are different needs, and one is not inherently better or worse than another. However, they are different, and so many of their ideas will conflict. For example, if you are assiduously dedicating yourself to one path, and then do the same with another path which contains thoughts which contradict those in the first, conflict is inevitable. The end result means that in order to harmonize the dissonance you will have to reinterpret certain ideas, not only of the Course, but of the other paths. Thus, a disservice is done to both spiritualities. It is thus possible that pursuing other paths along with the Course comes from an unconscious fear of what *A Course in Miracles* is teaching. Therefore you dilute the Course's message by focusing on another path, a subtle yet common ego technique of defending against its teachings. Thus, if we feel *A Course in Miracles* is our path, then that is what we should practice; that is where our dedication should be. And to reiterate an earlier point, if we believe after a while that the Course is not for us, then we shall find another path to follow.

Save time for me [Jesus] by only this one preparation, and practice doing nothing else.

Jesus is basically saying that the only preparation that we need is to accept that there is nothing we need do. We do not need to do any other elaborate rituals or practices. In fact, there are sections in the text preceding this one which state that we do not have to prepare ourselves for the holy instant (text, pp. 355,357; T-18.IV.1-5; T-18.V.2-3). Therefore, the only preparation that Jesus asks of us throughout *A Course in Miracles* is to recognize that "I need do nothing." This does not mean that *behaviorally* we do not do anything. The statement refers rather to the fact that we do not *have* to do anything because the problem has already been solved for us. Not only that, the statement also emphasizes that there is no problem outside of us that requires action; the problem is within our minds.

The ego sets up a world in which there are continual problems, and then we spend the rest of our time expending great effort trying to solve a problem that is in reality a pseudo-problem. This is one of the means used by the ego to keep us from realizing that there is only one problem, and that problem, again, is in our minds—our belief in separation.

"I need do nothing" is a statement of allegiance, a truly undivided loyalty. Believe it for just one instant, and you will accomplish more than is given to a century of contemplation, or of struggle against temptation.

This is a reference to our undivided loyalty to the content of *A Course in Miracles*. This loyalty can include Jesus, expressing our commitment to accepting his love and the specific means he has provided us to attain this. Moreover, as is explained in paragraph four of this section, we do not have to fight against sin through contemplation or struggles against external temptations. Since sin is nothing more than an illusory thought in our minds, we need simply change our minds by recognizing that we need do nothing because nothing happened that needs correction.

The two sections which we have just considered serve as an introduction to what *A Course in Miracles* sees as one of its major purposes: the saving of time through the healing of relationships. Discussion of this time-saving is the heart of Part II: the miracle and its role in the plan of the Atonement.

Chapter 6

THE MIRACLE

By way of introducing the concept of the miracle, I refer to chart 6, the spiral. This was part of a personal message Helen had received,[9] another way of Jesus' helping her understand the relationship between time and eternity. It is very similar to chart 5, but here the tiny dip now has become a spiral. It was explained to Helen that time was like a downward spiral that *seems* to break the solid line of eternity. In other words, the spiral represents the thought of separation which we believe has shattered Heaven. In reality that solid line is unbroken: Heaven is unchanged, as is its Son; the relationship between Creator and creation remains as unified as it always was. The spiral represents what we *believe* we accomplished. An advantage to seeing time as a spiral, instead of a tiny dip, is that the image lends itself to our experience of time's going on and on.

If we imagine ourselves at different points on the spiral the line looks different to us, suggesting that our view of Heaven and God are continually changing based upon where we believe we are: as always, projection makes perception. Along the spiral everything is a distortion of what truth is. This then represents the ego's first law of chaos, that truth is relative, and is different for everyone (text, p. 455; T-23.II.2:1-2). The "miracle," thus, pertains to the Holy Spirit's reinterpretation of our experience on that spiral in order to correct the misperceptions in our mind.

Thinking about some of the ways our brains automatically correct the distortions of the body will help in understanding what a miracle does on another level. Physiologically, our brains automatically correct distortions in what seems to be

---

9. For a more complete discussion of this message, see my *Absence from Felicity: The Story of Helen Schucman and Her Scribing of "A Course in Miracles,"* pp. 130-31. See Related Material at the end of this book.

the objective world. For instance, the image that is cast on our retina is really upside down, and our brain very early on in our earthly life corrects that error, so that instead of perceiving the world upside down we "perceive" it right side up. The misperceptions of the body are thus automatically corrected. Famous perceptual experiments on closure provide other examples: A group of circles is shown to a person, and one of the circles is incomplete, containing a tiny little break. Most people do not perceive the break and see the circle as whole. In reading a page in a book where the last word is "the" and the first word on the following page is also "the," most people will not perceive the double word, automatically correcting what they have seen. Having gone through the "agonies" of proofreading *A Course in Miracles*, I can attest to this. Only very recently was I told about an error that I had never even *seen*: the word "search" was spelled without an "r," but my brain automatically supplied the missing letter.

These examples of the brain's spontaneous corrections for the eye's misperceptions are analogous to how the Holy Spirit teaches us along the spiral. We are continually misperceiving Heaven and God, because we make Him into an image of our punitive egos. The Holy Spirit therefore teaches us to forgive, correcting our misperceptions of God and each other.

We begin our study of the miracle and the plan of the Atonement with a brief reflection on that lovely summary in the workbook defining a miracle (p. 463; W-pII.13). As we read this, it would be helpful to keep in mind the spiral of time and its relation to the unbroken line of eternity.

A miracle is a correction. It does not create, nor really change at all. It merely looks on devastation, and reminds the mind that what it sees is false.

This passage points out that the miracle pertains to the second level on which *A Course in Miracles* is written. It does not refer to Heaven at all, but deals only with the spiral. Its function is to correct the way that we perceive. An aim of the Course is to have our minds automatically correct what the body appears to see. An important point here is that the miracle does not do anything, *literally*; there is nothing that has to be done. We simply *un*do the mistakes the ego has done. And thus the statement here that the miracle (which really means our minds joined with the Holy Spirit) simply looks at the devastation the ego has made, reminding us that we *can* make another choice and identify with the Holy Spirit's truth instead of the ego's falsity.

It [the miracle] undoes error, but does not attempt to go beyond perception, nor exceed the function of forgiveness. Thus it stays within time's limits. Yet it paves the way for the return of timelessness and love's awakening, for fear must slip away under the gentle remedy it brings.

We shall see this idea also expressed in the text. The miracle occurs within time; it does not abolish it, but collapses it and therefore saves us time. When all of time has been corrected and undone by the miracle, it disappears, and the reality of our eternal state as God's Son is restored to our awareness. The miracle thus undoes all the errors of the ego, leaving the split mind sinless, the state *A Course in Miracles* calls the real world (which we will talk about in Part III). At that point, then, our personal ego world of attack and separation disappears.

A miracle contains the gift of grace, for it is given and received as one. And thus it illustrates the law of truth the world does not obey, because it fails entirely to understand its ways. A miracle inverts perception which was upside down before, and thus it ends the strange distortions that were manifest.

The miracle changes the misperceptions in our wrong mind, which reflects the purpose of *A Course in Miracles*. As it states in two places:

This is a course in mind training (text, p. 13; T-1.VII.4:1).

The purpose of the workbook is to train your mind in a systematic way to a different perception of everyone and everything in the world (workbook, p. 1; W-in.4:1).

Returning to our spiral—as we move about its different sides, reflecting our many-faceted daily experiences, we continue to experience things differently. The goal of *A Course in Miracles*, therefore, is to straighten out our misperceptions so that the spiral becomes a straight line; in other words, so that we perceive everything in the same way. This is the meaning of the New Year's prayer that comes at the end of Chapter 15 in the text: "Make this year different by making it all the same" (text, p. 306; T-15.XI.10:11).

Now is perception open to the truth. Now is forgiveness seen as justified.

Forgiveness is the home of miracles. The eyes of Christ deliver them to all they look upon in mercy and in love. Perception stands corrected in His sight, and what was meant to curse has come to bless.

The miracle shifts our identification with the ego's perceptions. Rather than seeing people as our enemies who have victimized us, or whom we believe we have victimized, we see everyone as sharing the same blessings of the Holy Spirit. The miracle does not awaken us from the dream, but corrects our mistaken belief that we are already awake, although in truth we remain asleep. The miracle affects and changes *only* what is within the illusion, and thus prepares the way for our awakening. What is beyond the dream is not its concern. Forgiveness, of course, is the means of the miracle, and expresses this shift in terms of how we perceive each other; the specialness we had made to curse, now becomes the classroom in which we learn to bless. In the inspiring words of "For They Have Come":

Where stood a cross stands now the risen Christ, and ancient
scars are healed within His sight. An ancient miracle has
come to bless and to replace an ancient enmity that came to
kill (text, p. 522; T-26.IX.8:4-5).

**Each lily of forgiveness offers all the world the silent
miracle of love. And each is laid before the Word of God,
upon the universal altar to Creator and creation in the
light of perfect purity and endless joy.**

This hardly needs commentary. The passage is a beautiful
rendering of the role of the miracle and forgiveness, the lily of
course being the Course's symbol for the latter. The altar refers to the place in our minds where we choose God or the ego.
Here it is the altar of the oneness of God and Christ.

**The miracle is taken first on faith, because to ask for it
implies the mind has been made ready to conceive of what
it cannot see and does not understand.**

The very fact that we would ask for a miracle, which means
asking the Holy Spirit's help to shift our perception of someone or something in the world that we have attacked, implies
that there must be a part of our mind that is choosing not to
identify with the ego. This part is what we have referred to as
the decision maker, that aspect of the split mind that chooses
whether to identify with the ego or the Holy Spirit. Even
though we cannot fully understand what lies beyond the ego,
we can nonetheless become aware that the conflict and pain
we are experiencing is not what we truly want. Rather, we
really want "the other way" that Bill Thetford and Helen
Schucman agreed to find together. In terms of the image in
chart 3, asking for a miracle means saying that we want to look
at a different picture; we are tired of feeling victimized, unhappy, guilty, and anxious. At last we want something else.

**Yet faith will bring its witnesses to show that what it rested
on is really there. And thus the miracle will justify your
faith in it, and show it rested on a world more real than**

what you saw before; a world redeemed from what you thought was there.

The fact that we choose the miracle will bring witnesses that will show us that the Source of the miracle is truly present. Even though we do not yet understand or experience the peace of Heaven, we can at least begin to know that there is a state of peace in this world which is possible of attainment. Note too the statement that the miracle redeems the world from the sin we *thought* was there. In other words, the world itself is not changed (or redeemed), simply our thinking about it. As the text states:

> Therefore, seek not to change the world, but choose to change your mind about the world. Perception is a result and not a cause. And that is why order of difficulty in miracles is meaningless. Everything looked upon with vision is healed and holy (text, p. 415; T-21.in.1:7-10).

Miracles fall like drops of healing rain from Heaven on a dry and dusty world, where starved and thirsty creatures come to die. Now they have water. Now the world is green. And everywhere the signs of life spring up, to show that what is born can never die, for what has life has immortality.

This first sentence echoes the expression in the manual, referred to earlier (p. 104 above), of the world's weary hopelessness (manual, p. 3; M-1.4:4-5). And yet, there is hope indeed in such a dreary and dismal place: not that the world will change (to restate this important point), but that we can learn how to perceive the world differently. It is not our bodies that starve and thirst, but our minds that yearn for the Love of God that alone can nourish them. Thus the miracle restores to our awareness our true life as Christ, a life that has never died.

The image of the desert, implied here, is beautifully foreshadowed in the following passage from "The Little Garden,"

describing the mind's shift from separation and attack to joining and love, using the symbols of the desert and garden:

> In your tiny kingdom you have so little!...Look at the
> desert—dry and unproductive, scorched and joyless—that
> makes up your little kingdom. And realize the life and joy that
> love would bring to it from where it comes, and where it
> would return with you.
>
> The Thought of God surrounds your little kingdom, wait-
> ing at the barrier you built to come inside and shine upon the
> barren ground. See how life springs up everywhere! The
> desert becomes a garden, green and deep and quiet, offering
> rest to those who lost their way and wander in the dust. Give
> them a place of refuge, prepared by love for them where once
> a desert was....And under its beneficence your little garden
> will expand, and reach out to everyone who thirsts for living
> water, but has grown too weary to go on alone (text, pp. 365f;
> T-18.VIII.8:4,6-7; 9:1-4,8).

Turning to the text now, we shall examine a few of the
miracle principles that specifically talk about the miracle's
relationship to time (text, pp. 1,2,4; T-1.I).[10] Let us begin
with principle 13:

**13. Miracles are both beginnings and endings, and so they
alter the temporal order. They are always affirmations of
rebirth, which seem to go back but really go forward. They
undo the past in the present, and thus release the future.**

It is impossible to understand this principle, and a number
of the others, without understanding the concepts which are
represented by the image of the carpet in chart 2. Here again,
the Course is talking about the miracle as it operates within a
world of linear time. This does not mean that time actually is
linear, but since this is what we believe, this is where the

---

10. For a more detailed analysis of the fifty miracle principles, the reader
may consult my *The Fifty Miracle Principles of "A Course in Miracles."*
See Related Material at the end of this book for additional information.

correction is needed. In relation to the carpet of time in chart 2, we are all stuck somewhere on this carpet, and the process is to return to the left-hand side of the carpet: Heaven, God, and Christ. Within the world of time, the world of illusion, it seems as if it is a very long journey. Thus, when the Course says that the miracle saves time, it refers to the saving of time within the illusion of this journey, and within this illusion, it does seem as if undoing our guilt would take an extremely long time. In a cute play on words later on, Jesus makes the same point regarding the need to guard our fear thoughts: "You may feel that at this point it would take a miracle to enable you to do this, which is perfectly true" (text, p. 27; T-2.VII.1:8).

Let us assume, for example, that there is a massive chunk of guilt that is associated with a particular problem, a particular way in which we have felt victimized by someone that seems to justify our anger at this person. Let us say, within the normal course of events on this carpet, it would take several lifetimes to work through this problem and/or relationship. The miracle, if we choose to let it, enables us to undo that massive chunk of guilt in the context of the specific relationship, and truly to forgive that person in this lifetime. Successfully forgiving that chunk of guilt is what saves the time by undoing the past and releasing the future. Reflected here, therefore, is the idea that guilt exists in the past—we feel guilty because of something we believe we have done or have failed to do, the meaning of sin. Our guilt is projected onto the future, where we believe we deserve to be punished. We then forget that *we* are the ones who projected our guilt, and so now believe that people are victimizing us unfairly.

Thus, the miracle reflects the change of mind that enables us to let go of our guilt, the belief in our past sinfulness. This then frees the Holy Spirit to work through us in the sense that we are now allowing the extension of His Love to occur. In the words of Lesson 194: "I place the future in the Hands of God" (workbook, p. 360; W-pI.194). This is not possible as long as we hold on to the ego's guilt. It *is* possible, of course, when we let go of the guilt, and that is what releases the future. The "beginning and the ending" that is referred to can be understood as the beginning and the ending of a relationship. The "beginning" would be the special relationship that the ego has made real, while the "ending" is the forgiveness of that relationship—making it holy. We move now to principle 15:

15. Each day should be devoted to miracles. The purpose of time is to enable you to learn how to use time constructively. It is thus a teaching device and a means to an end. Time will cease when it is no longer useful in facilitating learning.

The point here is that the ego made time as a way of trapping us, reinforcing our belief that separation and guilt are real, and so our fear of punishment is justified. The Holy Spirit, though, uses time in His own way within the illusion, so that He teaches us something else. As a way of clarifying this idea, let me read a passage from Chapter 2 in the text. This is a very important idea in terms of understanding why on one level Jesus speaks about time as an illusion, with the world already over, and yet on the other level, within the context of our experience here, he speaks about it as if it were real. The context of this passage, and what follows it, is the use of magic, and specifically its medical forms. Magic, incidentally, is understood by the Course to be anything that attempts to solve our problems by addressing their external manifestations, rather than their source (guilt) within our minds. Jesus is teaching here that the use of magic is not evil or sinful; the importance of the form of help lies in the *purpose* for which it is used.

> The value of the Atonement does not lie in the manner in which it is expressed. In fact, if it is used truly, it will inevitably be expressed in whatever way is most helpful to the receiver. This means that a miracle, to attain its full efficacy, must be expressed in a language that the recipient can

understand without fear. This does not necessarily mean that this is the highest level of communication of which he is capable. It does mean, however, that it is the highest level of communication of which he is capable *now*. The whole aim of the miracle is to raise the level of communication, not to lower it by increasing fear (text, pp. 20-21; T-2.IV.5).

This ties in with what I said in Part I—that the Course is coming to meet a specific need that we have now, but it is not the highest level of communication of which we are capable. Clearly, however, it is the highest level that we can accept at this point in human history, when we are still so preoccupied with fundamental ego self-centeredness, greed, attainment of pleasure, and rampant specialness. Jesus very specifically meets us where we are, and provides us with his gentle correction of forgiveness to help us along our journey home.

We have obviously made time very real, which is quite apparent in our contemporary Western world with its near obsession of saving time: fast food, fast travel, and the yearning for fast fixes, be it through drugs, sex, or instant acquisition of wealth. Thus, we need a thought system that comes within that framework, and teaches us that the purpose is to save time through the miracle. Hence, *A Course in Miracles* talks about the miracle as canceling out the past and releasing the future. In reality, none of this is real since it has already happened and has already been undone. As we discussed in Part I, we are sitting outside of time, as the observer, reliving what has already occurred (chart 3). Again, this emphasis on saving time is not the highest level of communication we are capable of understanding, but it is the highest level which we are capable of understanding *now*.

Another way of saying the same thing is that one of the reasons for the world being such a great trap is that we have forgotten the relationship between cause and effect, and the power of our minds that literally made up this world. We believe in the reality of the physical world because we repressed the fact that we made it up. A major focus of *A Course in*

Miracles' teaching is to restore to the mind the awareness of
the power that it has of being the cause of all illusions. To restate a passage quoted earlier (p. 85 above):

> The miracle is the first step in giving back to cause [the mind]
> the function of causation, not effect (text, p. 552; T-28.II.9:3).

Returning to principle 15: time is used by the Holy Spirit
as a "teaching device" not because it is real, but because it is
a means whereby we can learn. When we have learned our lessons time will disappear. As time was not made by God, it is
not eternal, lasting only as long as the dream that gave rise to
it is accorded reality. Now let us look at principle 48:

**48. The miracle is the only device at your immediate dis-
posal for controlling time. Only revelation transcends it,
having nothing to do with time at all.**

The miracle, then, is the only device that controls, undoes,
and saves us time. It is a very important device at our disposal,
as students of the Course, whereas revelation entails a sudden
shift to One-mindedness, being a direct communication from
God to us, transcending time entirely. The miracle entails a
shift from wrong- to right-mindedness; thus it saves us time
but does not abolish it. The miracle *corrects* our mistakes; revelation transcends them.

We turn now to the second section of Chapter 1, paragraph
six (text, p. 6; T-1.II.6), which summarizes many of the miracle principles, particularly the ones that discuss the miracle's
time-saving properties. In fact, it is an elaboration of principle
47, which I quote below. As we go through this passage, it
would be helpful to keep in mind the image of the carpet in
chart 2. Referring to the middle hyphenated line in the chart,
which represents the dividing line on the carpet of time, there
are two points, "A" and "B." "A" represents the point at which
we believe we are, let us say stuck with a problem of guilt in
a relationship. Within the normal span of time it would take a

thousand years to work this guilt through. In other words, we would have to re-experience the same pattern as it is on this video tape, over and over again. The miracle lifts us above the carpet vertically, carrying us *back closer* to the beginning of time at point "B," where we gently come down to the carpet. This is a metaphorical way of describing how the miracle saves us time. In the instant in which we choose the miracle and forgive, we skip over the "thousand years" it would have taken us to let go of our grievances of being unfairly treated.

Within the context of chart 3, the "saving of time" can be understood as the amount of time it would take us to press the happy dream button of the Holy Spirit, rather than the nightmare dream button of the ego, choosing only those video tapes that are healing and forgiving. Finally we note that the miracle is timeless, insofar as it does not obey the laws of time yet it occurs in "an out-of-pattern time interval." Thus, the miracle actually occurs outside of time, though is experienced within it. This is its paradoxical nature, as is seen in principle 47:

47. The miracle is a learning device that lessens the need for time. It establishes an out-of-pattern time interval not under the usual laws of time. In this sense it is timeless.

We begin now with Chapter 1, section II, paragraph 6:

The miracle minimizes the need for time. In the longitudinal or horizontal plane [a linear view of time] the recognition of the equality of the members of the Sonship appears to involve almost endless time.

Because the Holy Spirit's purpose for time is to undo guilt, by His having us undo guilt more quickly, our need for time lessens. Within the illusion of time, the recognition that the Father and the Son are one, and that the Sonship is one within Itself, would seem to take an endless amount of time, with the end a long way off. As is said later in the text (p. 30; T-2.VIII.2:5), the process could take millions of years. It seems that way to us because of the tremendous amount of guilt and fear that appears to be present in the world, let alone in our individual special relationships.

However, the miracle entails a sudden shift from horizontal to vertical perception. This introduces an interval from which the giver and receiver both emerge farther along in time than they would otherwise have been. The miracle thus has the unique property of abolishing time to the extent that it renders the interval of time it spans unnecessary.

Instead of going back in a linear way on the carpet we are lifted above the carpet by the miracle. That is what is meant by "vertical." The giver and receiver of the miracle (i.e., forgiveness) now go from point "A" to point "B." It is thus not necessary to experience that interval of a thousand years, since once the lesson is learned, that time is no longer needed. Its purpose—the Holy Spirit's—of undoing guilt has been fulfilled, and future experience of time is unnecessary.

There is no relationship between the time a miracle takes and the time it covers.

A miracle takes only an instant, what *A Course in Miracles* calls a "holy instant," and yet the time that it covers, as we see on the chart, could be a thousand years. This seems to defy all the laws of logic, only because our laws of logic deal with a linear view of time. The workings of the miracle make much more sense if we realize that time is nothing more than a "sleight of hand," a magic trick that the ego has played on us, as discussed earlier (see above, p. 11). Time, however, can be viewed in a totally different way—as collapsed in one instant. The Course does not require, as we have seen, that we understand the metaphysics of time; it merely asks that we understand the importance of choosing a miracle.

The miracle substitutes for learning that might have taken thousands of years. It does so by the underlying

recognition of perfect equality of giver and receiver on which the miracle rests.

The lack of difference between giver and receiver is a major underlying dimension of the miracle. The workbook says "To give and to receive are one in truth" (workbook, p. 191; W-pI.108): there is no separation between us; we are all the same. From the perspective of the spiral we considered in chart 6, it appears as if we are all different, and our perception is distorted and changing from one moment to the next. In reality, however, all things are the same, since illusions differ only in form; their content remains one.

The miracle shortens time by collapsing it, thus eliminating certain intervals within it. It does this, however, within the larger temporal sequence.

The miracle removes the time interval between "A" and "B" on chart 2, and thereby collapses time. The miracle does not abolish time, however, for it is experienced within the illusion of its temporal sequence. Therefore, the whole purpose of the miracle, as of *A Course in Miracles* itself, is to save us time.

Q: That line which says "the miracle substitutes for learning that might have taken thousands of years" seems to imply that if everything happened simultaneously in one instant, the miracle would eliminate the need to work toward correcting relationships one by one. Saying that "thousands of years" will be collapsed by the miracle seems to imply that one whole chunk of guilt involving a certain type of victimization pattern, would be collapsed through all incarnations linearly.

A: Correct. In fact, if you think of this in terms of a computer having all these programs of victimization, when you ask for a correction you are actually pressing the *delete* button, thereby canceling *all* victimization programs. That is why, in a sense, we need an image of a carpet because that expresses the linearity that we believe in. However, in order to understand better how the miracle works, a holographic non-linear image conveyed by the computer illustration is preferable. There is a nice passage in the text illustrating this idea of saving time through forgiveness:

> Your brother first among them will be seen, but thousands stand behind him, and beyond each one of them there are a thousand more. Each one may seem to have a problem that is different from the rest. Yet they are solved together (text, p. 537; T-27.V.10:4-6).

Let us move next to section V of Chapter 1, paragraph two (text, p. 10; T-1.V.2):

The basic decision of the miracle-minded is not to wait on time any longer than is necessary. Time can waste as well as be wasted. The miracle worker, therefore, accepts the time-control factor gladly.

This second sentence is obviously a pun. Translators of the Course have a most difficult time with that line, because they do not understand the English idiom "wasting time," which has no parallel in other languages. The basic thrust in that line is that we could use time on our behalf by regarding the world of linear time as a classroom in which we learn that there is no time. The mention of the "time-control" factor looks forward to the next chapter, where Jesus discusses our need to turn over to him all that does not matter, placing our egos under his control, so that he may then guide us in what does matter (text, p. 25; T-2.VI.1:3). And then later he reminds us that "time and space are under my control" (text, p. 29; T-2.VII.7:9). This means that when we turn our minds over to him, his love can then direct us within the illusory world of time and space to learn our lessons of forgiveness through the miracle. And thus "viewing time" is saved for us, for Jesus is now our video tape guide instead of the ego.

Q: Would this perhaps imply that procrastination is an ego device—that time can waste our ability or that time debilitates us?

A: Yes, and in that sentence we find an inverted subject and predicate. We talk about wasting time, but this says that time wastes.

He [the miracle worker] recognizes that every collapse of time brings everyone closer to the ultimate release from time, in which the Son and the Father are one.

This looks ahead to Lesson 158, which as we have seen, states that the time when the revelation that the Father and the Son are one has already occurred. The main idea in this paragraph is that all minds are joined. That is why the answer to the question in the manual, "How many teachers of God are needed to save the world?" is "one" (manual, p. 30; M-12.1:1). Because the mind of Jesus is totally healed, the mind of the Sonship is healed as well. The Atonement principle has been proven to be true. But we are reminded in the Course that the Holy Spirit holds that healing thought—any loving thought of the Kingdom—for us, until the time we are ready to accept it (e.g., text, pp. 100,153,196; T-6.V-C.1; T-9.II.3; T-11.VIII.2). We cannot avoid our responsibility to accept the truth that is already present in our minds. Thus, while we believe we are within the dream, our minds still have to be healed; but on another level, because minds are joined, if Jesus' mind is healed then everyone else's mind is healed too.

Equality does not imply equality *now*.

Within the illusion of time, some people will seem to be closer to returning home on the carpet than others. Some will have more highly developed spiritual abilities than others; that is a fact within the world that cannot be denied. Nor is it denied by *A Course in Miracles*. Thus, for example, the manual speaks of teachers, advanced teachers, and Teachers of teachers. The last category of course includes Jesus, who within the world of time is more advanced than any of us. But that is only within the illusion of time. As he says:

> There is nothing about me that you cannot attain. I have nothing that does not come from God. The difference between us now is that I have nothing else. This leaves me in a state which is only potential in you.
>
> "No man cometh unto the Father but by me" does not mean that I am in any way separate or different from you except in time, and time does not really exist (text, p. 5; T-1.II.3:10-4:1).

Similarly, later in the text Jesus reminds us not to deny our experience of guilt within the dream of time:

> You are not guiltless in time, but in eternity (text, p. 221; T-13.I.3:2).

Our next discussion takes us to the second section of Chapter 2 (text, p.16; T-2.II.5):

The Atonement was built into the space-time belief to set a limit on the need for the belief itself, and ultimately to make learning complete. The Atonement is the final lesson. Learning itself, like the classrooms in which it occurs, is temporary.

We made space and time in the instant the ego seemed to occur, and at that same instant God "gave" the Holy Spirit as the Correction, the principle of the Atonement. This then becomes the limit to the ego's world of time, and establishes the fact that the mistake has been healed. (Later in Chapter 2, as quoted earlier, Jesus speaks of the Atonement [or the Holy Spirit] as being the limit God set on the Son's ability to miscreate [text, p. 18; T-2.III.3:3].)

A Course in Miracles uses metaphors of the classroom all the way through—its very title is pedagogical. Thus, the

Course describes the world of time and space as a classroom. When we take a class in a university and pass it, then we no longer need it. The situation is the same here. The Atonement is the final lesson, and the *total* acceptance of the Atonement for oneself is the final recognition that the separation from God never happened. When we have finally learned this lesson the classroom disappears, as does the ego itself.

The ability to learn has no value when change is no longer necessary. The eternally creative have nothing to learn. You can learn to improve your perceptions, and can become a better and better learner. This will bring you into closer and closer accord with the Sonship; but the Sonship itself is a perfect Creation and perfection is not a matter of degree. Only while there is a belief in differences is learning meaningful.

Learning cannot exist in Heaven, where there is only perfection. Learning is required only within this world. In terms of chart 6, we believe we are on the spiral, and so we have to learn that the spiral is not our true home. When, again, we finally learn our lesson the spiral disappears. Our learning can occur because the Holy Spirit has joined us on the spiral to help us correct and straighten out our misperceptions. "The Sonship" refers to the unity of Christ, of which we are a part. In the carpet analogy in chart 2, the unity of Christ is represented on the left side. As we go towards the left on the chart, say from point "A" to point "B," and still further back, we get in closer and closer accord with the oneness of the Sonship. As the final lines in the passage state, it is only within the imperfect and miscreated world of time and space that we find degrees, a misbelief that necessitates our learning. Once we have totally learned our lessons, all that remains in our minds is the pure experience of our oneness with Christ and with God. Until that time, however, learning is necessary to help us unlearn the ego's thought system of differences.

Evolution is a process in which you seem to proceed from one degree to the next. You correct your previous missteps by stepping forward.

This statement makes sense when you consider that evolution proceeds linearly through time. Similarly, almost all people talk about their spiritual life as a journey that also proceeds linearly through time. *A Course in Miracles* uses this image as well; although, as we have already seen, it teaches on another level that the journey "without distance" has already been completed, and in fact, never was. In this sense, then, our carpet of time in chart 2 would not apply. The actual "movement" of the journey is backwards, proceeding from right to left instead of the more conventional linear view from left to right. This is implied in the next line from the text:

This process is actually incomprehensible in temporal terms, because you return as you go forward.

We experience ourselves as evolving, but we are really returning to the Heaven we believe we left. In chart 6 time is portrayed as a downward spiral, and this vertical axis is actually a better model than the horizontal one of the carpet. Elsewhere, *A Course in Miracles* talks about the separation as a ladder, where we are on the bottom rungs, and the Holy Spirit leads us up the ladder the separation led us down (text, p. 553; T-28.III.1:2). Thus, we are going back to the place from which we started, but again, which we never truly left.

This view is different, incidentally, from that of the noted French Jesuit, Teilhard de Chardin, who envisioned the process of biological evolution as being essentially completed, and that we are moving spiritually toward what he termed the Omega Point, when we recognize that we are all one. However, from his perspective as a paleontologist, he conceived of this process as an evolutionary development, proceeding over time. The contrast is clear with *A Course in Miracles*, where the healing of the mind has *already* occurred. The process is one of accepting the Atonement that has already been accomplished.

The Atonement is the device by which you can free yourself from the past as you go ahead. It undoes your past errors, thus making it unnecessary for you to keep retracing your steps without advancing to your return.

This is clear when we look again at chart 2: how the miracle (in this case the Atonement) saves us time by lifting us above the carpet of time vertically, thus freeing us from the past as we proceed ahead, making it unnecessary for us to re-trace our steps as we advance on our return home. If we think of this in the light of our analogy in chart 3, this means that we do not have to replay the same video tape or re-experience the same victimization nightmare. The Atonement undoes our past errors which really are the errors of guilt, the errors which we are holding on to in our mind.

In this sense the Atonement saves time, but like the miracle it serves, does not abolish it. As long as there is need for Atonement, there is need for time. But the Atonement as a completed plan has a unique relationship to time. Until the Atonement is complete, its various phases will proceed in time, but the whole Atonement stands at time's end. At that point the bridge of return has been built.

If we think of the Atonement as the Holy Spirit, we can see Him standing outside of time with us (the observer), awaiting our decision to awaken from the dream. That is what is meant by saying that the Atonement proceeds in time, "but the whole Atonement stands at time's end." There is a wonderful passage in the workbook that makes the same point, speaking of the Holy Spirit:

> Our Love awaits us as we go to Him, and walks beside us showing us the way. He fails in nothing. He the end we seek, and He the means by which we go to Him (workbook, p. 440; W-pII.302.2).

Our next group of passages deals with the Course's distinction between time and eternity, stating how both are in our minds. If we think of the observer in chart 3, the ego represents time and the Holy Spirit represents eternity. Both thoughts are in our minds, and we can choose which one we will identify with. We will start with the Introduction to Chapter 10 in the text (p. 168; T-10.in.1):

Nothing beyond yourself can make you fearful or loving, because nothing *is* beyond you.

The split mind contains all illusions which are then projected from the mind (the observer), and yet still remain within, since "ideas leave not their source." Thus, *everything* is within our minds, nothing outside: the inner and the outer are one and the same. A similar teaching is found in Lesson 70, "My salvation comes from me":

The seeming cost of accepting today's idea is this: It means that nothing outside yourself can save you; nothing outside yourself can give you peace. But it also means that nothing outside yourself can hurt you, or disturb your peace or upset you in any way (workbook, p. 118; W-pI.70.2:1-2).

And from the text:

Nothing can hurt you unless you give it the power to do so (text, p. 402; T-20.IV.1:1).

Nothing you made has any power over you unless you still would be apart from your Creator, and with a will opposed to His (text, p. 441; T-22.II.10:2).

Time and eternity are both in your mind, and will conflict until you perceive time solely as a means to regain eternity.

Deep down, we all share the belief that we are in conflict with God. This is the basic ego belief and one of the major ideas expressed in "The Laws of Chaos" (text, pp. 455-60; T-23.II). We shall continue to remain in conflict until we let the Holy Spirit reinterpret time for us, so it is no longer seen as an attack on God, which was the reason it was made in the first place. Rather, the Holy Spirit can help us see time as a learning device that can teach us that the attack on God never occurred. At that point, then, time is no longer to be seen in conflict with eternity; in other words, the spiral has become a straight line because all is perceived as the same. That corrected perception speeds us back home.

You cannot do this as long as you believe that anything happening to you is caused by factors outside yourself.

As long as we believe that we are victims of a world that God made, or that was made by forces outside of our minds, we shall continue to perceive the world of time and space as real. We must then believe the ego's attack on God is real, which, because of the dynamic of projection, means that we believe that God attacked us back and threw us out of Heaven. As *A Course in Miracles* states about the ego's thought system regarding God, in two very powerful passages:

> Nor will God end His vengeance...for in His madness He must have this substitute for love, and kill you...(text, pp. 457-58; T-23.II.13:3).

> If this [sin] were so, would Heaven be opposed by its own opposite [the ego], as real as it. Then would God's Will be split in two, and all creation be subjected to the laws of two opposing powers, until God becomes impatient, splits the world apart, and relegates attack unto Himself (text, pp. 515-16; T-26.VII.7:3-4).

At that point, of course, it is impossible to see time as kind, because we are already perceiving the world as cruel, i.e., as the result of God's vengeance on us.

You must learn that time is solely at your disposal, and that nothing in the world can take this responsibility from you.

This reflects one of the more basic teachings of *A Course in Miracles* that we give time, not to mention the world, power over us. We give people power to hurt and to victimize us, and that makes time into an enemy rather than the friend it can be when the Holy Spirit reinterprets it for us. Concurrently, the Course would have us become aware that *we* are responsible for how we use time within the illusion, and that no one else can be held responsible for its effects on us—time is at our disposal, not the other way around as the ego would have us believe. The world, in its origins and by its very nature, is therefore the ego's attempt to obscure the mind's responsibility for its own projections. It is this responsibility that must be accepted if our minds are to be healed and time seen as our ally in the Atonement.

Now let us move to the last paragraph of Chapter 10 (text, p. 178; T-10.V.14):

Arrogance is the denial of love, because love shares and arrogance withholds. As long as both appear to you to be desirable the concept of choice, which is not of God, will remain with you.

As long as we believe that there is a choice in the world, between God and the ego, and that *we want both of them*—sometimes we want the arrogance of the ego, sometimes we want the Love of God—then we are going to remain in conflict. We are reminded of the series of three workbook lessons:

> "The world I see holds nothing that I want."
> "Beyond this world there is a world I want."
> "It is impossible to see two worlds."
> (workbook, pp. 227-32; W-pI.128,129,130)

Once again, it all comes down to choice. Choosing is illusory since in the absolute unity of Heaven choice among different options is impossible. However, within the split mind, once the idea of choice between God and the ego entered in the dream, learning to choose between the Holy Spirit's Atonement and the ego's atonement *is* meaningful:

> Learning is an ability you made and gave yourself. It was not made to do the Will of God.... Yet you will learn them [the Holy Spirit's lessons], for their learning is the only purpose for your learning skill the Holy Spirit sees in all the world (text, p. 601; T-31.I.5:1,5).

While this is not true in eternity it *is* true in time, so that while time lasts in your mind there will be choices.

This is another way in which the Course contrasts the world of time and the world of eternity. Once again, there is no choice in Heaven. The concept of free will, as we ordinarily think of it, has no meaning in Heaven since we are a part of God and therefore cannot have a will apart from His. Therefore, we *cannot* choose to be apart from Him. Only in a dualistic dream world in which God and His Son are separate does the concept of free will have meaning. Heaven, however, is a non-dualistic state in which God and Christ are unified, and so Their Will is one. As *A Course in Miracles* states:

> God shares His Fatherhood with you who are His Son, for He makes no distinctions in what is Himself and what is still Himself. What He creates is not apart from Him, and nowhere does the Father end, the Son begin as something separate from Him (workbook, pp. 237-38; W-pI.132.12:3-4).

The same idea is expressed in an earlier lesson:

> Then close your eyes upon the world you see, and in the silent darkness watch the lights that are not of this world light one by one, until where one begins another ends loses all meaning as they blend in one (workbook, p. 230; W-pI.129.7:5).

The concept of free will, however, *is* meaningful when re-phrased to signify that our will is free. But it does not mean free will on the level of choice, because the Son of God cannot choose to be other than what God created Him to be. Free will here thus means freedom of will: the Will of God and His Son cannot be imprisoned by the illusions of the ego. As the Course says:

> *The Kingdom is perfectly united and perfectly protected, and
> the ego will not prevail against it. Amen* (text, p. 54;
> T-4.III.1:12-13).

And later:

> And Heaven itself but represents your will, where everything
> created is for you....How wonderful it is to do your will! For
> that is freedom. There is nothing else that ever should be
> called by freedom's name. Unless you do your will you are
> not free. And would God leave His Son without what he has
> chosen for himself?...God would not have His Son made
> prisoner to what he does not want. He joins with you in will-
> ing you be free....Your will is boundless; it is not your will
> that it be bound. What lies in you has joined with God Him-
> self in all creation's birth....Think not He wills to bind you,
> Who has made you co-creator of the universe along with
> Him. He would but keep your will forever and forever limit-
> less (text, p. 585; T-30.II.1:8; 2:1-5,8-9; 3:4-5; 4:4-5).

Therefore, choice and decision have meaning only within
this world which seems to be outside God. Here, we do seem
to be able to choose either the ego or the Holy Spirit. In the
real world, where choosing ends, there is only the reflection of
Heaven: the Holy Spirit's Love.

**Time itself is your choice. If you would remember eternity,
you must look only on the eternal.**

In this world, we look on the eternal not in terms of God or
spirit, which cannot be perceived. We look on the "eternal" as
it is translated for us by the Holy Spirit, which means to look
on the face of Christ, to look on someone with total forgiveness, to see everyone and everything as the same. That is what
A Course in Miracles means by phrases such as "the reflection
of holiness" and "heralds of eternity." As the workbook states:

> God has no name. And yet His Name becomes the final
> lesson that all things are one, and at this lesson does all
> learning end. All names are unified; all space is filled with

truth's reflection....Experience must come to supplement the Word. But first you must accept the Name for all reality, and realize the many names you gave its aspects have distorted what you see, but have not interfered with truth at all....And though we use a different name for each awareness of an aspect of God's Son, we understand that they have but one Name, Which He has given them (workbook, p. 338; W-pI.184.12:1-3; 13:2-3; 14:1).

If you allow yourself to become preoccupied with the temporal, you are living in time. As always, your choice is determined by what you value. Time and eternity cannot both be real, because they contradict each other. If you will accept only what is timeless as real, you will begin to understand eternity and make it yours.

This refers to the ego's use of time which involves focusing on the sins of the past which are reinforced by our guilt, and then projected into the future, leading us to believe that we will be punished. This of course is part of the ego's plan to bind us to *its* world, thereby causing our attention to be distracted from the Holy Spirit's world of forgiveness, which is His equivalent of Heaven's eternal Love. In this world we do choose time because that is where we believe we are, but it is the Holy Spirit's interpretation of it which becomes for us a reflection of the eternity of Heaven. It is all a question of our choice. In the above passages, choice is regarded as being between time and eternity; in other places it is between the ego and the Holy Spirit, or a miracle and a grievance. Clearly, in our experience in this world we cannot truly choose the timeless, which is not knowable here. Thus, again, Jesus is referring to the expressions of the timeless in this world, which can be thought of as forgiveness, being "the reflection of God's Love on earth" (workbook, p. 99; W-pI.60.1:5).

We turn now to the first section in Chapter 13 in the text. This section contains the passage from which I modeled the idea of the carpet of time. It is the only place in *A Course in Miracles* that actually refers to the "carpet." We begin with the third paragraph (text, p. 221; T-13.I.3).

As you look upon yourself and judge what you do honestly, you may be tempted to wonder how you can be guiltless.

This is true of all who begin to consider the enormity of their own feelings of worthlessness and inadequacy. The idea of being guiltless seems absolutely impossible. But of course, this is exactly the judgment the ego would have us make. In fact, it is its original judgment of us. For it is the belief in our inherent guilt that necessitated the making of the world as a defense against God's inevitable punishment for the sinfulness that can never be eradicated: the sin that was committed "cannot be done without. The stain of blood can never be removed" (manual, p. 43; M-17.7:12-13). Now Jesus is telling us, in a line I have already referred to, that we do not have to consider ourselves guiltless in order to be healed:

Yet consider this: You are not guiltless in time, but in eternity.

This extremely important line, which I have already quoted, is aimed at those students who strive to make themselves perfectly free of all special relationships, and then feel guilty that they have not achieved their goal. Jesus is saying very clearly that within the world of time, the world of duality, we *are* guilty, and that we will experience all the things that go with guilt—anger, depression, anxiety, and sickness. That is why we have come to this world, as the text later explains:

> Concentrate only on this [your willingness], and be not disturbed that shadows [i.e., guilt] surround it. That is why you came. If you could come without them you would not need the holy instant (text, p. 355; T-18.IV.2:4-6).

And from the teacher's manual:

Do not despair, then, because of limitations [i.e., of the body]. It is your function to escape from them, but not to be without them (manual, p. 61; M-26.4:1-2).

Therefore, in eternity we are guiltless; in time, where we believe we are, we are guilty by definition because time was made out of guilt. And so we are not asked to be perfect here, but simply to have the willingness to become perfect through learning how to forgive ourselves for, or to escape from, the limitations imposed by our thought system of sin, guilt, and fear.

You have "sinned" in the past, but there is no past. Always has no direction.

Here we find Level One and Level Two expressed in two succinct sentences. "Direction" obviously implies a contrast between the place where we are and the place to which we are going, and this has meaning only within a world of form. "Always," which is a synonym for eternity, is non-dualistic and therefore has no contrast or direction.

Time seems to go in one direction, but when you reach its end it will roll up like a long carpet spread along the past behind you, and will disappear. As long as you believe the Son of God is guilty you will walk along this carpet, believing that it leads to death. And the journey will seem long and cruel and senseless, for so it is.

This journey is the world of time, "long and cruel and senseless." It is the road of guilt, the fabric of the carpet. When we totally accept the Atonement for ourselves and undo our belief in the reality of guilt, the need for time is over and so the carpet rolls up and disappears.

In the above passage Jesus is setting up a syllogism that is typical of his presentation in the Course:

> If I am guilty, I am in time.
> I am guilty.
> Therefore, I am in time (or at least experience time as real).

He also teaches:

> If I am in time, I must be guilty.
> I am in time (or at least I believe I am).
> Therefore, I must be guilty.

To remove ourselves from the prison of time, therefore, we must undo guilt by shaking up our belief in the reality of time and space. That is the role of forgiveness, and teaching us to make this choice is the purpose of *A Course in Miracles*.

The journey the Son of God has set himself is useless indeed, but the journey on which his Father sets him is one of release and joy.

Earlier in the text Jesus says that "the journey to the cross should be the last 'useless journey'" that we take (text, p. 47; T-4.in.3:1). Aside from the obvious references to his own crucifixion, Jesus uses the term as a symbol for the ego thought system of suffering, sacrifice, and death. While the ego's journey is therefore useless and goes nowhere, the Holy Spirit's journey for us leads away from the dream of death— symbolized by the cross—by awakening us. This really is not a journey because, to state it again, the journey has no distance (text, p. 139; T-8.VI.9:7) and is already over. However, it is a journey to us because of our experience as temporal and spatial beings. Thus, the journey is the process of undoing this ego identity, joyfully releasing the memory of who we truly are.

The Father is not cruel, and His Son cannot hurt himself. The retaliation that he fears and that he sees will never touch him, for although he believes in it the Holy Spirit knows it is not true. The Holy Spirit stands at the end of time, where you must be because He is with you.

There is a Voice within our minds always telling us that God can never punish us, that our fears are unfounded and not justified. But the ego's voice seems to drown out the Holy Spirit's, and its voice of fear continually screams that God will most definitely punish us, if not immediately, then certainly in the future. The seeming paradox, that the Holy Spirit is at the end of time with us, while He is still present with us on the journey, is understandable in light of our previous discussion that time is already over, even though we experience ourselves as being here. This is similar to the statement (referred to earlier) that we were with Jesus when he arose (manual, p. 86; C-6.5:5); i.e., that when he awakened from the dream and stood at time's end, we were with him, at the same time that he remains with us in the dream. Since minds are joined, we must be with him because the Sonship is unified, even though it remains possible for us to believe we can separate ourselves from that thought of unity.

He has already undone everything unworthy of the Son of God, for such was His mission, given Him by God. And what God gives has always been.

Thus, again, the Holy Spirit is at the end of time, reflecting God's loving presence in our minds. Our true reality is Christ, and to restate the important line, we remain "at home in God, dreaming of exile" (text, p. 169; T-10.I.2:1). The healing of the separation has already been completed, the carpet has already been rolled back. The problem remains, however, that we sit in front of the screen watching something that we still believe is real.

The final line of that paragraph, "And what God gives has always been" seems to be a statement of doctrine in agreement with the traditional theology of the Church, namely, that the Holy Spirit was always with God. *A Course in Miracles* teaches something quite different, however: the Holy Spirit was created and given by God as the Answer to the separation: the Atonement. This could be understood on two levels, as most things are in the Course. Since the Holy Spirit is part of God and an extension of God's Love, He has always been; but His specific function as Messenger to the separated Son and communication link between God and His Son occurred after the separation, and thus belongs to the dream. However, as mentioned above, such discussion of the Holy Spirit is metaphorical and should not be taken literally, as if God *gave* an Answer to a problem that does not exist.

You will see me as you learn the Son of God is guiltless.

The "me" of course is Jesus, and what keeps him hidden from us is guilt. When he says, for example, that he stands within the holy relationship (text, p. 385; T-19.IV-B.5:3-4; 8:3), this does not mean that he does not stand in a special one. As he is in our minds, his love is always with us. But the special relationship is the home of guilt, and it is guilt that will keep hidden from us the person who represents guiltlessness for us. Guilt thus acts as a veil that keeps the light of our guiltlessness, held for us by Jesus, absent from our experience. Incidentally, this statement should not be taken to suggest that we would literally "see" Jesus. Rather, it should be understood as an expression of vision, which is an attitude of the mind and is not perceptual. In Hamlet's phrase, we would see Jesus in the "mind's eye."

He has always sought his guiltlessness, and he has found it. For everyone is seeking to escape from the prison he has made, and the way to find release is not denied him. Being in him, he has found it. *When* he finds it is only a matter of time, and time is but an illusion.

This idea makes sense when we consider that the seeming separation has already ended, and the right-minded part of the split mind knows this on one level although the rest of the split mind has not actually accepted it as yet. What we have believed we have done has already been undone; we *have* found the way out of prison, and but await our acceptance of what is always there. Thus, it is only a matter of time that we choose the inevitable.

The Holy Spirit is within the split mind, always telling us that the dream is over. Our situation, because of our identification with the ego, leads us to choose nightmares instead of happy dreams. We prefer to be right rather than to be happy (text, p. 573; T-29.VII.1:9). The process of changing our minds seems to take time, but again, time is only an illusion. One can see, incidentally, that passages such as this one make no sense without some understanding of the underlying metaphysical teachings on the fundamental unreality of time; more specifically, the idea that time has ended, and that we merely re-experience what has already gone by.

For the Son of God is guiltless now, and the brightness of his purity shines untouched forever in God's Mind. God's Son will always be as he was created. Deny your world and judge him not, for his eternal guiltlessness is in the Mind of his Father, and protects him forever.

This first line obviously seems to contradict what we just read in paragraph three that the Son of God is guilty now. But the "now" in that passage refers to the world of time. Here, "now" refers to the timeless present, the part of time that is the window to eternity. The Son of God is guiltless now because time has already ended; we are guiltless in terms of our true identity as Christ. As observers in front of the television screen, listening only to the Holy Spirit, we are guiltless, but when we choose to view dreams of guilt instead, we re-experience those events as if they were happening to us now.

If guiltlessness is in the Mind of the Father, it must be in our minds, too, because the Holy Spirit's Love is the bridge that joins all our minds in one. Judging another or ourselves erases that innocence from our awareness, for judgment obviously means separation. Thus, our ego's fear of the joining, marking the end of the thought of separation, leads us to choose judgment as the means of "protecting" ourselves from the unifying Love of the Holy Spirit, reflected in this world by forgiveness. The great importance of giving up judgment as the prerequisite to peace is a major theme in the Course, as seen in the following statement:

> You have no idea of the tremendous release and deep peace that comes from meeting yourself and your brothers totally without judgment. When you recognize what you are and what your brothers are, you will realize that judging them in any way is without meaning. In fact, their meaning is lost to you precisely *because* you are judging them (text, p. 42; T-3.VI.3:1-3).

Let us skip to paragraph seven (text, p. 222; T-13.I.7):

As you perceive the holy companions who travel with you, you will realize that there is no journey, but only an awakening.

We can interpret "holy companions" in different ways. They could be understood as our creations who have never left us. However, it would be more to the point here to regard them as all our brothers and sisters who walk along the same path we do. We have to remember again that there is no journey. It is an awakening from the dream, which means that in seeing ourselves as observers joined with the Holy Spirit we will awaken from the dream, for we shall no longer be seeing separation or duality. The "holy companions" referred to here are similar to the "mighty companions" spoken about in the fourth stage of the development of trust (manual, p. 10; M-4.I.6:11), who when we are ready to continue on our journey, go beside us.

The Son of God, who sleepeth not, has kept faith with his Father for you. There is no road to travel on, and no time to travel through. For God waits not for His Son in time, being forever unwilling to be without him. And so it has always been. Let the holiness of God's Son shine away the

cloud of guilt that darkens your mind, and by accepting his purity as yours, learn of him that it *is* yours.

The "Son of God" refers to the Christ in us. One might also understand this as Jesus, who represents for all of us the Son of God or Christ that we truly are. Or, it could be understood that the "Son of God" is the Holy Spirit we "perceive" in our brother, representing Christ (or the Son of God) for us.

The limitations of the carpet analogy are quite apparent in this passage, for the analogy really does not hold here. At this point, the kaleidoscope image (chart 3) works better as it emphasizes the non-linearity of time. And so, our ego's assertions of time and separation to the contrary, we have never been without God. The dispelling of the cloud of guilt is what *A Course in Miracles* means by forgiveness. As we begin to see with the vision of Christ, the light of holiness in our brother instead of the darkness of guilt, we embrace the same vision for ourselves. In truth, of course, the perceived guilt and holiness in another is only the reflection of what we have first made real in ourselves. But since we have made real for ourselves a world of duality, the process of forgiveness must also appear to us in that dualistic form.

You are invulnerable because you are guiltless.

This is a key line, but it takes us away from the topic of time. The theme expressed here is that if I am guiltless, then there is no guilt in me that demands punishment, which means I cannot be hurt. My body can be hurt, but without guilt I remember my Identity as spirit and *not* my body. Pain is non-existent, as Jesus demonstrated from the cross. Thus we can say that the two basic ideas in forgiveness are our invulnerability and guiltlessness.

You can hold on to the past only through guilt. For guilt establishes that you will be punished for what you have done, and thus depends on one-dimensional time, proceeding from past to future. No one who believes this [i.e., that we

are guilty] can understand what "always" means, and
therefore guilt must deprive you of the appreciation of
eternity. You are immortal because you are eternal, and
"always" must be now. Guilt, then, is a way of holding past
and future in your mind to ensure the ego's continuity.

It is guilt that keeps us rooted in this world. It keeps us on
the carpet because it teaches us that the sinful past is real; and
guilt demands that we be punished in the future. This dynamic
obviously establishes the linearity of the ego's time, which is
one-dimensional because it goes in one direction: the past
through the present to the future; sin through guilt to punishment. This passage also explains why we have so much
difficulty in understanding what *A Course in Miracles* is saying about time. It is because our guilt roots us in one-
dimensional time, preventing our understanding that time is
not real, and that everything has all already happened and is in
fact over—we are not even here.

For if what has been will be punished, the ego's continuity
is guaranteed. Yet the guarantee of your continuity is
God's, not the ego's. And immortality is the opposite of
time, for time passes away, while immortality is constant.

Accepting the Atonement teaches you what immortality
is, for by accepting your guiltlessness you learn that the
past has never been, and so the future is needless and will
not be.

A little later on we will see how the Course will talk about
continuity again in terms of the ego's continuity versus God's
or the Holy Spirit's. For now we can simply note the distinction between the ego's continuity through guilt, and God's
continuity through love which is ensured through the Holy
Spirit's presence in our split minds.

The remainder of this passage is another example of how
A Course in Miracles moves from Level Two back to Level
One: we learn that we are guiltless by forgiving others. By

learning *they* are not guilty, we are really learning that *we* are not guilty. If we are not guilty there is no sin, and that means there is no past, for sin only has meaning in the past. Sin is what holds the past in our minds, and that is why psycho-analysis, for example, can never truly heal. Its focus on the past makes the past real, and thus sin and guilt are real as well. How then can the ego be undone after it has been made real?

The future, in time, is always associated with expiation, and only guilt could induce a sense of a need for expiation. Accepting the guiltlessness of the Son of God as yours is therefore God's way of reminding you of His Son, and what he is in truth. For God has never condemned His Son, and being guiltless he is eternal.

This first sentence is a subtle correction of the Christian teaching, also found in other religions, of the need to expiate sin or atone for it. Once we believe sin must be atoned for, we have fallen into the trap of believing that sin is real. We must then correct in the future what we have done in the past, which establishes linear time as real. True Atonement undoes guilt simply by moving past it to the guiltlessness underneath. That is what *A Course in Miracles* means by the Holy Spirit looking past errors to the truth. In an early passage in the text, Jesus explains vision:

> Spiritual vision literally cannot see error, and merely looks for Atonement. All solutions the physical eye seeks dissolve. Spiritual vision looks within and recognizes immediately that the altar has been defiled and needs to be repaired and protected. Perfectly aware of the right defense it passes over all others, looking past error to truth (text, p. 18; T-2.III.4:1-4).

Thus, our forgiveness of each other is the means through which God reminds us that we are guiltless as His children. This is the Holy Spirit's plan of the Atonement: I acknowledge the guiltlessness of the Son of God in you, and this awareness, shared with you in my mind, teaches me that that guiltlessness is what I am as well.

Let us move now to section VI, "Finding the Present," paragraph four (text, p. 234; T-13.VI.4):

Time can release as well as imprison, depending on whose interpretation of it you use. Past, present and future are not continuous, unless you force continuity on them.

This reiterates what we have been saying: time in the hands of the ego imprisons us further in sin, guilt, and fear; while to the Holy Spirit time is a classroom in which we learn that that unholy trinity is non-existent. Within the world of illusion, past, present, and future are continuous. The guilt of my past then determines my present actions, which must always involve some fear of the future. However, time is not continuous, for everything happened in that one instant. The purpose of time, as we have seen many times, is to confuse us about this fact. An anonymous quotation from the *National Geographic* summarized it this way:

Time is nature's way of keeping everything from happening all at once (March 1990, p. 109).

You can perceive them [past, present, and future] as continuous, and make them so for you. But do not be deceived, and then believe that this is how it is.

Yet, this is what we all do. We misperceive reality, and then seek to justify it. We erect a myriad number of philosophies, psychologies, and theologies to prove that the misperception is true. A prominent example of this dynamic, frequently cited in *A Course in Miracles* itself, is traditional Christian theology. It begins with the premise that our past sins are real, present guilt justified and sometimes even healthy, and unless atoned for by a life of suffering and sacrifice we shall be deservedly punished in the future for our sins. This theology, which of course is really the *effect* of the underlying belief in sin that is accepted as divinely ordained and therefore objectively true, then becomes the proof that we are sinful. The circularity of this reasoning, however, is never examined, and thus can never be corrected. As the text says of this mistake:

> If the crucifixion is seen from an upside-down point of view, it does appear as if God permitted and even encouraged one of His Sons to suffer because he was good....Yet the real Christian should pause and ask, "How could this be?"...It is unwise to accept any concept if you have to invert a whole frame of reference in order to justify it. This procedure is painful in its minor applications and genuinely tragic on a wider scale (text, p. 32; T-3.I.1:5,8; 2:2-3).

For to believe reality is what you would have it be according to your use for it *is* delusional.

The word "delusional" here is deliberate as that is the word denoting psychotic people who have delusions of reality. They make the world into what they want it to be, as we all do on another level. Making the reality of Heaven an illusion, and the illusion of the world reality, we thus all become insane, as *A Course in Miracles* so frequently states. The ego begins with a belief in sin, guilt, and fear, and then makes up a world of time and space to reinforce that belief, and thus circularly "proves" that sin, guilt, and fear are real. While there is certainly a difference in this world between the delusions of the psychotic and the delusions we non-psychotics all share, dynamically the delusions remain the same. As workers in mental hospitals sometimes like to comment: the only real difference between the patients and the staff is that the latter have the keys to the wards.

You would destroy time's continuity by breaking it into past, present and future for your own purposes.

The reality of time is that it is holographic, but we have broken it up into a past, present, and future. The only real dimension is timelessness. The closest we come to that in this world would be the holy instant. In terms of chart 2 this means that when we choose a miracle, we are lifted above the one-dimensional world of time and space by the Holy Spirit.

Q: Another problem involved in our understanding of this is that no one has ever personally experienced time as *a*dimensional or continuous in that way, and written about that experience using scientific categories. There are accounts of mystics and others who have used drugs to induce altered states of consciousness, but there do not seem to be any accounts of personal experiences expressed in strictly scientific categories. Wouldn't such descriptions help us to understand what the Course is saying?

A: They could, and we are moving rapidly towards a reconstruction of our understanding of time. The new physics is helping us get closer to that point by breaking down our old conceptions of linear time. As I have said at other times, I believe *A Course in Miracles* is ahead of its time, pardon the pun. For its ideas to be fully accepted in the world, as the ideas of the Bible have been, for example, the Course must await the world's "catching up" in terms of sufficiently developing its own thought systems to be able to incorporate concepts such as we are discussing here.

You would anticipate the future on the basis of your past experience, and plan for it accordingly. Yet by doing so you are aligning past and future, and not allowing the miracle, which could intervene between them, to free you to be born again.

Obviously, this does not mean being born again in the fundamentalist Christian sense of proclaiming Jesus Christ as one's Lord and Savior. By our choosing to have a happy dream, rather than the ego's nightmares, we undo the ego's "birth" that substituted for our birth as Christ, and are reborn into the real world. This "rebirth" is the precondition for awakening from the dream of separation to re-experience our birth as a creation of God.

The theme of planning for the future will be discussed at length later (Chapter 8) when we look at some passages in the workbook. It is an important theme because we do plan all the time, and this planning is always based on our past experience, which is another subtle way the ego makes its world of past, present, and future very real to us. The early workbook lessons point out to us just how much emphasis we place upon the past. Throughout, *A Course in Miracles* stresses that all we really see are projections of the past. We then make the future to replicate the past, thus ignoring the present. The miracle would free us from the ego's prison house of time, and have us live only in the present moment. In our experience, this means that we see others as they are, brothers or sisters in Christ, not as we would have them be.

The miracle enables you to see your brother without his past, and so perceive him as born again. His errors are all past, and by perceiving him without them you are releasing him.

This is what the Course means by "seeing the face of Christ," i.e., not seeing the sins of another's past. Anything we may have accused ourselves of doing, or that we may have accused another of doing in the past, we now gladly see as a call for love. This call can only occur in the present, and reflects our call for love as well. "His errors are all past" means they are non-existent, for by seeing others without those errors, we are attesting that they have had no effect. As we have already seen, if another's errors (i.e., sins) have no effect, then they cannot be a cause, and therefore do not exist. By demonstrating to others this fact of the Atonement, we demonstrate that their sins are corrected and undone, "atoned for." Thus do we free them from their terrible burden of guilt, just as we are freeing ourselves, as the next sentence says:

And since his past is yours, you share in this release. Let no dark cloud out of your past obscure him from you, for truth lies only in the present, and you will find it if you seek it there. You have looked for it where it is not, and therefore have not found it.

The image of a cloud is frequently used in the Course, and usually represents our guilt. And of course, it is my own dark cloud of guilt that I project onto you, believing it is truly there. Thus, I do not see you as you are: I cannot see the light shining in you because *my* dark cloud of guilt is obscuring it.

This passage also expresses the important theme that runs throughout the Course: seeking and finding. If guilt is what I am looking for, then that is what I shall see. If I look for the truth about you in the past, and therefore conclude that you are a sinful person because you have hurt me and others, I can never know the real truth about you. In fact, I am actually denying your reality by believing that its truth lies in the past. And this of course is the ego's whole purpose; namely, to confuse us as to where truth is found. By projecting the problem outside of our minds onto someone else, the solution must be found outside of our minds as well. We thus continually seek after the truth, but never find it because we are looking in the wrong place. It is the miracle that enables us to seek *and* find, as we now see:

Learn, then, to seek it where it is and it will dawn on eyes that see. Your past was made in anger, and if you use it to attack the present, you will not see the freedom that the present holds.

This then is the function of the miracle: to see the sin, not in our brother's past, nor in our own, but rather in the present moment when we decided to make it real. In that moment of choice was the past and all of time made real as well, becoming a prison house from which we could never escape. The miracle holds the key that opens our prison cell, and releases us to the freedom of the present. It is in our looking at our decision to be sinful in the present that we are able, at last, to recognize the illusory nature of what we chose. This allows us to choose again—to be "born again"—and accept the truth of God's Love that is also present in our minds.

Judgment and condemnation are behind you, and unless you bring them with you, you will see that you are free of them. Look lovingly upon the present, for it holds the only things that are forever true. All healing lies within it because its continuity is real.

The light that shines in each of us is what we can lovingly behold in the present, when we, through the miracle of forgiveness, unlock the chains of judgment and condemnation. In this passage we also find Jesus juxtaposing the Holy Spirit's view of the continuity of time with the ego's. The Holy Spirit sees the only continuous time as the present, the "now" we all share because we are all of one mind. The ego, however, breaks the present up into past, present, and future thereby fulfilling its aim of keeping us separate. Thus, the ego's version of continuity is one of its principal defenses against the Holy Spirit's healing, which lies only in the present.

It [healing] extends to all aspects of the Sonship at the same time, and thus enables them to reach each other. The present is before time was, and will be when time is no more. In it are all things that are eternal, and they are one. Their continuity is timeless and their communication is unbroken, for they are not separated by the past. Only the past can separate, and it is nowhere.

That is what is meant by "When I am healed I am not healed alone" (workbook, pp. 254-56; W-pI.137). All minds are one in the present; that is the window to eternity: it is the only time that is real. The present, which contains the Love of God, existed before the error, and will always be. Chart 5 attempts to illustrate this: the solid line represents the eternal that existed before the dip seemed to be, and will also be there when the dip is gone. It is time—past, present, future—that manifests the ego's belief in separation and resultant fragmentation of the Sonship. Thus, time is an illusion, a dream in our minds that has no reality. Reality is totally unaffected by the ego's dream of time. Indeed, the past *can* separate, but only in a dream. The continuity of eternity remains as it always is.

Let us now turn to Chapter 15 in the text (p. 280; T-15.I). The first section, "The Two Uses of Time," is primarily about how the ego uses time. We are going to study only the first two paragraphs.

Can you imagine what it means to have no cares, no worries, no anxieties, but merely to be perfectly calm and quiet all the time? Yet that is what time is for; to learn just that and nothing more. God's Teacher cannot be satisfied with His teaching until it constitutes all your learning. He has not fulfilled His teaching function until you have become such a consistent learner that you learn only of Him. When this has happened, you will no longer need a teacher or time in which to learn.

In other words, thinking of ourselves as the observers sitting in front of the video screen, when we hear only the Holy Spirit's Voice and choose to view only His tapes, we will no longer need Him because we will have learned the lesson. At that point, we no longer need time either. This first sentence echoes the stated goal of *A Course in Miracles*, which is the attainment of peace; not knowledge or Heaven, but the real world. At that point learning ceases and the Holy Spirit has fulfilled His function. All video tapes are gone, as the Holy Spirit's have corrected and undone the ego's. Only the Love of God exists now in the Son's mind, and all his thoughts and actions but reflect this Love. Choice is done, for he has made the one and only choice there ever was, thus canceling out the others.

One source of perceived discouragement from which you may suffer is your belief that this takes time, and that the results of the Holy Spirit's teaching are far in the future. This is not so.

There are several other places in the Course that mention this. For example, in the text Jesus says in an aforementioned passage, "let me remind you that time and space are under my control" (text, p. 29; T-2.VII.7:9). He means by this that time is not linear, space is not real, and that if we let him teach us his lesson we could learn very quickly. Then time would be collapsed, a notion we discussed earlier in relation to the miracle; a concept not understandable to anyone living in a state of duality consciousness, of temporal awareness.

If we look at the problem of guilt and time from the ego's point of view, it will seem as if the process of undoing our guilt is endless, because our guilt seems so enormous; but that way of thinking is another subtle trap of the ego. As we saw in Part I, the workbook asks the rhetorical question: "Why wait for Heaven?" (workbook, p. 347; W-pI.188.1:1). This is very helpful to keep in mind when we are choosing hell. When we are angry, upset, depressed, or guilty it is very helpful to realize that it is merely a choice; all we have to do therefore is make another one. The process sounds simple, but it is certainly not easy. What we must remember is that there is another Voice inside us that continually calls to us and says, "My brother choose again."

For the Holy Spirit uses time in His Own way, and is not bound by it. Time is His friend in teaching. It does not waste Him, as it does you.[11]   And all the waste that time seems to bring with it is due but to your identification with the ego, which uses time to support its belief in destruction. The ego, like the Holy Spirit, uses time to convince you of

---

11. This sentence was inadvertently omitted from the first edition of *A Course in Miracles.*

the inevitability of the goal and end of teaching. To the ego the goal is death, which *is* its end. But to the Holy Spirit the goal is life, which *has* no end.

The ego teaches us that we are guilty, separate, victimized, that the body and death are real, the world real, and thus existence here is absolutely fruitless, pointless, and impossible. Both the Holy Spirit and the ego use time to fulfill their own teaching goals. But since the goals are diametrically opposed, the means used differ as well; the ego's means is attack, and the Holy Spirit's is forgiveness.

Q: Would you elaborate on "death is the ego's end"?

A: In the ego thought system, the ultimate outcome of guilt or self-hatred is for one to be killed or to die. Even more to the point, the phrase means that if guilt demands punishment, the ultimate punishment for the body, which is the symbol of our sin, would be death. Thus the ego's goal is clearly death, which remains the most powerful witness to the reality of the ego. This idea is echoed in the Adam and Eve myth, where the two sinners are condemned by God to a life of pain and suffering, culminating in death: "For dust you are and to dust you shall return" (Gn 3:19). *A Course in Miracles*, however, describes the Holy Spirit's version of death, wherein when the body's

> usefulness is done it is laid by, and that is all. The mind makes this decision, as it makes all decisions that are responsible for the body's condition (manual, p. 31; M-12.5:6-7).

And in the pamphlet "The Song of Prayer"[12] comes this beautiful description of death:

> Yet there is a kind of seeming death that has a different source. It does not come because of hurtful thoughts and raging anger at the universe. It merely signifies the end has

---

12. Foundation for Inner Peace, Glen Ellen, CA, 1978.

come for usefulness of body functioning. And so it is discarded as a choice, as one lays by a garment now outworn.

This is what death should be; a quiet choice, made joyfully and with a sense of peace, because the body has been kindly used to help the Son of God along the way he goes to God. We thank the body, then, for all the service it has given us ("The Song of Prayer," p. 16; S-3.II.1:8-2:2).

Now we turn to the last paragraph in this section, which makes the same point we have been considering (text, p. 283; T-15.I.15):

Time is your friend, if you leave it to the Holy Spirit to use. He needs but very little to restore God's whole power to you.

We are so accustomed to seeing time as an enemy. Certainly in terms of human life, time *is* our enemy: we grow old, become weaker, and ultimately die. In fact, Freud taught that from the moment we are born we are in the process of dying. From the ego's point of view this of course is absolutely correct. Our life from birth is an inevitable journey to death.

Q: Like the idea that things are constantly in a state of decaying, in the process of falling apart?

A: Yes, and that is how the universe is seen too. Time thus must be seen as an enemy because it brings the death of the body, which we believe is our self. As the workbook teaches:

The body is a fence the Son of God imagines he has built, to separate parts of his Self from other parts. It is within this fence he thinks he lives, to die as it decays and crumbles. For within this fence he thinks that he is safe from love. Identifying with his safety, he regards himself as what his safety is (workbook, p. 415; W-pII.5.1:1-4).

Time, again, fulfilling the ego's purpose, becomes our indomitable foe, our only hope being to somehow stave off the inevitable defeat for a while. However, if given over to the Holy Spirit, time becomes our friend, fulfilling His holy purpose of becoming the classroom in which we learn the lesson that there is no time.

He Who transcends time for you understands what time is for. Holiness lies not in time, but in eternity. There never was an instant in which God's Son could lose his purity. His changeless state is beyond time, for his purity remains forever beyond attack and without variability. Time stands still in his holiness, and changes not. And so it is no longer time at all. For caught in the single instant of the eternal sanctity of God's creation, it is transformed into forever.

Just as guilt lies in time, holiness lies in eternity. When it fulfills its purpose of leading us there, time becomes holy, serving the Holy Spirit's purpose of forgiveness. Joining with this purpose occurs within the holy instant, the interval outside of time in which we choose to use time to awaken from the dream, rather than remaining within it. Thus there is a line in the text that says, "At no single instant does the body exist at all" (text, p. 362; T-18.VII.3:1). This is a reference to this holy instant, which reflects the timelessness of eternity. In that instant, where there is no time, there can be no body, no sin, and no death. Attack is impossible, for there are no bodies with which to attack, or by which to be attacked. And change is impossible, for the Son of God's Identity as the changeless Christ is held for him in all its purity by the Holy Spirit's Love. Chart 5 illustrates that the tiny dip or tick of time has no effect upon the eternity in which dwells our Self as Christ.

The title of the chapter in which this section comes is "The Holy Instant," and is the first place in the Course which fully presents Jesus' teachings on the holy instant. Stated another way, the holy instant is when we choose the miracle which, as we have seen, lifts us above time. Thus it becomes a herald of eternity, a window to eternity, a reflection of our holiness in Heaven. Time's purpose thus has been transformed from an imprisoning agent to a liberating one, and our minds are freed at last to melt into God.

Give the eternal instant, that eternity may be remembered for you, in that shining instant of perfect release. Offer the miracle of the holy instant through the Holy Spirit, and leave His giving it to you to Him.

Jesus is urging us to ask the Holy Spirit's help to choose a miracle instead of a grievance, to join instead of to attack, to look at the happy dream on our VCRs instead of the nightmare. We are asked, in fact, to leave everything to Him. Our job is simply to ask for the miracle. The extension of the miracle through us, as we have already pointed out, is His responsibility. As Jesus says in the text regarding forgiveness:

> Extension of forgiveness is the Holy Spirit's function. Leave this to Him. Let your concern be only that you give to Him that which can be extended. Save no dark secrets that He cannot use, but offer Him the tiny gifts He can extend forever (text, p. 449; T-22.VI.9:2-5).

Now we will move to Chapter 22, the section "Your Brother's Sinlessness," paragraph eight, line four (text, p. 440; T-22.II.8:5-6):

Whose function is to save, will save. *How* He [the Holy Spirit] will do it is beyond your understanding, but *when* must be your choice.

This is a direct extension of what we just talked about. Our only responsibility is to choose the miracle. How the Holy Spirit will extend His miracle through us is not our concern. Our only concern is choosing it. As we have seen, the miracle's expression has already happened, for that particular video tape has already been filmed and is in the computer's memory bank of our minds. What remains is that we *learn* to choose it. Thus, *when* we press that button is our choice.

For time you made, and time you can command. You are no more a slave to time than to the world you made.

The delusion of the world is that we are subject to forces beyond our control: we cannot control the ravages of time upon our bodies; we cannot control what people do to us. This belief leads us to identify with an image of the perfectly innocent victim we all believe we are. As we approach the final veil of unforgiveness that separates us from God's Love, described in "The Obstacles to Peace," we are asked to look truly at the ego's thought system, for the first time:

> It seems to you the world will utterly abandon you if you but raise your eyes. Yet all that will occur is you will leave the world forever. This is the re-establishment of *your* will. Look upon it, open-eyed, and you will nevermore believe that you are at the mercy of things beyond you, forces you cannot control, and thoughts that come to you against your will (text, p. 392; T-19.IV-D.7:1-4).

Jesus thus is telling us that we can choose to change our minds and choose a different kind of experience, recognizing that our decisions are the determiners of our distress and the causes of our *experiences* of victimhood. We are slaves only to our own choices.

Q: That is a very heavy line: "For time you made, and time you can command." How many people in this world have ever had an experience of commanding time?

A: Very, very few. That is the purpose behind passages such as these: to teach us the truth that is belied by our experience. We can see again the revolutionary teaching of *A Course in Miracles*, that literally says that the entire world is an illusion. Our experience of time and space exists only in our minds, and therefore we have the power to change the experience. Thus, there is a deeper metaphysical idea involved here as well, for this means that we can literally change time. The way we learn how to do that is by choosing what appear to be the little miracles in everyday living.

Let us move now to Chapter 25, section III, paragraph six (text, p. 488; T-25.III.6):

Everyone here has entered darkness, yet no one has entered it alone. Nor need he stay more than an instant.[13] For he has come with Heaven's Help within him [the Holy Spirit], ready to lead him out of darkness into light at any time.

The context of these statements is our linear view of time. When we are born into this world, which *is* a world of darkness, we are not alone, although our physical self has been suddenly thrust from its home in the mother's womb. The Holy Spirit remains within our minds. Thus, while our physical experience is that we are born into this world alone, separated from our mother and increasingly forced to fend for ourselves, the truth is that we are not alone, for the Holy Spirit's loving presence is within our minds as well.

The time he chooses [to be led out of darkness] can be any time, for help is there, awaiting but his choice. And when he chooses to avail himself of what is given him, then will he see each situation that he thought before was means to justify his anger turned to an event which justifies his love.

We find the same idea expressed over and over again: we do not have to wait for future happiness, for it can be right now. This is a very practical and specific expression of the Course's basic idea that at any given moment we can choose the Holy Spirit instead of the ego. We then can see that what

---

13. This sentence was inadvertently omitted from the first edition of *A Course in Miracles*.

the ego had interpreted as a situation involving a victim and victimizer, now has been changed to our experiencing two equal children of God, each calling for the love they have denied. Despite the *form* of what seems to be happening, this remains the truth. And this truth awaits our mind's recognition that *we* are doing this to ourselves. This is expressed very powerfully in the following passage:

> The secret of salvation is but this: That you are doing this unto yourself. No matter what the form of the attack, this still is true. Whoever takes the role of enemy and of attacker, still is this the truth. Whatever seems to be the cause of any pain and suffering you feel, this is still true. For you would not re-act at all to figures in a dream you knew that you were dreaming. Let them be as hateful and as vicious as they may, they could have no effect on you unless you failed to recognize it is your dream (text, p. 545; T-27.VIII.10).

We turn now to section VI, "The Special Function," the middle of paragraph five (text, p. 493; T-25.VI.5):

Forgiveness is the only function meaningful in time. It is the means the Holy Spirit uses to translate specialness from sin into salvation. Forgiveness is for all. But when it rests on all it is complete, and every function of this world completed with it. Then is time no more. Yet while in time, there is still much to do. And each must do what is allotted him, for on his part does all the plan depend.

This of course refers to the end of time, when everyone has completed his or her part of forgiveness in the plan of the Atonement. We shall consider this theme in depth in Part III. The theme of having much to do in this world is expressed in Lesson 169, already discussed, where Jesus is speaking about the metaphysical dimensions of time. He then suddenly breaks off by saying that there is no way we can understand these ideas, and so we should rather speak of what we *can* understand: forgiveness. There remains much that we have to do, which of course is forgiving our special partners. We all must complete our parts, otherwise the plan is incomplete. That is the meaning of Lesson 186: "Salvation of the world depends on me."

He [each Son] *has* a special part in time for so he chose, and choosing it, he made it for himself. His wish was not denied but changed in form, to let it serve his brother and himself, and thus become a means to save instead of lose.

When the carpet rolled out and we chose that one instant when terror took the place of love, at that same instant we chose all of our special love and special hate partners, all the ways that we would experience the victim and victimizer scripts of the ego. Thus, content and form occurred simultaneously, since sequential time is illusory. Within the same illusory instant the Holy Spirit undid the mistake—content and form. Thus, these special relationships now became our special function. Stated another way, along with the collection of ego tapes of hatred, viciousness, separation, and death, is its counterpart: a different way of looking at the world. Our egos desired to be special, and this original desire now manifests in our special relationships. When we choose to identify with the Holy Spirit, this same wish to be special assumes the *content* of our call for help, and thus the *form* now serves the Holy Spirit's loving answer to us of forgiveness. Incidentally, the word "form" in the last sentence of the above passage has the *meaning* of "content," yet another example of Jesus' inconsistent use of language (form), yet remaining consistent with meaning (content).

The final passages in the text that we will look at are in Chapter 26, the section "The Immediacy of Salvation" (text, p. 519; T-26.VIII.1). We begin with the first paragraph of this section:

The one remaining problem that you have is that you see an interval between the time when you forgive, and will receive the benefits of trusting in your brother.

We find the same idea mentioned earlier: we still believe in the reality of time and the enormity of the task of letting go of our guilt. We believe there is a tremendous amount of time required between the moment that we choose forgiveness and the moment that we receive the benefits of the Holy Spirit, meaning the benefits of letting go of our guilt and experiencing the peace that comes from truly trusting in each other. To reiterate the earlier quoted line:

> You have no idea of the tremendous release and deep peace that comes from meeting yourself and your brothers totally without judgment (text, p. 42; T-3.VI.3:1).

We believe that we must sacrifice our present happiness to atone for our sins in order to ensure our future happiness, a belief which stems ultimately from the dynamic that guilt demands punishment. This does not allow us to realize that we can be happy *now*. And while this process seems to take time, in truth it takes but an instant, the holy instant wherein we have chosen the Holy Spirit's Love and forgiveness as our guide, rather than the ego's guilt and fear. The holy instant of course takes no time at all, as it occurs in the dimension of timelessness.

This but reflects the little you would keep between you and your brother, that you and he might be a little separate [that little gap of separation that this portion of the text talks about]. For time and space are one illusion [separation], which takes different forms.

We hold on to the idea that we are separate from each other, and in so doing hold to the idea that the separated world of time and space is real. Time and space consist of the one illusion of being separate, and are, in fact, but different forms of this same thought. Jesus now proceeds to talk about this illusion's two different forms, the basic fabric of our existence here.

If it has been projected beyond your mind you think of it as time.

The "it" refers to the illusion of separation, so the line may be read as: "If separation has been projected beyond your mind you think of it as time." This is the illusion of the linearity of time's past, present, and future, leading to a view that what happened a thousand years ago is different from what is happening now, different also from what will happen a thousand years from now. Thus, we manifest the illusion of separation by breaking up time and making its segments separate, distorting time's true continuity, revealed to us by the holy instant.

The nearer it [separation] is brought to where it is [the mind], the more you think of it in terms of space.

This means we now think that you and I are inhabiting the same dimension of time, but we are still separate because we are inhabiting different spaces. Thus we find different variations of the same basic idea of being separate. One variation is that we are separate in time, so I am separate from the ancient Greeks, the prehistoric people, and the dinosaurs, and I am separate from whatever forms we believe will evolve in the future. Another variation is to say we share the same dimension of time, but we are still separate because we are separate physically. Jesus is teaching us here that there is no difference between saying that you and I are physically separate, and saying I am separate from people living in different periods in history. They are simply different forms of the same idea. And so it is that our rootedness in separation makes it impossible for us to believe that we can be healed now, as we now read, skipping a paragraph:

Salvation *is* immediate. Unless you so perceive it, you will be afraid of it, believing that the risk of loss is great between the time its purpose is made yours and its effects will come to you.

Unless we choose to accept the holy instant *now*, we will continue to sustain the ego's illusory thought system that teaches us to fear the vengeful punishment of God's Love. Thus our only salvation is to suffer pain and sacrifice now, so as to appease His wrath and hopefully be saved sometime in the future. Skipping a few lines, we read:

Time is as neutral as the body is, except in terms of what you see it for.

And so again we see that once the ego made time to suit its purpose of attacking eternity, it becomes neutral in our experience within the dream of our being here. Thus, time can either continue to serve the ego's purpose of maintaining the illusion of our sinful past, guilty present, and fearful future, or the Holy Spirit's purpose of undoing this insane belief through forgiveness. Purpose is the only criterion for meaningfully evaluating any aspect of the physical world.

Let us turn now to paragraph six (text, p. 520; T-26.VIII.6:1-2):

The working out of all correction takes no time at all. Yet the acceptance of the working out can seem to take forever.

Once again we see the metaphysical and experiential levels expressed together. To work out the correction from our position outside of time as the observer (chart 3) we need only change which buttons we are going to push, thereby deciding that time is an illusion we no longer wish. This takes no time at all because it has already happened. We needed only an illusory instant in which to believe the ego, and now need only the illusory holy instant to undo this mistaken choice. However, it seems to take a tremendously long time *within* the world of illusion. Within the illusion of time the Atonement seems to be a tremendously long process, and the end a long, long way off. However, in reality, to state it once again, salvation occurs in just an instant, because it has already been accomplished in an instant.

Let us shift now to the workbook and look at a couple of passages which are going to say essentially the same thing we have been discussing. We begin with paragraphs thirteen and fourteen from Lesson 136, "Sickness is a defense against the truth" (workbook, p. 252; W-pI.136.13-14). The preceding line states that what God wills for us must be received. This expresses the idea that giving and receiving are the same, and thus what God has given us we have already received and cannot lose. This is the context of the passages we examine now.

It is this fact that demonstrates that time is an illusion. For time lets you think what God has given you is not the truth right now, as it must be.

If God has given us creation, and has given us Himself, then we are that creation, the extension of that Self, and thus cannot be separate from Him. Time, however, tells us that we *are* separate. Even if in our best moments we believe we are really separate now, but will be rewarded in Heaven when we die, we still labor under the same illusion—that there is a gap between where we are and where God or Heaven is. The reality is that the world of time is a dream, and we remain awake with God and one with Him.

The Thoughts of God are quite apart from time. For time is but another meaningless defense you made against the truth. Yet what He wills is here, and you remain as He created you.

Remember that this lesson's context is that sickness is a defense against truth. *We* made up time as a defense against the truth of eternity, and so this line is another very clear statement of the Course's teaching that neither God nor the Holy Spirit made time. The Holy Spirit simply reinterpreted time for us. The truth is that we are not separate from God in time or space, for we remain one with Him, as He created us.

Truth has a power far beyond defense, for no illusions can remain where truth has been allowed to enter. And it comes to any mind that would lay down its arms, and cease to play with folly.

Truth has entered our minds via the Holy Spirit, and so all we need do is accept and identify with His presence, at which point the whole illusion of time disappears. We are thus asked to "cease to play" with what is elsewhere described as the childish toys of sin (text, pp. 578,589; workbook, p. 409; T-29.IX.6:2-3; T-30.IV.4:6-11; W-pII.4.5:2). Sin, the bedrock of the ego's thought system, appears so serious to us. Yet in truth sin is as silly as any game a child plays, with no more reality than the make-believe world of children's toys or our sleeping dreams. Thus we read, for example:

> The wearying, dissatisfying gods you made are blown-up children's toys. A child is frightened when a wooden head springs up as a closed box is opened suddenly, or when a soft and silent woolly bear begins to squeak as he takes hold of it. ...But *you* are not endangered. You can laugh at popping heads and squeaking toys, as does the child who learns they are no threat to him....All illusions that you believe about yourself obey no laws. They seem to dance a little while, according to the rules you set for them. But then they fall and cannot rise again. They are but toys, my child, so do not grieve for them (text, p. 589; T-30.IV.2:1-2; 3:5-6; 4:3-6).

How would an army act in dreams? Any way at all. It could be seen attacking anyone with anything. Dreams have no reason in them. A flower turns into a poisoned spear, a child becomes a giant and a mouse roars like a lion. And love is turned to hate as easily. This is no army, but a madhouse. What seems to be a planned attack is bedlam (text, p. 431; T-21.VII.3:7-14).

It [truth] is found at any time; today, if you will choose to practice giving welcome to the truth.

The truth of God's eternal presence in us, and of our eternal presence within as Christ, can come in any instant. All that is necessary is that, as the observers of these insane dreams, we change what we want to experience. At the moment we change that desire, it has already happened. As the wonderful line in the workbook says: "We are concerned only with giving welcome to the truth" (workbook, p. 469; W-pII.14.3:7). Changing our mind and welcoming what is already there is thus our only true desire.

Now we will move to the first paragraph of Lesson 138, "Heaven is the decision I must make" (workbook, p. 258; W-pI.138.7:1-2). This lesson states the idea that Heaven is a choice. But it is a choice to accept what we already have, not what we must yet attain: Heaven is already in us.

So we begin today considering the choice that time was made to help us make. Such is its [time] holy purpose, now transformed from the intent you gave it...

Clearly this does not mean that the Holy Spirit made time, but simply that He reinterprets what *we* made. We made time to attack God, reflecting our choice for hell, while the Holy Spirit reinterprets time as an aid to choose Heaven. Similarly, the Course elsewhere describes the Holy Spirit's "making" of the world:

> There is another Maker of the world, the simultaneous Corrector of the mad belief that anything could be established and maintained without some link that kept it still within the laws of God; not as the law itself upholds the universe as God

created it, but in some form adapted to the need the Son of
God believes he has.... There is another purpose in the world
that error made, because it has another Maker Who can rec-
oncile its goal with His Creator's purpose (text, pp. 487-88;
T-25.III.4:1; 5:1).

I am emphasizing this point because often students of the
Course will take these lines as well as others out of context, to
maintain that Jesus is teaching us that God or the Holy Spirit
made time. This would be a gross misreading of what the
Course really means, which is that time is "transformed from
the intent you gave it"; an intent of murder and hell. Given to
the Holy Spirit, time is reinterpreted and transformed as a
means out of hell. Thus, we are once again speaking of purpose, and its shift from the ego's to the Holy Spirit's. The
sentence from the workbook would actually read better if
there were a colon instead of a semicolon after "gave it." Let
me read it punctuated that way:

**Such is its holy purpose, now transformed from the intent
you gave it: that it be a means for demonstrating hell is
real, hope changes to despair, and life itself must in the end
be overcome by death.**

This then is the meaning we gave to time. If we change our
minds, the Holy Spirit is able to teach us that time is unreal.
Time therefore becomes a classroom in which we learn that
Heaven is what we truly want. In fact, Heaven is what we truly
are; and hell, despair, and death are the illusions.

Let us move to Lesson 194, "I place the future in the Hands
of God" (workbook, p. 360; W-pI.194.4). I already read
briefly from this passage in another context, but I shall repeat
it now and then continue. I begin with the fourth paragraph,
another clear expression of how the Holy Spirit and *A Course
in Miracles* use our illusions of time to teach us that there is no
time.

God holds your future as He holds your past and present. They are one to Him, and so they should be one to you.

This reflects the true continuity of time, that it is all one. The entire range of time, spanning billions of years, is nothing more than one single illusory instant.

Yet in this world, the temporal progression still seems real. And so you are not asked to understand the lack of sequence really found in time. You are but asked to let the future go, and place it in God's Hands. And you will see by your experience that you have laid the past and present in His Hands as well, because the past will punish you no more, and future dread will now be meaningless.

If we bring our guilt to the Holy Spirit—our illusions to the truth, our darkness to the light—He can take them away from us. Once again, we see that *A Course in Miracles* is asking us to turn over the guilt from the past, which not only frees us from the belief in our sinfulness, but correspondingly also frees us from our fear that the future will punish us. Future dreads thus become meaningless. That is why if we have no guilt in our minds, we cannot be afraid. Fear comes only from the unconscious belief that we deserve to be punished for the sins of the past.

Release the future. For the past is gone, and what is present, freed from its bequest of grief and misery, of pain and loss, becomes the instant in which time escapes the bondage of illusions where it runs its pitiless, inevitable course. Then is each instant which was slave to time transformed into a holy instant, when the light that was kept hidden in God's Son is freed to bless the world.

The light of Christ was kept hidden by the clouds of guilt in which we enshrouded ourselves, and onto which we also projected our sins, seeing them in others rather than ourselves.

The phrase "pitiless, inevitable course" reflects the manual's previously mentioned description of the world as weary, hopeless, and despairing (manual, p. 3; M-1.4:4-5).

Q: Could it also be tied into cause and effect, or action and reaction, because it says it is an inevitable course?

A: Yes, once we choose the sin and guilt of the past, we must inevitably see the world as a hostile, dreary prison house from which there is no escape. Despair is the inevitable effect of sin. Acceptance of the cause as true automatically makes the effect true as well.

This passage also reflects the very important emphasis placed in the Course on our not having to seek after the light, but rather to remove the interferences to the natural extension of this light through us. In the context of the love that has been buried within our minds, the Course states, as we have already seen (see p. 28 above):

> Your task is not to seek for love, but merely to seek and find all of the barriers within yourself that you have built against it. It is not necessary to seek for what is true, but it *is* necessary to seek for what is false (text, p. 315; T-16.IV.6:1-2).

And then in another passage:

> The course does not aim at teaching the meaning of love, for that is beyond what can be taught. It does aim, however, at removing the blocks to the awareness of love's presence... (text, intro.; T-in.1:6-7).

Now is he free, and all his glory shines upon a world made free with him, to share his holiness.

This sentence summarizes the basic message of *A Course in Miracles*: as we forgive each other, we are set free. Since we, as separated Sons of God, are all ultimately part of the one ego mind, a mind of unforgiveness or guilt, true forgiveness undoes this guilt as one, and so we are all free and healed together. The next chapter specifically deals with this issue.

Chapter 7

GUILT: THE EGO'S USE OF TIME

Before moving to the next group of passages, let me first comment further on the ego's use of time. We have been discussing time on Level Two, which is not the metaphysical view we considered in Part I. The context here is that everything that the ego made, and continues to use, is a defense against God. Perhaps the most powerful of these defenses is time, which was made by the ego as a way to protect itself from its perceived threat of eternity. In this connection, guilt is the ego's most effective device to ensure that we believe in time, because as we will see from some of the passages we are about to study, it is guilt that tells us that the sins of our past have occurred and are real. This then means that the punishment which guilt tells us we deserve is to be feared in the future. In this way the ego makes both past and future real, which securely anchors its version of time as it obscures the present, the window to eternity.

One of the prominent ideas we find in many if not all of the world's spiritualities, both East and West, is that because time is real, salvation must adhere to the laws of time. Thus in the West, and particularly in Christianity, people are taught that the way to atone for the sins of the past is to sacrifice and suffer now in the present, so that the rewards of Heaven will be secured in the future. This clearly reinforces the ego's defense of time's linearity. The Eastern parallel to this notion is the law of karma, also heavily based on the idea that time is linear. This Eastern view maintains that we have to work through our sins of the past by successive reincarnations, which is another way of saying that our salvation rests in the future.

Clearly, one of the major emphases that we find throughout *A Course in Miracles*, as we have already discussed, is that salvation is now. It is the now that is represented by the observer in chart 3. We do not work out our salvation through the events *within* the kaleidoscope, the right-hand side of the chart. We work it out by choosing, beyond time, to let go of all that appears to be in time. The Course is not talking about the same kinds of things that we find, for example, in Gestalt Therapy, which also emphasizes the here and now. The Course's "here and now" is on a much deeper level. It is not primarily concerned about simply living in the present and letting go of the past, a process that is still focused on the body, although that *is* a significant part of the process. Its ultimate goal is letting go entirely of our notion of time. That is why the Course continually places emphasis on salvation being *now*, within the holy instant that directly leads us out of time's linearity. At that point the entire defensive nature of time collapses and the ego itself disappears, "into the nothingness from which it came" (manual, p. 32; M-13.1:2).

The passages that we will look at now reflect this distinctive way of regarding time. We begin with paragraph four of "The Function of Time" in Chapter 13 (text, p. 229; T-13.IV.4):

The ego has a strange notion of time, and it is with this notion that your questioning might well begin.

As Jesus does in many other places in the Course, he is asking us to *look* at the ego's thought system with him. Two other prominent examples follow, including one we have already cited in Part I:

> Be not afraid to look upon the special hate relationship, for freedom lies in looking at it....In looking at the special relationship, it is necessary first to realize that it involves a great amount of pain (text, pp. 313,317; T-16.IV.1:1; T-16.V.1:1).

> The "laws" of chaos can be brought to light, though never understood....Let us, then, look upon them calmly, that we may look beyond them, understanding what they are, not

what they would maintain [in other words, not trying to make sense of the world, but rather trying to understand the ego's motivation in upholding the illusion that there is a world that is "upheld" by certain laws]. It is essential it be understood what they are for, because it is their purpose to make meaningless, and to attack the truth. Here are the laws that rule the world you made. And yet they govern nothing, and need not be broken; merely looked upon and gone beyond (text, p. 455; T-23.II.1:1,4-7).

In this particular set of passages Jesus is asking us to examine the ego's manipulative use of time through guilt and fear. Once we understand these dynamics and realize guilt's purpose, we can step back and realize we are not guilty for the reasons we think. All that has happened is that we played the ego's tape rather than the Holy Spirit's, having rooted ourselves in a belief that guilt and fear were real and justified. The problem is never what we think we are guilty or fearful of, but rather that we have *chosen* to become a slave to time's guilt and fear. Thus, understanding the ego's use of time allows us to make another choice, and this then allows us to take a major step towards becoming free of the imprisoning nature of the ego's thought system.

Returning now to Chapter 13 in the text (text, p. 229; T-13.IV.4:2):

The ego invests heavily in the past, and in the end believes that the past is the only aspect of time that is meaningful. Remember that its emphasis on guilt enables it to ensure its continuity by making the future like the past, and thus avoiding the present. By the notion of paying for the past in the future, the past becomes the determiner of the future, making them continuous without an intervening present. For the ego regards the present only as a brief transition to the future, in which it brings the past to the future by interpreting the present in past terms.

199

We have discussed the ego's continuity sufficiently so we do not have to review its dynamics in great detail. "Continuity" according to the ego is the linking of past and future, which becomes a defense against the "true" continuity of the present which leads continuously to Heaven. The ego's continuity, on the other hand, is *its* Heaven, which is merely hell. The more prominent psychological theories, almost all ultimately derived from Freud, are examples of this. Such theories typically maintain, in one way or the other, that the child is the father of the man; i.e., what happens in the past imprisons us and determines what the future will be. It is as if our past experiences carved out our future in stone, whose core can never be changed, simply dressed up differently. Everything then is perceived through the filter of our guilty past.

"Now" has no meaning to the ego. The present merely reminds it of past hurts, and it reacts to the present as if it *were* the past. The ego cannot tolerate release from the past, and although the past is over, the ego tries to preserve its image by responding as if it were present.

The reason of course that "now" has no meaning is that in the holy instant, that *is* now, we let go of the guilt of the past and the fear of the future that had obscured the ongoing presence of the Holy Spirit. Thus, saying that the ego is not able to tolerate the release from the past is no different from saying the ego is afraid of love, or that the ego is afraid of forgiveness. The attraction of guilt then becomes the way in which the ego protects itself from the Holy Spirit's Love, for our acceptance of that Love does mean the end of its thought system.

It [the ego] dictates your reactions to those you meet in the present from a past reference point, obscuring their present reality. In effect, if you follow the ego's dictates you will react to your brother as though he were someone else, and this will surely prevent you from recognizing him as he is.

200

The opening statement foreshadows later discussions of specialness, and especially the section "Shadows of the Past" in Chapter 17. Once we see through the filter of the past, we cannot see the light of Christ that shines in others. Rather, we shall see around them only a shadow of the guilt which *we* have put there. We put it there because we have projected it from our minds as a magical attempt to escape from the guilt of *our* past. An example of this is people who have unresolved problems with their fathers, and with authority figures in general, who then see any authority figure as if that person were their father. The ultimate origin of the authority problem of course is our belief in the separation from God, the only Authority. See, for example, the last two sections of Chapter 3 in the text for a discussion of this important topic (text, pp. 41-46; T-3.VI,VII).

And you will receive messages from him out of your own past because, by making it real in the present, you are forbidding yourself to let it go. You thus deny yourself the message of release that every brother offers you *now*.

The "message of release," which is the message of forgiveness, is that there is no past because there is no sin and no guilt. That is the crucial factor because it is guilt that holds the ego's system of time together. Therefore, in my choice to see another is my choice to see myself: guilty or innocent, imprisoned or free.

Q: The brain probably has been programmed over eons of evolution to constantly react to the past. In fact, all thought seems to deal with that. What method could we use to overcome this pattern of action-reaction?

A: Krishnamurti frequently spoke about that. The first step is to recognize, at least intellectually, exactly what the purpose of time is from the ego's point of view. On a practical level, when we start getting angry, which means that we are already caught in the midst of the ego's thought system, we should step back as quickly as we can and look at ourselves being caught. This is what the "little willingness" is about; there is really no other way. The idea is to try and stop the ego reaction as close to its starting point as possible.

This process, incidentally, is similar to the Buddhist practice of stepping back and watching our thoughts, and is extremely helpful as an exercise. We are not trying to stop the thoughts, but simply stepping back and watching them. Consequently, the power of those thoughts is diminished because their power lies in *not* looking at them. If we are stepping back and watching ourselves becoming upset, the part of us that is watching cannot be the part that is upset. This initiates the process of weakening our identification with the ego. *A Course in Miracles* explains that we have no choice but to choose *either* the ego or the Holy Spirit as our guide. There are no other alternatives, and we cannot *not* choose. As the text explains:

> ...you *cannot* make decisions by yourself. The only question really is with what you choose to make them. That is really all.... You will not make decisions by yourself whatever you decide. For they are made with idols or with God. And you ask help of anti-Christ or Christ, and which you choose will join with you and tell you what to do (text, p. 584; T-30.I.14:3-5,7-9).

The ego tries to teach us that once the anger starts, it is a chain reaction that must follow its course to the end, and then only at some future point—a few hours, a day or two later, etc.—is it over and we are back to normal again. In a sense, of course, we are still a prisoner because we remain victimized by the anger until sometime in the future when we shall be peaceful again. And so this approach is still rooted in a linear view of time, affirming the idea that we are prisoners of our past learning.

The way out of this prison, once again, is simply to stop the reaction as quickly as possible. Admittedly, it is very difficult to do that, at least at first. But if it were easy, Jesus would not talk about the difficulty as often as he does. Stepping back and watching ourselves go through the process is helpful even if we cannot stop it. It is better to watch oneself go through it than to be one hundred percent in it. That is progress indeed. And when we can look at our ego attacks calmly and gently, i.e., with the gentle love of Jesus or the Holy Spirit beside us, we have in effect completed our part in the process of forgiveness. It is the looking with this love beside us that constitutes the three steps in forgiveness I have discussed elsewhere.[14]

We continue now with the middle of paragraph six in "The Function of Time" (text, p. 229; T-13.IV.6:6):

The ego would preserve your nightmares, and prevent you from awakening and understanding they are past.

This could be thought of in terms of our sitting before the screen having two buttons to push, the nightmare and happy dream buttons. The ego continually reinforces the idea that our nightmare world is reality: sin and guilt are the facts, and our punishment is deserved. As we have seen, this is the basis of the past and future dimensions of the ego's system of time, what the ego would have us choose rather than the Holy Spirit's button which teaches that the only moment is now. His teaching is that forgiveness, not fear, is our reality in this world. At the point of the right choice we enter into the happy dream, which eventually leads to our awakening.

Q: Sometimes people who feel lonely in their present situation spend a lot of their time reminiscing about their childhood, or the childhood of their children, etc. Would that be a way of using their past to keep their ego dreams intact?

---

14. See, for example, *Forgiveness and Jesus*, Fourth Edition, pp. 55-61.

A: Absolutely. That is what the Course means by fantasies, and fantasies are always a defense against a reality with which we do not want to deal. We thus retreat by returning to memories of the past—either painful memories which then enable us to say: "I was a victim and that is why I am so unhappy," or pleasant memories which lead to: "Things were wonderful then," which of course they never truly were. But believing that our past was happy enables us to feel just as miserable as when our past was terrible, for we become justified in our current experience of victimhood by the contrast with our wonderful past. The ego will trap us regardless of the dream's form.

Let us skip to the next paragraph (text, p. 229; T-13.IV.7):

It is evident that the Holy Spirit's perception of time is the exact opposite of the ego's. The reason is equally clear, for they perceive the goal of time as diametrically opposed. The Holy Spirit interprets time's purpose as rendering the need for time unnecessary. He regards the function of time as temporary, serving only His teaching function, which is temporary by definition.

This is a common structure of many of the sections of the text, where the ego's view is juxtaposed with the Holy Spirit's. The ego's purpose is to teach us that time is real, while the Holy Spirit's purpose is to teach exactly the opposite. The final sentence is actually a play on words. Time's function is temporary because it is not going to last. It is also temporary because it occurs within time, by definition. The purpose of time, which is forgiveness, was given by the Holy Spirit in answer to the ego's purpose of time, which is guilt.

We continue with a passage partially quoted earlier.

His emphasis is therefore on the only aspect of time that can extend to the infinite, for *now* is the closest approximation of eternity that this world offers. It is in the reality of

"now," without past or future, that the beginning of the appreciation of eternity lies. For only "now" is here, and only "now" presents the opportunities for the holy encounters in which salvation can be found.

We are still operating within the second level, within the illusory nature of this world where time is seen as linear—past, present, and future. But the Holy Spirit helps us use that linearity to forgive the past, let go of the fear of the future, and then to retain the present. Thus, we are clearly not talking about eternity, which is independent of time, but rather the steps within the dream that will lead us to Heaven. One other point: as I mentioned before, this should not be confused with the Gestalt emphasis on the present, the "here and now," because this is seen only within a linear, "this world" context. *A Course in Miracles*, on the other hand, speaks about using the "now" to lead us beyond time entirely. In addition, the purely psychological approach to valuing the present emphasizes our feelings: we live with our feelings in the present. The Course's understanding is that feelings are not the key factor, but rather are the effects of the *thoughts* that give rise to those feelings.

Q: Actually, is it not true to say that the feelings that we are experiencing supposedly in the now, according to Gestalt therapists, really are the past according to the Course? They are not really occurring in the present, for the real "now" is only the moment when we join with someone.

A: Right. The Gestalt view is still inherently placed within this world, because the feelings it emphasizes occur within the body, which does automatically make the past real. The Course's view is radically different of course. However, it should be said that the Gestalt emphasis on the "here and now" was a helpful correction of the Freudian understanding of the present being imprisoned by the past.

Q: In other words, are you saying that the first step of being able to step back and watch yourself do something is more in line with the psychological model, but that true forgiveness will enable you to go to the next step of recognizing that the thoughts and feelings expressed are not really you at all?

A: Yes, that is exactly what I am saying. It is the gentle looking at the ego, with the Love of the Holy Spirit beside us, that vaults us from the ego's world to God's, thereby freeing us from the tyranny of feelings—good and bad—altogether.

The ego, on the other hand, regards the function of time as one of extending itself in place of eternity, for like the Holy Spirit, the ego interprets the goal of time as its own.

Later on, Chapter 15 discusses the ego's use of hell, which is really the continuation of itself (text, pp. 280-81; T-15.I.3-7). The use of the word "extending" here is interesting to note, because of its application to the ego. Almost always, *A Course in Miracles* employs "extending" for the Holy Spirit. This passage is an exception, and it provides a nice example of how Jesus is not rigidly consistent in terms of form, though strictly consistent in terms of content.

The continuity of past and future, under its direction, is the only purpose the ego perceives in time, and it closes over the present so that no gap in its own continuity can occur. Its continuity, then, would keep you in time, while the Holy Spirit would release you from it. It is His interpretation of the means of salvation that you must learn to accept, if you would share His goal of salvation for you.

The Holy Spirit uses time, as does the ego, but the Holy Spirit's purpose in using time is to free us from it, whereas the ego's purpose is to root us even further in its world. We all would want to share the Holy Spirit's goal of salvation because there is a part of us that is deeply miserable in the world that we have made. However, we must first unlearn the ego's lessons that time will protect us from the vengeance of eternity. Thus, our minds must first choose to accept the Holy Spirit's truth of His gentleness. Practicing forgiveness is the means by which we unlearn the ego's teachings that salvation is separation, and then join with the Holy Spirit and with each other as we journey together through time to our goal: first the holy instant, and then our home in eternity.

You, too, will interpret the function of time as you interpret yours.

If we decide that our function is to attack, separate, and maintain the ego, then of course we will see time as a means to achieve those ends. If, on the other hand, we say that our function here is to forgive, then time will be seen as a means of fulfilling that function. Once again, we decide first in our minds what we want, and then think and behave accordingly: projection makes perception (text, pp. 231,415; T-13.V.3:5; T-21.in.1:1).

If you accept your function in the world of time as one of healing, you will emphasize only the aspect of time in which healing can occur. Healing cannot be accomplished in the past. It must be accomplished in the present to release the future.

In the psychoanalytic tradition, as well as in other psychological systems, healing is always directed toward the past. We go back to the hurts and the frustrations of the past to release them, and that is what heals us in the present. Of course, all that has occurred is that the past has been made real and established as the cause of our present problems. The mind, which only exists in the present, is thus denied its power. Having been made impotent, the mind is unable to choose true healing and peace. The healing and peace that may result is spurious in the sense that it does not last; the real cause of the distress—the mind's guilt—has remained unexamined and therefore unhealed. On another level, of course, healing is facilitated any time two people join together in a desire to help and be helped. This healing, however, has nothing to do with the form of the help—in this case some application of psycho-analytic theory—but rather with the joining in the mind of therapist and patient. The Course's companion pamphlet on "Psychotherapy" discusses this:

> Healing is limited by the limitations of the psychothera-pist, as it is limited by those of the patient. The aim of the process, therefore, is to transcend these limits. Neither can do this alone, but when they join, the potentiality for transcend-ing all limitations has been given them. Now the extent of their success depends on how much of this potentiality they are willing to use....Progress becomes a matter of decision....But in the end there must be some success. One asks for help; another hears and tries to answer in the form of help. This is the formula for salvation, and must heal ("Psy-chotherapy," p. 7; P-2.III.2:1-4,6; 3:3-5).

This interpretation ties the future to the present, and ex-tends the present rather than the past. But if you interpret your function as destruction, you will lose sight of the present and hold on to the past to ensure a destructive future.

The first sentence of course refers to the Holy Spirit's inter-pretation with respect to what true healing does. Our future now becomes an extension of the healing of the present, which undoes the belief in past sin. The resultant peace now extends through us, both in the dimensions of time (from the present into the future) and space (to each other). If I believe, how-ever, that my function is to destroy, I will feel guilty. Focusing on the sins of my past, I will now project these onto the future. Inevitably, following the ego's law, these projections from my mind will return to attack me. As the text states:

> That is why those who project are vigilant for their own safety. They are afraid that their projections will return and hurt them. Believing they have blotted their projections from

their own minds, they also believe their projections are trying
to creep back in (text, p. 121; T-7.VIII.3:9-11).

Therefore, my guilt over thoughts to destroy the world demands that the world will then try to destroy me. These
projections of guilt, rather than an "objective" outer world, are
thus the basis of *all* fear. The Course continually emphasizes
that the ego's basic thrust is to destroy: Heaven, God, and
Christ. And this destruction originates and will end only in the
mind, despite its seeming appearances in the world.

**And time will be as you interpret it, for of itself it is
nothing.**

Like everything else in the world, time is neutral. Although
the ego made it as an attack, time becomes neutral insofar as
we have a choice whether to continue to use the things of the
world for the purpose of attack, or to use them as a means to
forgive attack.

Q: What if you happen to be career-oriented, seeing your
function as a gardener or mail carrier, instead of understanding
the association between a career and the two purposes that the
Course speaks of here?

A: For you then, time could be a means for removing you
from the terrible present you feel you are in. You may thus
long for the day when you can retire and be free of what you
perceive as the onerous job of being a mail carrier, gardener,
or whatever. Time then is experienced as a prison in the
present from which you have some future hope of escape, and
obviously time has been made quite real, being the means used
by the ego to "escape" from the painful "present."

Even if you love your job for its own sake, you still will
have the same fear, albeit in different form: "I love my job, but
what happens if I should lose it by injury, by firing, or through
retirement? What do I do then?" The pleasure which is associated with the form, experienced in the seeming present, is

vulnerable to change in the future, and now time is made real by becoming the enemy. In these examples time is not consciously thought of as destructive, but we can see that its underlying content is certainly not loving.

Q: Ultimately, living in time is an imprisonment, because its limitations restrict our true freedom of living in the present with the Holy Spirit. Yet there are so many ways in which we become rooted in this world. We get caught up so easily in the world's demand that we become someone, do something, advance our knowledge, etc. Is it possible actually to live in the world of time, and not get stuck in it by feeling like a prisoner or an alien?

A: Absolutely. Jesus did, and he has become the model we seek to emulate for our journey through time. In many of their writings, the Gnostics used the exact words we find in *A Course in Miracles* in terms of seeing ourselves as strangers, aliens, and prisoners in this world. These Gnostics could not wait until they escaped the world. But, you see, they also became stuck in the illusion of making the world of time and space real. That is why they ended up making the same kinds of mistakes we find in other religious movements.

The right idea, however, is to recognize that while we *are* strangers here, we can yet identify with the Holy Spirit's purpose for the world. Thus, our attitude shifts, and it becomes possible to be in this world and not suffer, not because the apparent sufferings of the world are denied, but rather because we realize that the body has a different meaning and purpose. Needless to say, this shift is not easy. It takes great willingness and learning to be first stuck in the body, and then realize that it can be seen differently. We have all allowed ourselves to be subject to the tremendous over-learning that has taught us that the body is to be used for attack and separation, and that in turn it will be attacked, suffer, sacrifice, and die. We are talking about a massive shift in how we think. Of this learning Jesus writes:

> No one...could ever doubt the power of your learning skill. There is no greater power in the world. The world was made by it, and even now depends on nothing else. The lessons you have taught yourself have been so overlearned and fixed they rise like heavy curtains to obscure the simple and obvious.... You have continued, taking every step, however difficult, without complaint, until a world was built that suited you. And every lesson that makes up the world arises from the first accomplishment of learning; an enormity so great the Holy Spirit's Voice seems small and still before its magnitude. The world began with one strange lesson, powerful enough to render God forgotten, and His Son an alien to himself, in exile from the home where God Himself established him (text, pp. 600-601; T-31.I.3:1-4; 4:3-5).

This process of re-focusing our thinking can be especially tricky because the ego will subtly burrow into anything, like a fifth column. Its motto then would be: "If you cannot lick them, join them." Thus, the ego takes a book such as *A Course in Miracles*, as egoless as any book could be, and it will still use it for ego purposes. As Jesus said of the care with which the Course was written:

> I have made every effort to use words that are almost impossible to distort, but it is always possible to twist symbols around if you wish (text, p. 33; T-3.I.3:11).

The ego is quite subtle in its workings, to say the very least.

Q: You are really speaking of the shift necessary to get us unstuck that cannot even be described in words. It almost seems to be a mysterious process, some kind of click, insight, or recognition that will shift us right out of our egos.

A: Yes, and this is because the shift occurs beyond our conscious experience. Remember that the issue, if you go back to chart 3, is not what happens in the circle on the right-hand side, but rather relates to the choice the observer makes that is ultimately beyond this world of time and space. The observer, once again, is outside of time and is not our consciously experienced selves. As we have all experienced and noted, this process is not easy. It is relatively simple to practice this Course, believing we are really doing what it says, when in fact we have not even begun to plumb its depths. It is not simply a process of loving everyone, even though such love is what Jesus is ultimately teaching. Learning to love as he did involves a massive thought reversal. When this task begins to appear overwhelming to us, it is always helpful to remember Jesus' assurance, as quoted earlier, that "the outcome is as certain as God" (text, p. 52; T-4.II.5:8).

Let us turn to Chapter 6 of the text, the section, "The Alternative to Projection," paragraph ten (text, p. 90; T-6.II.10). Here again the Course describes the difference between the Holy Spirit's use of time and the ego's, but now the difference is presented in another way.

The Holy Spirit uses time, but does not believe in it.

This statement is based upon the familiar biblical idea of being *in* the world but not *of* it: living in a world of forms and symbols, adhering to them, and yet recognizing their basic unreality. Perhaps the clearest expression of this theme is found in Lesson 184:

> It would indeed be strange if you were asked to go beyond all symbols of the world, forgetting them forever; yet were asked to take a teaching function. You have need to use the symbols of the world a while. But be you not deceived by them as well. They do not stand for anything at all....Use all the little names and symbols which delineate the world of darkness. Yet accept them not as your reality (workbook, p. 337; W-pI.184.9:1-4; 11:1-2).

When in the next chapter we discuss the passages in *A Course in Miracles* that refer to the Holy Spirit's plan for us, as well as His solving problems in the world, we will recognize that passages such as the above from the text are an example of how Jesus speaks to us in the Course in a way that we can understand. Thus the Holy Spirit is spoken of as a person Who, here, uses time, but does not believe in it. And so, what the ego made to serve its purpose the Holy Spirit can now use differently.

Coming from God He [the Holy Spirit] uses everything for good, but He does not believe in what is not true. Since the Holy Spirit is in your mind, your mind can also believe only what is true.

Again, the Holy Spirit uses everything in this world to teach us what truth and illusion are, but He does not believe in anything in this world because it is not the realm of truth. The world is either all true or all false, and what it is must therefore be the opposite of Heaven. Thus if God is true, the world must be completely false. The part of our mind (termed the right mind in the early chapters in the text) in which the Holy Spirit resides is the part that shares His recognition of what is true and what is false. In this world, on Level One, nothing is true. However, on Level Two, anything is true that reflects forgiveness and healing; falsity is anything that reinforces separation and attack. Recognition of this distinction comes from our right mind.

The Holy Spirit can speak only for this, because He speaks for God. He tells you to return your whole mind to God, because it has never left Him. If it has never left Him, you need only perceive it as it is to be returned. The full awareness of the Atonement, then, is the recognition that *the separation never occurred*. The ego cannot prevail against this because it is an explicit statement that the ego never occurred.

One could not ask for a clearer statement of the Atonement, and what the acceptance of the Atonement involves. We believe that we left God, but in reality the impossible has not happened. The fact that the word "perception" is used ("you need only perceive it as it is to be returned") tells us that Jesus is talking about this world. The perception of the mind's true reality is what the Course calls true perception or the real world. It is from that point that the end of time proceeds, culminating in God's last step. Thus, the acceptance of the Atonement is the denial of the ego's "fact" that the separation has truly occurred.

The final sentence of this passage is taken from the statement in Matthew's gospel in which Jesus tells Peter: "And I say also unto thee, That thou art Peter, and upon this rock I will build my church; and the gates of hell shall not prevail against it" (Mt 16:18, KJV). The ego cannot stop the recognition that the separation never occurred, because that truth is already present in our minds through the Holy Spirit. This truth of course carries with it the truth that the ego never occurred. This gospel allusion, by the way, appears frequently in the Course, as in this early reference in the text, cited earlier:

> *The Kingdom is perfectly united and perfectly protected, and the ego will not prevail against it. Amen.*
>
> This is written in the form of a prayer because it is useful in moments of temptation. It is a declaration of independence (text, p. 54; T-4.III.1:12-2:2).

The ego can accept the idea that return is necessary because it can so easily make the idea seem difficult.

Thus, one of the ego's basic techniques is exposed here. On one level, we would all acknowledge that what *A Course in Miracles* is asking us to do is difficult. But, saying that and allowing that "reality" to influence our acceptance of the Atonement in the present is to fall into the trap of making time real, the ego's ultimate purpose.

Q: That ego maneuver puts us right back into a state of becoming, blotting out the holy instant, doesn't it?

A: Right. That is why, as I said before, the Course emphasizes that salvation is now, which means that we can switch off that terrible ego tape we are watching on the video screen. The focus is thus always on the observer who is beyond time, not yet in eternity, but beyond time. From that position in our minds we can choose what aspects of time we will observe. The aspects of time the Holy Spirit counsels us to observe would be those of the happy dream.

Yet the Holy Spirit tells you that even return is unnecessary, because what never happened cannot be difficult.

This is where *A Course in Miracles* differs from the spiritualities of the world (almost all of them) that operate within a linear time frame, in which we undo the sins of the past through current actions, preparing us for the future—all of which makes time real. As the Course says in "I Need Do Nothing" (text, p. 363; T-18.VII.4:10-11), this does not mean that the other paths will not work, which they must if their goal is God. But they will take a much longer period of time because of the reality accorded the ego's temporal tricks.

However, you can *make* the idea of return both necessary and difficult. Yet it is surely clear that the perfect need nothing, and you cannot experience perfection as a difficult accomplishment, because that is what you are.

Even when we use the analogy of the carpet, as we do in the second chart, we are within the framework of the ego system because the carpet reflects a linear process; namely that we moved away from God in the beginning, and now we have to return. That is why, though it talks about a journey, *A Course in Miracles* very often reminds us that the journey is already over and that we *are* perfect in God. As mentioned earlier (see above, pp. 145-48), the first chapter of the text discusses this "return" in terms of the horizontal framework which is rooted in time, and the vertical one which transcends time and exists only in the present (the holy instant) (text, p. 6; T-1.II.6:1-3). The miracle, thus, is the sudden shift from the horizontal plane to the vertical one.

This is the way in which you must perceive God's creations, bringing all of your perceptions into the one line the Holy Spirit sees. This line is the direct line of communication with God, and lets your mind converge with His.

This would be an example of the spiral in chart 6, which we considered earlier. The spiral with all its curves represents the different ways in which we perceive, the shifting and changing patterns of our perceptual world. When our perceptions are aligned by the Holy Spirit's forgiveness so that everyone and everything are seen as serving the same purpose, the spiral becomes straightened out and there are no differences: everyone is seen as a brother or sister in Christ, calling out for love or expressing love. *All* situations are therefore seen as opportunities that help us to learn this lesson. The spiral thus represents the linear view of time: past, present, and future. Its complete straightening out symbolizes living only in the present moment, in the now that is one holy instant and the real world. At that point, we have a "direct line" to God since all interferences to His memory have been removed.

There is no conflict anywhere in this perception, because it means that all perception is guided by the Holy Spirit, Whose Mind is fixed on God.

In the original dictation there was some discussion between Jesus and Helen about the Freudian notion of fixation, which resulted in several puns. Briefly, fixation occurs when an unresolved problem in infancy becomes fixed in the psyche, and then everything else experienced by that person in the future harks back to that. The idea in this passage is that our minds should not be fixed on the past, but only on God. And so all of our experiences here would be understood in the light of God, and our behavior automatically guided by His Voice.

Only the Holy Spirit can resolve conflict, because only the Holy Spirit is conflict-free. He perceives only what is true in your mind, and extends outward only to what is true in other minds.

This is another of the Course's clear statements indicating that we cannot do this by ourselves. Any loving thought we have does not come from us, but from the Holy Spirit in our minds. Only that presence of Love is without conflict. This is another way of saying that unambivalent love is impossible in this world (text, p. 55; T-4.III.4:6). All of our love will have some aspect of conflict in it because we would not be in this world if we had not already made the conflict of the ego real. In fact, from the Holy Spirit's point of view that is why we are here: to undo this conflict.

However, even though pure love cannot be expressed in this world, it can be expressed from the Holy Spirit through us once we choose to forgive. Again, that is why we are here: to learn how to forgive. And so our being in the world and choosing our spiritual path already reflects a decision made in the mind to return to the Holy Spirit as our Teacher. The basic idea of *A Course in Miracles* therefore is that we learn to undo the guilt in our minds, which allows the Holy Spirit's perception to extend through us. At that point we perceive as real only the light of Christ in ourselves, and therefore in each other as well.

Turn back now to "Time and Eternity" in the text (p. 79; T-5.VI.1).

God in His knowledge is not waiting, but His Kingdom is bereft while *you* wait. All the Sons of God are waiting for your return, just as you are waiting for theirs. Delay does not matter in eternity, but it is tragic in time.

Because we believe that we have removed ourselves from the Kingdom, *we* are the ones who feel bereft and wait for our return; hardly God, Who *knows* that we never truly left. Thus, on the level of truth we are all in Heaven, yet within the dream we wait for our seemingly separated identities to return home. Delay in our return is "tragic" because of all the pain that this is causing us. If you look at chart 3 and think of our sitting in front of a screen continually choosing to watch horror movies of sacrifice and suffering, death and pain, *that* indeed is tragic. It is not tragic from the point of view of eternity, because we are already home in eternity, but it *is* tragic because of the nightmare dreams to which we are continually subjecting ourselves.

You have elected to be in time rather than eternity, and therefore believe you *are* in time. Yet your election is both free and alterable.

Here we are, looking at these films that depict a linear view of time, believing that we are really in the bodies we observe in those films. In truth of course we are only re-experiencing them in our minds. Yet we believe we are in time because we *chose* that it be so. Therefore, we can just as easily change our minds, the fundamental purpose of *A Course in Miracles* being to help us do just that.

You do not belong in time. Your place is only in eternity, where God Himself placed you forever.
Guilt feelings are the preservers of time.

This is one of the first places in the text which actually talks about guilt, which is treated in much greater depth later on, beginning with Chapter 13. Guilt, once again, preserves time by teaching us that we have sinned in the past, and therefore have to be fearful in the present of the punishment that our egos tell us is forthcoming. Guilt thus teaches us that we *do* belong in time, for we do not deserve to be with God in eternity.

**They [guilt feelings] induce fears of retaliation or aban-
donment, and thus ensure that the future will be like the
past. This is the ego's continuity. It gives the ego a false
sense of security by believing that you cannot escape from
it.**

This is the continuity of the ego system, with which we are
already familiar. And so we have still another illustration of
how the Course repeats itself over and over again, utilizing the
same themes throughout. The "false sense of security" is the
idea that within this system there is no escape. Thus the ego
believes that it is forever safe, provided of course that we remain within its thought system, which feeling guilty certainly
has us do.

**But you can and must [escape]. God offers you the conti-
nuity of eternity in exchange. When you choose to make
this exchange, you will simultaneously exchange guilt for
joy, viciousness for love, and pain for peace. My role
[Jesus] is only to unchain your will and set it free.**

The "continuity of eternity" comes to us through our
choosing the holy instant which, as we have seen, becomes the
window to eternity. That is the continuity of God's Love, of
Heaven shining through our minds, now healed by our acceptance of Jesus as our teacher. Through our "little willingness"
to turn our wills over to his, we undo the decision to separate
which was the original problem. He cannot accomplish this
for us without our choosing to join him. As he writes earlier in
the text:

> The correction of fear *is* your responsibility. When you
> ask for release from fear, you are implying that it is not. You
> should ask, instead, for help in the conditions that have
> brought the fear about. These conditions always entail a will-
> ingness to be separate (text, p. 25; T-2.VI.4:1-4).

**Your ego cannot accept this freedom, and will oppose it at
every possible moment and in every possible way. And as**

its [the ego] maker, you recognize what it can do because you gave it the power to do it.

This reflects the viciousness of the ego's last ditch stand, when we become increasingly committed to the freedom the Holy Spirit's forgiveness brings, instead of the ego's tyranny of guilt and attack. As the text states of the ego when we "respond to the Holy Spirit":

> The ego is, therefore, particularly likely to attack you when you react lovingly, because it has evaluated you as unloving and you are going against its judgment....This is when it will shift abruptly from suspiciousness to viciousness, since its uncertainty is increased....It remains suspicious as long as you despair of yourself. It shifts to viciousness when you decide not to tolerate self-abasement and seek relief....The ego will make every effort to recover and mobilize its energies against your release (text, pp. 164,166; T-9.VII.4:5,7; T-9.VIII.2:8-9; 4:5).

This viciousness is analogous to the "dark night of the soul" described by St. John of the Cross, the great sixteenth-century Spanish mystic.

Remember the Kingdom always, and remember that you who are part of the Kingdom cannot be lost. The Mind that was in me _is_ in you, for God creates with perfect fairness. Let the Holy Spirit remind you always of His fairness, and let me teach you how to share it with your brothers. How else can the chance to claim it for yourself be given you?

The second sentence of the above passage is reminiscent of St. Paul's statement: "Let this mind be in you, which was also in Christ Jesus" (Ph 2:5, KJV). Jesus is thus saying here that the mind of the Holy Spirit that was in him, and which represents the total undoing of specialness—i.e., that God has no exceptions and plays no favorites: has "perfect fairness"—is in each of us as well. In this sense there is no difference between ourselves and Jesus. What he lived out in such perfection we can learn from the Holy Spirit.

What we are discussing here can be seen very clearly in charts 2 and 3. As we have stated before, in that one instant when the ego made up the world of time and space (the carpet with the script rolled out), at the same time the Holy Spirit gave His correction. That correction was given for each and every circumstance, relationship, and situation that the ego made up. For every time I had an angry thought toward someone, there was also a correction in my mind from that very same instant. Blending symbols, we can say that on this carpet of time there is a frame-by-frame healing of the film containing all the ego's mistakes.

We can then place chart 2 into chart 3, and instead of seeing this process as linear, we understand it holographically, with all having occurred in that one instant. Then as we are sitting in the observer's chair, two voices speak to us: the ego telling us to continue to see ourselves as a victim; at the same time the Holy Spirit is urging us to return to that same situation as experienced through a vision of forgiveness. Instead of our attacking this person and/or seeing ourselves as victims of attack, we see this person as our brother or sister in Christ; instead of tapes of judgment and anger, we now have chosen to re-experience tapes of forgiveness. The situation in general is the same in form, but with a different content or purpose: fairness instead of specialness. That is the meaning of turning to Jesus for help: we remember God's "perfect fairness" that is already present in us, and allow Jesus to teach us the ending of specialness through forgiveness. By sharing this teaching with others, we come to learn it for ourselves.

The two voices speak for different interpretations of the same thing simultaneously; or almost simultaneously, for the ego always speaks first. Alternate interpretations were unnecessary until the first one was made.

Thus, even though this whole thing happened in an instant, there would not have been the Holy Spirit's correction if there had not first been the ego's mistake. And we see again that the Holy Spirit's correction script is essentially the ego's first script—of guilt and hatred—forgiven and seen differently. Therefore when Jesus speaks of the script having already been written, he is referring to the ego's script which came first. Only after the mistake was made does the Holy Spirit's correction apply.

Q: I think that the idea that the ego always speaks first can often be misunderstood. Doesn't it mean that without the ego there would not be a need for correction?

A: Yes, that is quite right. But this does not mean that if you meditate or pray, the first voice you hear will always be the ego. We would not even be meditating or praying if we first did not believe that we were here in the body, which of course is the ego's belief. And so our desire to pray is actually an answer to the prior mistaken belief that we are separate from God and are truly here in the world. These sentences therefore are referring to the larger process of correction we have been speaking about.

Now we will skip to the last paragraph of the section (text, p. 81; T-5.VI.12). The preceding paragraph spoke about the infinite patience that Jesus was taught by the Holy Spirit; that patience is the context of the passages we will read now.

Now you must learn that only infinite patience produces immediate effects.

The "immediate effects" occur when we shift from the ego's video tape to the Holy Spirit's. That shift can occur immediately, and its effect be experienced immediately. My patience in realizing that you have an ego that you are working through, that I have an ego that I am working through, and that neither one is real, enables me not to take any of it seriously and not to be trapped into believing the ego's view of time. In that holy instant when this shift occurs, I experience the "immediate effects": where before I was disquieted, angry, and upset, now I am at peace. Also, my insistence on a time frame in which salvation must be worked out is always an ego trap, for it makes time real. Therefore, I cannot dictate when the shift of the holy instant will occur; that is the Holy Spirit's function.

This is the way in which time is exchanged for eternity. Infinite patience calls upon infinite love, and by producing results *now* it renders time unnecessary. We have repeatedly said that time is a learning device to be abolished when it is no longer useful.

Seeing ourselves in the context of chart 3, we can suddenly shift from believing in the reality of the ego's video tapes of time, realizing at last that it is all an illusion, nothing more than a flimsy veil that sought to hide eternity. That veil is what Jesus parted by his demonstrating the power of love in the presence of seeming attack. Time *has* no power over eternity. Learning that lesson is therefore time's only purpose for us. When the lesson is learned, and we can stand in front of the video screen saying "I no longer want this," time ceases to have meaning and therefore will cease to exist.

The Holy Spirit, Who speaks for God in time, also knows that time is meaningless. He reminds you of this in every passing moment of time, because it is His special function to return you to eternity and remain to bless your creations there.

Within a linear view of time the Holy Spirit cannot complete His function until every last remaining Son of God has awakened from the dream. The statement of the Holy Spirit's returning to eternity and blessing our creations refers to this earlier passage in the text:

> When the Atonement is complete and the whole Sonship is healed there will be no call to return. But what God creates is eternal. The Holy Spirit will remain with the Sons of God, to bless their creations and keep them in the light of joy (text, p. 68; T-5.I.5:5-7).

Like so many other statements we have discussed, this should not be taken literally on the level of *form*. Rather, its message is the *content* of the eternal nature of love.

Chapter 8

THE HOLY SPIRIT'S PLAN

The next group of passages we will consider deals with the idea that the Holy Spirit has a plan for us. If these sections are taken out of context, they can certainly be taken to mean that the Holy Spirit does things for us in the world. I would like to explain this issue briefly now, and then use specific passages to discuss it further.

As we have already seen, *A Course in Miracles* uses the various symbols of the world, but teaches us something quite different from what these symbols usually represent. Lesson 99, the first set of passages we shall look at, talks about the plan of God. Earlier, when we discussed the notion of the future as it is presented in Lesson 194 ("I place the future in the Hands of God"), we saw that the Course teaches that there is no past, present, and future in God's Mind; for they are all one. But because we still believe in the temporal progression of time, Jesus approaches us in terms of this belief. This is what we will find in Lesson 99 as well.

As we have also seen in many, many places, the Course aims at correcting the misthinking of the world in general, and the Christian theological world specifically. One of the major points of the Christian theology of salvation is that God permits us to suffer in the present as a way of attaining future salvation. I heard one of the most striking contemporary descriptions of this principle from Mother Teresa, when she spoke of suffering as a kiss from God.

If you really think that position through, its implications are frightening. In one striking passage in the text, Jesus describes our world of suffering: "The world you see is the delusional system of those made mad by guilt. Look carefully at this world, and you will realize that this is so." He concludes his graphic description: "If this were the real world, God *would* be cruel" (text, p. 220; T-13.in.2:2-3; 3:1). However, within the thought system that Mother Teresa represents, that of the traditional Roman Catholic Church, the notion that God permits us to suffer out of His Love is a very comforting one. Since we all suffer, to believe that this is the Will of God—in fact is a kiss from God—can indeed on one level provide a measure of consolation. But on closer examination, this belief that God allows us to suffer now so that we will be happy in the future fits in very nicely with the ego's view of sacrifice as being its part of a special love bargain with God: we will suffer and sacrifice now so that God will welcome us back into His Kingdom later. It is quite apparent that most people, even those who were not brought up in a religious atmosphere, implicitly accept the idea that we suffer now so that we will have future peace. The Protestant work ethic, hardly restricted to Protestants of course, is a clear example of this kind of thinking.

Another common belief along these lines, which is seemingly reflected in a passage we shall soon examine, is that God will place blocks in our path so that we will stumble, fall, and suffer, only so we could learn His lessons and be released from pain later on. *A Course in Miracles*, in one sense, says the same thing, but makes it clear that this is not God's plan. Jesus does talk about how things will be difficult, but this is part of the ego's will, not God's. If we let the Holy Spirit join with us in our difficulties, He can then teach us the lessons which would help us most: "All things are lessons God would have me learn" (workbook, pp. 357-59; W-pI.193). It is essential to remember, though, that it is not God Who writes the script. God does not cause us to be punished; He does not put stones in our path, nor is our suffering a kiss from Him.

Therefore, it is in this context that these passages ought to be understood: they represent an attempt to correct the idea that God punishes us in the present or in the future. That is why the message takes the form it does. Basically, we will regard the plan, as it is presented in the following passages, as being on two levels. The first is the overall plan of the Atonement that undoes the separation; the second expresses the plan within the context of correcting our misconceptions that God punishes us and causes us to suffer.

Let us start with Lesson 99 in the workbook, paragraph four (workbook, p. 174; W-pI.99.4). From here on, incidentally, the entire workbook is written in blank verse.

What joins the separated mind and thoughts with Mind and Thought which are forever one? What plan could hold the truth inviolate, yet recognize the need illusions bring, and offer means by which they are undone without attack and with no touch of pain?

Both levels—the metaphysical and the practical—are reflected in this passage. The concept of the plan which holds the truth inviolate reflects the truth of Heaven, meaning that everything in this world is an illusion: Level One. The shift to Level Two occurs in the second part of the above sentence, which states that the plan at the same time recognizes the "need that illusions bring." In other words, the truth of Heaven has to be translated for us into the symbols and forms of this world of illusions. In fact, the Holy Spirit is described at one point as a translator:

> Laws must be communicated if they are to be helpful. In effect, they must be translated for those who speak different languages. Nevertheless, a good translator, although he must alter the form of what he translates, never changes the meaning. In fact, his whole purpose is to change the form so that the original meaning is retained. The Holy Spirit is the translator of the laws of God to those who do not understand them (text, p. 106; T-7.II.4:1-5).

The very fact that Jesus is talking about undoing illusions is saying that this level, where we experience illusions as real, is where they must be undone. So we operate within this world of illusions, except that what we do with them is not to attack but to forgive them.

What but a Thought of God could be this plan, by which the never done is overlooked, and sins forgotten which were never real?

The Holy Spirit holds this plan of God exactly as it was received of Him within the Mind of God and in your own.

The "plan of God," again, is the Atonement, acceptance of which is the recognition that the separation never occurred. Without sin, guilt, and fear of punishment, no defense is needed, and so the basis for sacrifice and special relationships is gone. The plan is nothing more than the presence of God's perfect Love in our minds, which being of God can never change and remains as it always is. Like a beacon of light in the darkness of our split minds, it calls us unceasingly to return to this light, which reflects the light of our Source.

The Holy Spirit is the presence of God's Love, the bridge between the split mind and the Mind of God. This bridge, automatically undoing the gap between God and His Son, *is* the Atonement. We find here, incidentally, the familiar idea of the Holy Spirit being "the communication link between God and His separated Sons" (text, p. 140; T-8.VII.2:2; see also text, pp. 88,171,250; T-6.I.19:1; T-10.III.2:6; T-13.XI.8:1).

It [the plan] is apart from time in that its Source is time-less. Yet it operates in time, because of your belief that time is real.

Again, we find both levels expressed. The first sentence is a typical Level One statement, reflecting the idea of the Holy Spirit (the plan of the Atonement) being part of God (our time-less Source), and therefore separate from the illusion. The second sentence reflects only the illusion, the Holy Spirit's perceptual function of being within our right minds, correcting our wrong-minded thinking. What is important here is the recognition that He is *perceived* as operating within the

228

framework of this world, joining us in the ego thought system that maintains that time and space are real. He joins with us to teach us ultimately that time and space are illusory.

The Holy Spirit's teaching is accomplished by His undoing the "glue" that roots us in this world of time and space. That "glue" is our guilt and our fear of God's punishment. In actuality, of course, the Holy Spirit does not "do" anything. Rather, He is simply a Thought in our split minds, the memory of God's Love that we carried into the dream when we fell asleep and began the dream of separation. Thus, His is a *presence* of Love and light that "calls" our attention back to the point in our minds when we chose the ego, allowing us the opportunity now to choose again. Our experience, however, can be that He is an *active* presence that actually does things for us.

Thus, the Holy Spirit operates within this temporal framework even though He knows that time and space are not real. However, He does not obliterate the belief in time and space, which would awaken us from the dream too rapidly, precipitating panic. Rather, the Holy Spirit changes our nightmare dreams to happy dreams. This results in the experience of remaining in the split mind, living within the world of time and space, but living only in the present, not the past or the future. What is thus undone is not the dream itself, but simply that part of the dream that holds our guilt and the belief that God will punish us. As the text says of the miracle:

> The miracle does not awaken you, but merely shows you who the dreamer is. It teaches you there is a choice of dreams while you are still asleep, depending on the purpose of your dreaming. Do you wish for dreams of healing, or for dreams of death? (text, p. 551; T-28.II.4:2-4)

Unshaken does the Holy Spirit look on what you see; on sin and pain and death, on grief and separation and on loss. Yet does He know one thing must still be true; God is still Love, and this is not His Will.

This is the Thought that brings illusions to the truth, and sees them as appearances behind which is the changeless and the sure.

The Holy Spirit does not deny our experience of pain, but His love immediately looks beyond it to the fear which caused it, and beyond that to the Love that is our only reality. This is a central idea in *A Course in Miracles*, and is stated even more explicitly in this important passage from the text:

> In gentle laughter does the Holy Spirit perceive the cause, and looks not to effects. How else could He correct your error, who have overlooked the cause entirely? He bids you bring each terrible effect to Him that you may look together on its foolish cause and laugh with Him a while. *You* judge effects, but *He* has judged their cause. And by His judgment are effects removed (text, p. 545; T-27.VIII.9:1-5).

Earlier in the text we are urged, whenever tempted to become upset by any aspect of the separated world, to remember these lines:

> When you seem to see some twisted form of the original error rising to frighten you, say only, "God is not fear, but Love," and it will disappear (text, p. 348; T-18.I.7:1).

Later on in the workbook this idea becomes part of the fifth review lesson that "God is but Love, and therefore so am I." This passage we are considering from Lesson 99 also looks forward to Lesson 187, which says:

> Nor can he fail to recognize the many forms which sacrifice may take. He laughs as well at pain and loss, at sickness and at grief, at poverty, starvation and at death (workbook, pp. 345-46; W-pI.187.6:3-4).

The "he" in this passage refers to the right-minded Son of God, to whose perception we all aspire. The laughter of course is not the derisive laughter of the ego, but the gentle laughter of the Holy Spirit, born of the awareness of the inherently illusory nature of the world and all its suffering. *We* judge the terrible effects of our belief in sin and separation, but the Holy Spirit's presence of God's Love "judges" the cause of sin as merely impossible. Fear is the basis of all the world's problems, and fear has already been undone by the Holy Spirit's Love.

By aligning our minds with the Holy Spirit, His perception becomes our own. Thus, we do not deny what our body's eyes see, but rather give what we see a different interpretation. As we have already observed, Jesus is the shining example of that principle. This gentle laughter as a response to the seeming reality of the perceptual world is the idea of the Atonement. We bring the illusions of the ego—our guilt, fear, and belief in separation—to the truth that we are all joined; and we look beyond the appearances of the darkness of the egos to the light of Christ that shines in us. The manual describes this shift in perception:

> The body's eyes will continue to see differences. But the mind that has let itself be healed will no longer acknowledge them. There will be those who seem to be "sicker" than others, and the body's eyes will report their changed appearances as before. But the healed mind will put them all in one category; they are unreal (manual, p. 24; M-8.6:1-4).

As we continue our discussion of the Holy Spirit's plan for us, let us turn to the workbook, Lesson 135, "If I defend myself I am attacked," paragraph eleven (workbook, p. 246; W-pI.135.11):

A healed mind does not plan. It carries out the plans that it receives through listening to Wisdom that is not its own.

This is one of the more frequently misunderstood and misapplied ideas in the Course, because many students stop with the first sentence and do not continue on with the second. They then conclude that because a healed mind does not plan, they therefore should throw away their date books and calendars, give up their insurance policies, and simply not plan anything at all—just live in the present moment. However, they neglect to read the next sentence, which clearly does not tell us *not* to plan. Rather, we are told to plan, but not by ourselves. The Holy Spirit's is the Wisdom we consult, and so we carry out the plans that are given us by Him.

It [the healed mind] waits until it has been taught what should be done, and then proceeds to do it. It does not depend upon itself for anything except its adequacy to fulfill the plans assigned to it. It is secure in certainty that obstacles can not impede its progress to accomplishment of any goal that serves the greater plan established for the good of everyone.

We are not being asked *not* to be active in the world, but simply not to act on our own. The "greater plan" is the plan of the Atonement, in which no one loses and everyone gains. The obstacles referred to consist of anything in this world that we believe is a problem. The older, more traditional way of regarding obstacles is that they are gifts from God, as we have already seen. Through suffering and working our way through these obstacles and problems, the ways God shows us His Love, we come to know His Will. The biblical book of Job is a very powerful expression of that kind of thinking.

Thus the Course is teaching us here that any of the obstacles we believe are present can be overcome by changing our minds about them. The meaning of forgiveness is not that we change other people or the world, but that we recognize that what bothers us is not outside of us. It is the way we perceive other people and the world that causes our disquiet. By removing the obstacles in our minds, which are different expressions of our own guilt, our minds are healed; and since minds are joined, the healing of our minds also heals the whole Sonship. That is the "greater plan" established for the good of everyone. Each of us fulfills the special function of forgiveness of our special relationships (text, p. 493;

T-25.VI.5). As the Course explains regarding the "secret of salvation," we are bringing all pain and suffering unto ourselves:

> This single lesson learned will set you free from suffering, whatever form it takes. The Holy Spirit will repeat this one inclusive lesson of deliverance until it has been learned, regardless of the form of suffering that brings you pain. Whatever hurt you bring to Him He will make answer with this very simple truth. For this one answer takes away the cause of every form of sorrow and of pain. The form affects His answer not at all, for He would teach you but the single cause of all of them, no matter what their form. And you will understand that miracles reflect the simple statement, "*I* have done this thing, and it is this I would undo" (text, pp. 545-46; T-27.VIII.11).

Let us skip now to Lesson 135, paragraph seventeen (workbook, p. 247; W-pI.135.17):

Defenses are the plans you undertake to make against the truth.

This lesson deals with defenses, as does the next lesson, set in the context of sickness. It begins by first making sin real by telling us that "we have a problem," and then proceeding to erect a defense (the world and the body) to protect ourselves from this ego-invented and therefore non-existent problem. Meanwhile, the ego has tricked us into believing that all of our energies should be directed at resolving the reflections of this problem, which incidentally could manifest either internally (psychological) or externally. And all the while the problem of sin and guilt (itself a defense against God's Love) is kept hidden and protected in our minds.

For example, let us say I have a specific phobia. I start off by saying that this is a real problem, and that I am going to devise a way to protect myself against this. It could be either by my avoiding the object of the phobia, or through the dynamic of counter-phobia—going against the phobia, thereby trying to prove that I am not afraid of it. The crucial idea is that we set the whole situation up. We define the problem and then decide what the answer is. As we saw earlier, the section "I Need Do Nothing" teaches that I am not to do anything on my own (at least if I truly wish to be happy). I do not first define a problem and then say I have to do something about it. I rather let the Holy Spirit guide me, allowing Him to help me realize that the problem is not as I perceive it at all. My one problem is believing that I am separate. Thus, in terms of the phobia, while on the one hand I may seek to remove the phobic symptoms through some form of what the Course would call magic—e.g., psychotherapy, behavioral modification, or medication—on the other hand I seek to remove the *cause* of the phobia, which is the guilt in my mind stemming from my decision to be separate.

Their [defenses] aim is to select what you approve, and disregard what you consider incompatible with your beliefs of your reality. Yet what remains is meaningless indeed. For it is your reality that is the "threat" which your defenses would attack, obscure, and take apart and crucify.

We do not realize that our ego self-image, which in its origin is sinful, guilty, and weakened, requiring continual defense, is itself a defense. The real threat is not the outside world, nor any thoughts we feel are potentially harmful to us; the real threat for the ego is the truth of who we are. This theme is also picked up again in the next lesson which talks about sickness as a defense against truth. If we think of ourselves back in the observer's chair (chart 3), we would realize that the nightmare tapes we repeatedly replay, over and over again, are tapes that contain some aspect of our guilt, the hatred of ourselves that has to be defended against.

Sometimes the form of the defense is to attack other people, leading us to become nasty and vicious. Other times the defense comes in the form of making ourselves sick. And sometimes our defenses seem not to work at all, and we become flooded with anxiety, terror, guilt, and depression. The result is still the same, however, because even if we are flooded with anxiety and depression, the idea that we are guilty egos is being reinforced.

Thus, even when the ego's defenses do not seem to be working, they really are, at least from the ego's point of view. We always try to select those defenses we believe will work better than others. In reality, though, none of them can truly succeed in bringing us peace. The very fact that we need to choose certain aspects of our world to relate to reflects our belief there is something weakened inside of us that has to be protected. This obviously makes the whole ego system real.

What could you not accept, if you but knew that everything that happens, all events, past, present and to come, are gently planned by One Whose only purpose is your good.

This can be taken to mean that the Holy Spirit acts in this world and plans our external lives for us. If we recall what we discussed earlier about the metaphysics of time, we can see that this obviously cannot be the case, because on this level there is no past, present, and future. In other words, everything has happened already. In addition, as we have just seen, the Holy Spirit does not deal in the world of form or effects (the problems of the world), but only with the content or cause (the mind's belief in the reality of sin).

Let us again consider ourselves as the observers sitting before a screen. We have a collection of ego nightmare tapes, and then a counterpart collection containing the Holy Spirit's correction for all the mistakes. Both the problem and answer occurred simultaneously in that split second. This passage thus is telling us that as we sit in the observer's chair, the Holy Spirit is within our minds whispering, "You will feel better if you play My tapes of joining, forgiveness, and healing, rather than the ego's tapes of condemnation and judgment." This thought of forgiveness constitutes the Holy Spirit's plan. The words seem to suggest that the Holy Spirit operates in time, but this is to correct the notion that God or the Holy Spirit will act to punish us, making us suffer either out of love so that in the end we can attain the Kingdom, or as an expression of Their vengeful wrath, justified because of our sins against Heaven.

Another analogy is that of sitting in a movie theater watching the images come and go on the screen. Dust falls into the projector and lands on the film as it passes through, and casts a black image on the screen, marring the scene. We do not seek to fix, change, or clean the screen, because there is nothing there to fix. Rather we go to the source of the problem, the dust on the film. Similarly, as we have seen, the Holy Spirit does not deal with the effect, the projection onto the screen of our lives, but rather His Love undoes the cause, the guilt in our minds. As our minds are cleaned, our perception is cleaned as well, and all pain and suffering—nothing more than a projection of what is in our minds—is undone as they disappear back into the nothingness of sin and guilt which is their origin.

Lest a student of the Course be confused about the Holy Spirit's "plan," thinking it might include painful events, the following lines are offered:

Perhaps you have misunderstood His plan, for He would never offer pain to you. But your defenses did not let you see His loving blessing shine in every step you ever took.

This means that the Holy Spirit has taken the ancient script of pain and suffering and has changed it around for us; not in form but in content. Our only choice is which tape we are going to view. Therefore, the reason that Jesus emphasizes that things are gently planned is not that the Holy Spirit plans things for us—this could not be because everything has already happened, let alone the fact that He looks only to the cause, and does not see the effects that are not there. The purpose of emphasizing the gentle planning of the Holy Spirit is to correct any misperception that He does not plan *gently*, but with anger and judgment.

Q: There is a part in the teacher's manual that sounds similar to this. Jesus says, "The past as well held no mistakes; nothing that did not serve to benefit the world, as well as him to whom it seemed to happen" (manual, p. 13; M-4.VIII.1:6).

A: That is expressing the same idea. But in interpreting this passage it helps to keep in mind the symbol of the dual highway in chart 2: the ancient script filled with pain and suffering and death, etc., and beneath it the correction. They both occurred simultaneously.

Q: If you do not have that insight in your mind, you can really misinterpret this and end up thinking: "Oh, that so and so in Heaven! Look at the events that He planned for today."

A: Unfortunately, that is what people do, ending up with the idea that the Holy Spirit's plan called for me to be raped or to lose my home, possessions, and loved ones, all to teach me that I am not my body. As the saying goes: "With friends like this, who needs enemies?" It does not seem to matter that there are so many other places in the three books that categorically refute that idea. Remember that the ego plan calls for making the Holy Spirit into a cruel and vindictive monster.

Q: It is similar to what some people do with lines in the Bible, such as the one which says that in order to follow Jesus you have to hate your mother and your father.

A: Unfortunately, it is true that lines such as these have been ripped from their context and used to justify all forms of ego thoughts, the exact opposite of their true meaning. A passage quoted earlier is worth recalling at this point. Referring to the traditional Christian belief that God demanded the suffering and sacrifice of His own Son, Jesus says: "Yet the real Christian should pause and ask, 'How could this be?'" (text, p. 32; T-3.I.1:8).

This next line is a beauty.

While you made plans for death, He led you gently to eternal life.

The ego script, which contains our plans for death, is turned around by the Holy Spirit. Our plans for death, which we think are really plans for life, are the defenses our egos set up to protect ourselves from God's punishment. In the midst of these, whether the defenses take the form of external problems, or are associated with our physical or mental distress, the Holy Spirit's loving presence still gently leads us home. A previously quoted sentence in the text reads: "In crucifixion is redemption laid" (text, p. 518; T-26.VII.17:1). In the heart of guilt's pain in our minds redemption is present as well, if we but make the decision to remove our finger from the ego's button and place it on the Holy Spirit's, thus shifting from video tapes of nightmares to those of happy dreams. The choice is always ours.

Your present trust in Him is the defense that promises a future undisturbed, without a trace of sorrow, and with joy that constantly increases, as this life becomes a holy instant, set in time, but heeding only immortality.

Despite all the "objective" misery of this world, or what seems to be the misery of being a prisoner in this world, there is another way of looking at this world: through the holy instant which leads us beyond the ego's perceptions. The world itself does not change, as we have already seen, but as our perceptions change, so do our attitudes about the world, for they are one. With this new meaning extended from our minds, the world has changed as well: cause and effect, source and idea, remain unseparated.

Q: What is the definition of "undisturbed" in this context?

A: It means undisturbed by ego thoughts. This is important. Even the most disturbing of world situations, as for example being a prisoner in Auschwitz, can have no effect on our inner peace providing we are perceiving the situation through the eyes of the Holy Spirit. The *cause* of all our distress and disturbance does not lie outside of us, but rather in our mind's choices. Remember the important passage from the workbook, cited earlier:

> The seeming cost of accepting today's idea ["My salvation comes from me."] is this: It means that nothing outside yourself can save you; nothing outside yourself can give you peace. But it also means that nothing outside yourself can hurt you, or disturb your peace or upset you in anyway (workbook, p. 118; W-pI.70.2:1-2).

Therefore, though still living in the world of time, through choosing the peace of the holy instant we are obeying the loving law of eternity, reflected here in our forgiveness of each other and of ourselves.

Let no defenses but your present trust [the emphasis is on *present* trust, which is repeated from the beginning of the paragraph] direct the future, and this life becomes a meaningful encounter with the truth that only your defenses would conceal.

Without defenses, you become a light which Heaven gratefully acknowledges to be its own. And it will lead you on in ways appointed for your happiness according to the ancient plan, begun when time was born.

We could think of defenses in this context as clouds of guilt, a metaphor that is prominent in the early workbook lessons as well as in the text. When those clouds of guilt are taken away, the light of Christ that is already in us is allowed to shine. And so, at the instant time was born and the ego script emerged, the ancient plan of the Holy Spirit was born as well. It seems to occur *in* time, but in reality it is *beyond* time. The "plan" calls for our recognizing in every situation an opportunity to forgive and heal our minds. Thus, we are reminded in the text:

> When you meet anyone, remember it is a holy encounter. As you see him you will see yourself. As you treat him you will treat yourself. As you think of him you will think of yourself. Never forget this, for in him you will find yourself or lose yourself. Whenever two Sons of God meet, they are given another chance at salvation. Do not leave anyone without giving salvation to him and receiving it yourself (text, p. 132; T-8.III.4:1-7).

Identifying with this plan, then, our lives become "meaningful encounters with the truth." It is the ego's fear of this truth that its illusory arsenal of defenses serves to uphold.

Your followers will join their light with yours, and it will be increased until the world is lighted up with joy. And gladly will our brothers lay aside their cumbersome defenses, which availed them nothing and could only terrify.

As we choose to forgive and let go the clouds of guilt that obscured the light of Christ in our minds, that light shines forth into the minds of everyone, as theirs shines forth as well. Thus does the circle of Atonement grow (text, pp. 262-64; T-14.V). Perhaps the ultimate expression of this vision is at the very end of the text, in the context of Jesus' prayer to our Father:

> I give You thanks for what my brothers are. And as each one elects to join with me, the song of thanks from earth to Heaven grows from tiny scattered threads of melody to one inclusive chorus from a world redeemed from hell, and giving thanks to You (text, p. 622; T-31.VIII.11:4-5).

There is a parallel passage in the text at the end of the section "Entering the Ark" (text, p. 404; T-20.IV.8). It basically says the same thing, but in a different way. We turn to this now:

You may wonder how you can be at peace when, while you are in time, there is so much that must be done before the way to peace is open.

This expresses the aforementioned inevitable feeling of Course students as they begin to appreciate the enormity of the ego system, tending to say, "My God, how could this ever be undone?" There is another passage in the text, already partially quoted, which conveys the same message:

Readiness is only the beginning of confidence. You may think this implies that an enormous amount of time is necessary between readiness and mastery, but let me remind you that time and space are under my [Jesus] control (text, p. 29; T-2.VII.7:8-9).

The idea mentioned earlier is important here: we do not have to be perfect, and need not have mastered something in order to be ready to perform it. Readiness does not mean mastery. Very, very few have mastered this thought system, but that does not mean that people are not ready to practice it. However, if we think that undoing our guilt is impossible, or if we feel overwhelmed by this task and think it would take a tremendous amount of time to learn to forgive, Jesus steps in at that point to remind us that time and space are under his control and therefore the miracle has the power to shorten time. In other words, the miracle can help us suddenly shift from the nightmare of the ego to the happy dream of the Holy Spirit. Once again, it seems as if it is an enormous and an impossible task, but that is because we believe that time is real.

Perhaps this seems impossible to you. But ask yourself if it is possible that God would have a plan for your salvation that does not work. Once you accept His plan as the one

function that you would fulfill, there will be nothing else the Holy Spirit will not arrange for you without your effort. He will go before you making straight your path, and leaving in your way no stones to trip on, and no obstacles to bar your way.

We can recognize in this passage the significance of the Course's use of words, the repetition of certain words like "obstacles." The risk of misinterpretation is considerably lessened if we recognize that the message here is a correction for another way of thinking. We have considered this before. The traditional view was that God placed stones in our path, and through the process of overcoming these obstacles we found His Love. Jesus is telling us here that the situation is the other way around. The phrase "making straight your path" is biblical, John the Baptist's words taken from Isaiah. This could be thought of in terms of chart 6, which portrays the ego's crooked path in the form of a spiral. The Holy Spirit's path is a straight line that overcomes all the ego barriers of separation. Now, again, this seems to suggest that the Holy Spirit arranges things for us, that He works out the future. This could not be the case, however, if time is an illusion.

To make the point once again, these passages are presented to us precisely because we *do* believe that time is real, and therefore, just as we are asked to "place the future in the Hands of God" (workbook, p. 360; W-pI.194), we are also asked here to trust that the Holy Spirit will take care of things for us. Therefore, the way He helps us is by *reminding* us that we can change our minds, change our viewing channel to re-experience the happy dreams of forgiveness rather than nightmares. This does not mean that He does things in the world, because as the Course stresses again and again, there is no world, just as there is no future, but only the scripts that have already been completed.

Thus, the Holy Spirit operates in our minds within the illusion that there is time, that there are things that have to be done and obstacles to be overcome. But that is only because that is where we believe we are. Earlier in the text, as we have seen, Jesus asks us to ponder the question, "Who is the 'you' who are living in this world?" (text, p. 54; T-4.II.11:8). He is teaching us that this "you" is not our real Self at all, and that we have to be vigilant in recognizing how the ego masks our true Identity that is held for us by the Holy Spirit.

Nothing you need will be denied you. Not one seeming difficulty but will melt away before you reach it. You need take thought for nothing, careless of everything except the only purpose that you would fulfill.

This is a reference to the portion of the Sermon on the Mount in Matthew's gospel that asks us to consider the lilies of the field and the birds of the sky, all of whose needs are met by God. This seems to suggest that God satisfies our bodily needs as we experience them in the material world. But, once again, Jesus could not mean that literally because elsewhere in the Course he explains that God does not even know about this dream (e.g., text, pp. 53,364; T-4.II.8:6; T-18.VIII.4:1-2). Moreover, we have already discussed that the Holy Spirit does not deal with effects, but only their cause in our minds. That is why it is essential to keep in mind the context in which *A Course in Miracles* presents itself. Passages should not be taken out of context so that they mean what we want them to mean, violating the overall thought system.

To say that nothing we need will be denied us, that not one difficulty but will melt away, seems to suggest also that the future is real and that we are on a temporal journey. As we have already seen, the Course uses language like this because of our strongly embedded belief that time is a linear process. In many other places Jesus says that the journey is already over. Consequently, the Holy Spirit does not change anything in the world because "there is no world" (workbook, p. 237; W-pI.132.6:2); we are not going through things for the first time. However, His loving presence does seem to "speak" to our dreaming minds to change what we are experiencing. The trap is that we forget that we are not the people on the screen, but simply the observers.

Q: Would you discuss this a little further? Again, how are we supposed to take this passage?

A: This passage should be taken as a correction for the idea that the Holy Spirit punishes, that He makes things difficult and brings us suffering. This is the main idea; but the language used to convey this idea is the language which can be understood by minds imbued with the belief that time is linear. The workbook lesson about placing our future in the Hands of God, as we have seen, uses the language that reflects the belief that time is linear to convey the message that the Holy Spirit is sitting with us in the observer's chair, urging us to choose to replay tapes of relationships He has already healed for us. Our experience in this world can be that He has done this for us—that He has made straight our path and removed obstacles. In truth, however, we have merely accepted the correction already present in our minds through the Holy Spirit.

The idea that we need take thought for nothing except the only purpose that we would fulfill, refers to forgiveness. It is important to recognize that a passage such as this could be used to justify talk about the Holy Spirit's magic tricks—He gives parking spots, heals cancer, provides money when needed, and in general works everything out so that all needs are met. If this were really the case, it would confirm the belief that the world of time and space is real by virtue of the Holy Spirit's intervention in it. *A Course in Miracles* uses language like this, still once again, because we believe we are in this world, but such usage should not be misread to justify "magic" (the Course's term, as we have seen, for the attempt to solve a problem in the mind through physical measures). The Holy Spirit's "interventions" are simply the reminders in our *minds* that we have only a single problem, and His Love has already solved it for us.

Q: Could the idea that "you need take thought for nothing" be understood to say that ultimately we do not have to be concerned about the basic daily problems of living, what we should wear and what we should eat, for example? Does it mean that because we will not have the need to make ourselves suffer, we inevitably will have what we need? We will not have to focus on anything as an end in itself?

A: Yes, that is what is implied. The crucial word in your question is "concerned." It is not that we do not pay the electric bill, or provide for our loved ones and for ourselves. It is simply that we will not interpret such material needs through the eyes of guilt and deprivation. This projection is the source of all our concerns and perceived problems, which become very effective distraction devices as we all know.

A Course in Miracles is a blend of the ideal with the practical, metaphysical principles with our everyday experience. The confusion enters into students' minds when they confuse these two levels. Thus, again, people may say: "The Holy Spirit told me to leave my job; I do not have any money but I know that the Lord will provide for me." That clearly is not what Jesus means by this. He is telling us rather that we will no longer be concerned with things that are not truly problems, but rather will recognize what our true problems are. The Course's purpose is to help us gradually to recognize that our only function is to heal our own minds, and only that is important: *"The sole responsibility of the miracle worker is to accept the Atonement for himself"* (text, p. 22; T-2.V.5:1). Jesus is certainly not suggesting that we do this apart from the form and symbols of the world; his Course does not advocate removing ourselves from the world, but rather that we shift how we perceive the world:

This course remains within the ego framework, where it is needed. It is not concerned with what is beyond all error because it is planned only to set the direction towards it. Therefore it uses words, which are symbolic, and cannot express what lies beyond symbols (manual, p. 73; C-in.3:1-3).

And earlier in the manual, regarding the question of changing one's life situation, we read:

Changes are required in the *minds* of God's teachers. This may or may not involve changes in the external situation.... It is most unlikely that changes in attitudes would not be the first step in the...training (manual, p. 25; M-9.1:1-2,4).

The Holy Spirit thus interprets our words and symbols differently, yet does so within their context. Elsewhere Jesus explains how the Holy Spirit does not take our special relationships away from us, but transforms them (text, p. 333; T-17.IV.2:3); the form or symbol remains, but the content has been changed from guilt to forgiveness.

Q: Are there any other reasons for this type of misunderstanding? People have become involved in some pretty horrendous situations and then concluded that the Holy Spirit set up those situations to teach His lessons. For example, as you have already said, a woman who had been brutally raped sincerely believed that the Holy Spirit sent this rapist to her so she could forgive him.

A: The misinterpretation comes because people read what their egos want them to read, so that they will fail to understand the larger context in which these passages occur. That is why I have spoken of these passages in the greater context of time. Perhaps the greatest preparation for working with *A Course in Miracles* is common sense. Common sense, let alone the Course's theory, would tell us that rape could never be the Holy Spirit's will, that suddenly walking out on our jobs, leaving a family without visible means of support, was not the Holy Spirit's will. Indeed, He might guide us to leave a job. However, in situations in which denial is involved, leading us to use other people so as to avoid taking responsibility for our own scripts, it is clearly the ego's guidance we are following. There is, again, no question that a person could be guided, as part of his or her Atonement path, to leave a particular situation. But if so, peace would be the result, not sacrifice. The Holy Spirit is not a magical bird who takes care of our problems. That is why I have been prefacing these passages by emphasizing how essential it is to understand that the Course's teachings are a correction. Once their purpose is understood, without misinterpretation or misapplication, the teachings are thoroughly consistent and make much more sense.

As that [purpose] was given you, so will its fulfillment be. God's guarantee will hold against all obstacles, for it rests on certainty and not contingency. It rests on *you*. And what can be more certain than a Son of God?

Forgiveness is the purpose given us by the Holy Spirit, which thus allows our minds to be healed. And since it *was* given us, its fulfillment is guaranteed as well, requiring only our inevitable decision of acceptance. The ancient script of the ego occurred within the dream, but the ancient script of forgiveness occurred as well. The "you" that certainty rests upon is the *real* Self, the Christ in us, and Its Love merely waits for our certain return to the home we never truly left.

PART III

THE END OF TIME

INTRODUCTION TO PART III

In this final Part, we will consider the Course's ideas about the real world, the Second Coming, the Last Judgment, and then God's last step, which within the Course's presentation come sequentially. Clearly, however, the sequence is illusory, for these final "steps" correct and undo a belief in time that never was. These stages are nonetheless helpful for us who still believe we are in time, for they serve to reverse the ego's steps of the descent into its hell. We begin with the real world, the attainment of which is the learning goal of *A Course in Miracles*.

Chapter 9

THE REAL WORLD

We begin with the beautiful summary of the "real world" found in the workbook (workbook, p. 433; W-pII.8.1). We could actually devote a whole book to this topic, as *A Course in Miracles* contains so many references to it. But we will confine ourselves to just three, one from each Course book. But before we begin, some additional comments.

To state it again, Heaven is not the goal of the Course, the real world is. Within the context of our discussion related to chart 3, the real world is reached when we perceive only tapes of forgiveness and joining, after which all tapes disappear. Our perceptions in the real world are no longer distorted through the projection of our own guilt or belief in sin, but rather are now the extension of the Holy Spirit's Love. This Love is the goal of the Course, and places us at the end of the Atonement path.

It is important to realize that the real world remains part of the world of illusion, and thus is not Heaven. When *A Course in Miracles* talks about reality it is talking about Heaven, which is usually juxtaposed with the illusory world. But the phrase "the real world" refers to this world, albeit a forgiven one. As the workbook says at the beginning of the passage we shall now examine, "The real world is a symbol," which means it is not a fact. The only fact that is true is spelled with a capital "F," the Fact of God. So even though the real world is a symbol, it is not a symbol of sin or separation. It is the pure reflection, within the separated mind, of the reality and unity of Heaven. As such, the real world is not a reference to the physical world, but rather to the attitude of forgiveness that is now within the mind that has recognized its sinlessness. Now, to the workbook:

The real world is a symbol, like the rest of what perception offers. Yet it stands for what is opposite to what you made.

Chart 2 depicted the ego's and the Holy Spirit's scripts as a dual highway, the top part belonging to the ego, while the bottom is the Holy Spirit's correction, the exact opposite to what the ego has done. Therefore living in the real world can be likened to driving only on the Holy Spirit lane of the highway, where there is no longer any script at all. To state it once again, once the Holy Spirit's corrections have been accepted, the ego's mistakes have disappeared, making corrections unnecessary. As Jesus explains regarding his own role as teacher:

> I will teach with you and live with you if you will think with me, but my goal will always be to absolve you finally from the need for a teacher (text, p. 49; T-4.I.6:3).

Thus, once the guilt we made is replaced by its opposite—forgiveness—both disappear:

> This is the shift that true perception brings: What was projected out is seen within, and there forgiveness lets it disappear....seen within your mind, guilt and forgiveness for an instant lie together, side by side, upon one altar [the mind]. There at last are sickness and its single remedy joined in one healing brightness. God has come to claim His Own. Forgiveness is complete (manual, p. 82; C-4.6:1,7-10).

Your world is seen through eyes of fear, and brings the witnesses of terror to your mind. The real world cannot be perceived except through eyes forgiveness blesses, so they see a world where terror is impossible, and witnesses to fear can not be found.

The real world holds a counterpart for each unhappy thought reflected in your world; a sure correction for the sights of fear and sounds of battle which your world contains.

Each instant that we choose to be separate has already been healed through a decision of joining. For each time that we have attacked and held grievances against people, there has been a correction in which we have forgiven them. That is the counterpart for every unhappy thought we have had. The idea that each unhappy thought is reflected in the world is an expression of the dynamic of projection. And each unhappy thought has fear as its source, inevitably leading to an experience of the world as terrifying, and ourselves as vulnerable to its wickedness. On the other hand, accepting the Holy Spirit's correction allows His Love to extend through our minds, ultimately becoming reflected in the perception of the real world.

The real world shows a world seen differently, through quiet eyes and with a mind at peace. Nothing but rest is there. There are no cries of pain and sorrow heard, for nothing there remains outside forgiveness. And the sights are gentle. Only happy sights and sounds can reach the mind that has forgiven itself.

What is important here is understanding that the real world is not a denial of the world. We still live in a separated world of illusion, but although the body's eyes "see" the same things as before, the interpretations placed on what is "seen" is entirely different. In other words, our perception has been entirely corrected and so we simply see through the eyes of love.

Q: That line should not be taken literally then, "There are no cries of pain and sorrow heard"?

A: That is right. It does not mean that people are not crying in pain, but rather that we shall not hear it that way.

Q: So is it literal in one sense and in another sense not?

A: Right, it depends on which level you are speaking. The main point is to be sure that we are not engaged in denial: denying starvation in the world, the plight of an oppressed country, the people in the holocaust, or whatever. This passage should therefore not be taken to mean that these things are not happening. It means that we will look at such things differently, without giving them power to disturb our inner peace.

Q: Wouldn't it also be a mistake to think that the real world is some kind of a place different from this world?

A: Yes, of course. The real world, again, is an attitude, a state of mind. One can physically still be in Auschwitz, or hanging from a cross, but the mind will be totally at peace. And so the seemingly external situation is perceived through quiet and gentle eyes. Only kindness is experienced, for only kind thoughts remain in the mind.

What need has such a [forgiven] mind for thoughts of death, attack and murder?

This is an important statement, for Jesus is telling us that our ego self has a *need* for thoughts of death, attack, and murder, which means that they result from a decision we make. That certainly is not the way the world looks at attack, which in any of its forms seems so real. But this passage is teaching us that the problem is that we have an *investment* in believing in the reality of attack. We choose to make it real—which of course roots us in the body and in a world of separation, guilt, and fear—because that is what the ego wants. Choosing thoughts of attack really comes from a decision to remain in time, "safely" within the ego's world.

What can it [the forgiven mind] perceive surrounding it but safety, love and joy? What is there it would choose to be condemned, and what is there that it would judge against?

Again, this does not mean that we deny what happens in the world. We simply realize that what happens in the world cannot affect Who we really are. What Jesus taught us is that despite what seemed to be happening to him, he was surrounded by safety, love, and joy. Therefore he could not be in pain, nor perceive any part of the Sonship as separate from him. Nothing happened to him because there was nothing in his mind that demanded that something happen to him.

The section "Where Sin Has Left" (text, pp. 509-11; T-26.IV) is a beautiful rendering of the forgiven or the real world. There is an absence of sin, and if there is no sin there can be no guilt. And so there is no need to see oneself or others as condemned. Without guilt judgment is impossible and separation non-existent. A brief excerpt from this section follows:

> Forgiveness is this world's equivalent of Heaven's justice. It translates the world of sin into a simple world, where justice can be reflected from beyond the gate behind which total lack of limits lies....
>
> Forgiveness turns the world of sin into a world of glory, wonderful to see....There is no sadness and there is no parting here, for everything is totally forgiven. And what has been forgiven must join, for nothing stands between to keep them separate and apart. The sinless must perceive that they are one, for nothing stands between to push the other off (text, pp. 509-10; T-26.IV.1:1; 2:1,3-5).

The world it [the forgiven mind] sees arises from a mind at peace within itself. No danger lurks in anything it sees, for it is kind, and only kindness does it look upon.

In many places in the workbook, especially in these one-page summaries, a tremendous amount is expressed in each sentence, directly or by implication. We find this here as well. The world that we see arose from a conflicted mind that must inevitably project its conflict. And this is how the world was made. Forgiveness corrects this error, healing the conflict of believing we had attacked God. Peace replaces conflict, and another world arises from this loving thought. In other words, again, in the real world we see and experience the dream differently.

Moreover, if I am kind and can look only upon kindness, I shall no longer perceive danger. The second sentence is a causal statement: "No danger lurks in anything it sees," because "it is kind." Therefore, even if you are standing in front of me with a gun pointed at my head, if there is only kindness within me—there is no sin and no judgment—no matter what happens I know I am not in danger. If danger comes, it is the effect of an unkind thought. An unkind thought results from a belief in sin and guilt which demands I be punished. I must thus inevitably believe the world is a dangerous place. In the real world, regardless of what happens on the level of form, I remain at peace. We have seen many examples from World War II, again, of people who survived the concentration camps in a state of peace, despite the obvious physical dangers that were all around them. Their peace resulted from their choice to identify with love instead of attack. In this world we do not always have control over what is external to us, but we always have control over our thoughts and perceptions. These we *can* change.

The real world is the symbol that the dream of sin and guilt is over, and God's Son no longer sleeps. His waking eyes perceive the sure reflection of his Father's Love; the certain promise that he is redeemed. The real world signifies the end of time, for its perception makes time purposeless.

So we are now beginning to awaken from this nightmare dream. The purpose of time from the Holy Spirit's point of view is to undo sin. Once sin is undone, there is no further need for time. Thus we can say that the attainment of the real world is the necessary step towards ending our belief in the reality of time. While God's Love is not possible in this world, as seen in the aforementioned statement "No love in this world is without...ambivalence" (text, p. 55; T-4.III.4:6), Love's reflection *is* possible through the Holy Spirit's perception.

The Holy Spirit has no need of time when it has served His purpose. Now He waits but that one instant more for God to take His final step, and time has disappeared, taking perception with it as it goes, and leaving but the truth to be itself. That instant is our goal, for it contains the memory of God. And as we look upon a world forgiven, it is He Who calls to us and comes to take us home [God's last step], reminding us of our Identity Which our forgiveness has restored to us.

The "final step" is what the Course elsewhere calls God's last step, and we shall deal with that stage later. As time disappears so does perception, and knowledge then dawns upon our minds, restored at last to the awareness of the oneness of Heaven. That is the instant when our minds are fully healed because that is when we have totally accepted the Atonement for ourselves: we have undone our belief in the reality of guilt. The real world represents the completion of our individual paths. The final stages—the Second Coming, the Last Judgment, and the last step—as we will see, are really collective steps. In other words, when every separated fragment of the Sonship has healed its mind, at that point the Sonship is awakened as one. The real world expresses the individual completion of that path. That instant of healing is our goal. As we see the face of Christ in others the memory of God dawns on our minds, and we are home in the awareness of our perfect oneness with God and all creation.

Now we will move to the manual, the section called "How Will the World End?" (manual, p. 35; M-14). The central theme we have been considering is that total forgiveness and the attainment of the real world mark the ending of this world. It is the theme of this section as well.

Can what has no beginning really end? The world will end in an illusion, as it began. Yet will its ending be an illusion of mercy.

If we talk about the end of the world then we are implying that there must have been a beginning. We therefore would be saying that the world actually exists. This is one of the subtle ways the ego uses to make the world, and therefore itself, real. It is the same idea as when people talk about the resurrection of Jesus' body. If you say that his body resurrected then you are saying that his body must have died. If you are saying that his body died then you must be saying that his body lived, which is another example of the clever trap the ego sets to have us believe in the reality of its world. It is the same thing here: to talk about the ending of the world is to say that the world had to have a beginning and therefore that it, and the entire ego thought system, is real.

"Yet will its ending be one of mercy." This is intended as a correction for the traditional Christian view that the world will end in judgment, and clearly this judgment is not a good one if you are on the wrong team.

Q: Doesn't the book of Revelation say that the world is going to end in fire, the battle of Armageddon?

A: Yes; the Bible states that the world will end in a big conflagration and there will be a great deal of suffering. If you are on the "good team" then you will be okay. The Course is here stating that the world will end much differently; i.e., in "an illusion of mercy."

The illusion of forgiveness, complete, excluding no one, limitless in gentleness, will cover it, hiding all evil, concealing all sin and ending guilt forever. So ends the world that guilt had made, for now it has no purpose and is gone.

Here is another clear statement in the Course that forgiveness, too, is an illusion. The end product of the process of forgiveness is that no one is excluded, and so is guilt undone. This world, however, is upheld by guilt. Guilt made the world—a very clear statement of this important Course teaching—and is upheld by it. Therefore, when guilt is gone and forgiveness is complete, the world must disappear because its cause is gone. The world is the effect, and guilt or sin is the cause.

Let us skip to the second paragraph, the eighth sentence:

The world will end when all things in it have been rightly judged by His judgment. The world will end with the benediction of holiness upon it. When not one thought of sin remains, the world is over. It will not be destroyed nor attacked nor even touched. It will merely cease to seem to be.

This then is the vision of Christ, the Holy Spirit's true perception, and the real world. Moreover, this statement is a correction for the traditional Christian view of Armageddon. The words here obviously are carefully chosen. It is not that the world will merely cease to be; "It will merely cease to *seem* to be" because its existence is illusory. The world does not exist; it only *seems* to exist. Furthermore, as we considered at the end of Part II when we talked about the Holy Spirit's plan, *A Course in Miracles* makes it very clear in many passages, such as this one, that there is no world. However, Jesus does not constantly speak on that level. If he did, the Course would become extremely frustrating to us who believe that the world is real. There are enough passages in the Course which show us exactly what its metaphysical view is. But there are many other passages which speak of the world as if it were real, because, again, we are invested in believing in the reality of the world of time.

It is also important to note that the world is not destroyed or attacked, is not opposed in any way, since how can nothing be opposed or destroyed? The world is simply looked at through the eyes of Christ, and then its nothingness is understood and disappears. As the Course says regarding the transcending of the body:

Not through destruction, not through a breaking out, but merely by a quiet melting in (text, p. 362; T-18.VI.14:6).

Certainly this seems to be a long, long while away. "When not one thought of sin remains" appears to be a long-range goal indeed. But time stands still, and waits on the goal of God's teachers. Not one thought of sin will remain the instant any one of them accepts Atonement for himself.

Obviously, within our dream of time, it appears as if it will take a tremendous amount of time for sin to be undone and our minds healed. And so this passage makes no sense within a linear view of time. When we consider our individual egos and how long it will take to be totally free on that level, and then multiply that a billion-fold in terms of the world at large, the end of the ego would seem to be a long, long way off. However, this approach, we have already remarked, merely reinforces the illusion of time. What is helpful in understanding the Course's metaphysical view of time, especially in connection with chart 3, is that it points out how different the actual process of Atonement is. All we need do is press a different button and our entire experience changes.

It is as if you are watching a horror movie on the VCR, and then suddenly decide that you have had enough of this. You have thus changed your mind and so switch to a musical comedy instead. It does not seem to be this easy in our everyday lives because we are so rooted in believing we deserve to be frightened, punished, unhappy, and conflicted. But that is the problem: our *belief* that we deserve pain. Some other metaphysical systems teach that pain is what we attract to us. However, this approach merely makes the world real. It is not that we attract the pain to us. Rather, we simply choose to re-experience that tape of misery over and over again. All that is needed for the world of time to disappear for us as reality is to change our minds, to "change channels." When we consider the Last Judgment in Chapter 11 we shall return to the idea of the completion of the Atonement being "a long, long while away."

Q: That one sentence, "Not one thought of sin will remain the instant any one of them accepts the Atonement for himself," applies to Jesus, does it not?

A: It certainly could. He showed us that this entire world of experience, as shown in chart 3, is an illusion. But that certainly does not mean that we do not have to accept the Atonement for ourselves. That individual healed mind of Jesus demonstrated that the world is a dream, and now it remains for us to accept that truth.

Let us skip to the opening sentences of paragraph four:

The world will end when its thought system has been completely reversed. Until then, bits and pieces of its thinking will still seem sensible. The final lesson, which brings the ending of the world, cannot be grasped by those not yet prepared to leave the world and go beyond its tiny reach.

Jesus is stating here that within the world of time, the ending of the ego thought system occurs as a process. The "final lesson" is the total undoing of the belief in time, death, or any form in which the thought of separation is expressed. But it is impossible for us to understand how this is accomplished as long as we remain glued to our screens watching horror movies. Again, the crucial point is that a choice is involved: I have chosen to re-experience this particular form of the nightmare, and therefore can just as easily change my mind. And so, if we are watching a terrible movie on television, nobody is forcing us to continue with it. We can always change channels (or even turn the set off entirely). This is exactly the situation with our own experiences. We are always free to change how we are looking at something. In the language of *A Course in*

Miracles, the change occurs when we choose a miracle instead of a grievance. In the images we have been using here, we have changed buttons. We accelerate our Atonement process as we continue to choose the Holy Spirit's videos instead of the ego's.

Now we turn to the text, the section entitled "Forgiveness and the End of Time," paragraph two (text, p. 572; T-29.VI.2:1). This is a more poetic view of the end of the world.

Swear not to die, you holy Son of God!

The punctuation in this line is very important. If you place a comma after the word "swear" ("Swear, not to die you holy Son of God!"), the sentence would mean that we do not have to die, an interpretation that many Course students have made. We would be swearing not to die, meaning that we would remain alive in a physical body, promising never to die in this body. Thus, this understanding presupposes that the body lives, or better, that we live in the body, and thus we swear to become immortal in the body. Yet earlier Jesus clearly states that there is no life in the body:

> There is no life outside of Heaven. Where God created life, there life must be. In any state apart from Heaven [i.e., in the body] life is illusion. At best it seems like life; at worst, like death. Yet both are judgments on what is not life, equal in their inaccuracy and lack of meaning. Life not in Heaven is impossible, and what is not in Heaven is not anywhere (text, p. 459; T-23.II.19:1-6).

If the sentence were punctuated with a comma after "swear," then the interpretation I just gave would be justified. Clearly that interpretation is not the meaning here.

"Swear not to die" is talking about our decision to deny the reality of death as part of the ego thought system. When this passage is understood as it is written—"Swear not to die, you holy Son of God"—we are clearly exhorted to choose not to die, not to make death real, and not to make it a punishment for our sin. We are therefore asked to choose against our original promise to the ego to uphold its insane and murderous thought system. In a wonderfully evocative passage, this oath of fidelity to the ego is recalled, as we stand before the final obstacle to peace:

> And now you stand in terror before what you swore never to look upon. Your eyes look down, remembering your promise to your "friends." The "loveliness" of sin, the delicate appeal of guilt, the "holy" waxen image of death, and the fear of vengeance of the ego you swore in blood not to desert, all rise and bid you not to raise your eyes (text, p. 392; T-19.IV-D.6:1-3).

Therefore, rather than continuing to remain faithful to the ego's shabby and unholy image of ourselves, we swear allegiance to the Holy Spirit's evaluation: "you holy Son of God!"

You make a bargain that you cannot keep. The Son of Life cannot be killed. He is immortal as his Father. What he is cannot be changed. He is the only thing in all the universe that must be one.

The bargain that we cannot keep, again, is the bargain that we made with the ego, the bargain expressed by the laws of chaos that we must be killed because of our sins. That is the insanity of the ego system. However, the good news is that we are not the son of the ego, but the Son of Life (the capital "L" of course signifies God). We cannot be killed, but remain as changeless and immortal as our Source and Creator.

Here now is the beautiful rendering of the end of the ego's world:

What *seems* eternal all will have an end. The stars will disappear, and night and day will be no more. All things that come and go, the tides, the seasons and the lives of men; all

things that change with time and bloom and fade will not return.

This is a very clear and poetic statement that everything in this physical universe is going to disappear. Everything will have an end, which is the Course's logical argument as to why the eternal God could not have created it. In antiquity the Greeks, for example, worshiped the beauty of the stars, planets, sun, and the ordered movements of the heavenly spheres. Their attitude has been referred to as "cosmic piety." To the Greeks, these celestial forms were eternal and therefore a reflection of the perfection of God, and, in fact, these "heavenly bodies" were called living gods. However, we are learning here that all physical objects will disappear. Being form, they change; and if anything changes, it cannot be of God.

Where time has set an end is not where the eternal is. God's Son can never change by what men made of him.

"Where time has set an end" refers to death, because that is the end of our individual time on earth. Note that *A Course in Miracles* elsewhere does not say that the world will die, but simply, as we have already seen, that the world will disappear back into the "nothingness from where it came" (manual, p. 81; C-4.4:5). Therefore, we can never find the eternal in anything that is ephemeral and that dies, whether we are talking about an individual life or the physical cosmos. "God's Son can never change by what men made of him": what we have made of ourselves and of the world has no impact on who we really are. In the manual, Jesus exhorts us:

> Teacher of God, your one assignment could be stated thus: Accept no compromise in which death plays a part. Do not believe in cruelty, nor let attack conceal the truth from you. What seems to die has but been misperceived and carried to illusion. Now it becomes your task to let the illusion be carried to the truth. Be steadfast but in this; be not deceived

by the "reality" of any changing form (manual, p. 64; M-27.7:1-5).

He will be as he was and as he is, for time appointed not his destiny, nor set the hour of his birth and death. Forgiveness will not change him. Yet time waits upon forgiveness that the things of time may disappear because they have no use.

Despite the fact that this is all an illusion, time will still wait for the final illusion, forgiveness. When that purpose of attaining the real world is fulfilled, then time and its world will disappear.

This concludes our discussion of the real world, and we move now to the next phase, the Second Coming, the collective awakening of the Sonship from the dream.

Chapter 10

THE SECOND COMING

When *A Course in Miracles* talks about the Second Coming and Last Judgment it is important to remember the origin of these terms in traditional Christianity. I will therefore preface both of these chapters by reading passages from the gospels that set the stage for seeing how Christianity has understood these concepts. I will start with Matthew's gospel, which contains one of the more important references in the New Testament to the Second Coming, traditionally seen as the return to earth of Jesus after his ascension into Heaven. The images used by Matthew, incidentally, are based on the vision of the Old Testament prophet Ezekiel.

> If, then, they say to you [this is Jesus speaking about himself], "Look, he is in the desert," do not go there; "Look, he is in some hiding place," do not believe it; because the coming of the Son of Man [i.e., Jesus] will be like lightning striking in the east and flashing far into the west. Wherever the corpse is, there will the vultures gather.
>
> Immediately after the distress of those days the sun will be darkened, the moon will lose its brightness, the stars will fall from the sky and the powers of heaven will be shaken. And then the sign of the Son of Man will appear in heaven; then too all the peoples of the earth will beat their breasts; and they will see the Son of Man coming on the clouds of heaven with power and great glory. And he will send his angels with a loud trumpet to gather his chosen from the four winds, from one end of heaven to the other (Mt 24:26-31).

This is a clear statement of the traditional view of the Second Coming, which over the centuries has evoked great fear. Obviously, Jesus' return is not seen as a very peaceful event, and certainly not a forgiving one. The early Church actually did believe that Jesus was coming very quickly. It was only as the decades went by that they realized that he was not, and so the eschatological theology (pertaining to the end times) had to be modified. If you read the early letters of Paul, for example, you receive a definite sense of the imminent coming of Jesus, which changes in the later letters. It actually was a period of great disillusionment in the early Church.

Returning to *A Course in Miracles*, we have already seen that Jesus uses the phrase "Son of God" to express all of us as the one Christ, correcting the traditional understanding that only he was the Son of God. Jesus now does a similar thing with the phrase "Second Coming," which as we shall see presently, expresses the return to sense of the entire Sonship. Thus, similar to his resurrection, the Second Coming is explained by Jesus in the Course as a mental event, having nothing whatsoever to do with the physical world, let alone with his bodily return. Moreover, the Course's use of "Second Coming" contains none of the fear, judgment, and threat of punishment that is found in the biblical understanding. And this correction is the central idea behind Jesus' usage of it here.

We start with Chapter 4 in the text, paragraph ten in the section "This Need Not Be" (text, p. 58; T-4.IV.10):

The First Coming of Christ is merely another name for the creation, for Christ is the Son of God. The Second Coming of Christ means nothing more than the end of the ego's rule and the healing of the mind. I was created like you in the First, and I have called you to join me in the second.

These are very clear statements of the end of the ego, as well as Jesus' statement that he is no different from us. The First Coming of Christ is not the birth of Jesus, but rather is the creation of the Sonship of which he is a part. It was then that the ego's dream appeared to be born, necessitating the Atonement correction. When the Atonement is complete and the Sonship awakens from the dream, the Second Coming of

Christ dawns. And Jesus is asking us to join in that process with him, which he "undertook to begin" (text, p. 6; T-1.III.1:1).

I am in charge of the Second Coming, and my judgment, which is used only for protection, cannot be wrong because it never attacks.

Moreover, Jesus says he is in charge of the Atonement (text, p. 6; T-1.III.1:1), and the teacher's manual states that the Holy Spirit established Jesus as the leader of the plan of the Atonement (manual, p. 85; C-6.2:2). The meaning here is the same. Moreover, again, his judgment clearly lacks the implication of punishment or attack that is central to the traditional view. Jesus' judgment is simply that the separation never happened, and so our pain and suffering not only is not warranted, but is inherently non-existent, its cause of sin having been undone. Thus we are "protected" from the ego's thought system by the truth of the Atonement. We shall return to the notion of the absence of God's judgment in the following chapter on the Last Judgment.

Let us move now to Chapter 9, section IV, paragraph nine (text, p. 158; T-9.IV.9:3-4):

This [the Last Judgment] is the Second Coming that was made for you as the First was created. The Second Coming is merely the return of sense. Can this possibly be fearful?

The Second Coming is not God's doing in the usual sense, as it is the correction for the ego's thought that the First Coming (our creation by God) never truly happened. This separating God out from a process of correction that must be illusory is highlighted by the use of the word "made," juxtaposed with "created" in the same sentence.[15] The

---

15. In *A Course in Miracles*, "make" is reserved for the world of separation or its correction, while "create" refers only to the activity of spirit in Heaven (see, for example, text, pp. 29,39,49-50; T-2.VIII.1; T-3.V.2; T-4.I.9:3).

271

Second Coming therefore is the Holy Spirit's correction for the ego's plan. Part of the world of illusion, the Second Coming yet signifies the end of the world of illusion. Thus, the Second Coming was made for us by the Holy Spirit as the correction for the ego's belief in separation, its defense against the First Coming, which was our creation as Christ.

This correction becomes much more meaningful when we recall the passage from Matthew we have just read, which expresses a great amount of fear. To the *senseless* ego, the Second Coming and Last Judgment can indeed be fearful, and from the ego's point of view, justifiably so. The "return of sense" is the realization of the truth of the Atonement principle; namely that the separation has not happened, this world is unreal, and attack and judgment are not justified.

Let us turn to the workbook for another summary statement, "What is the Second Coming?" (workbook, p. 439; W-pII.9):

Christ's Second Coming, which is sure as God, is merely the correction of mistakes, and the return of sanity.

Jesus is telling us not to be fearful of the Second Coming. We are not going to see flames in the sky, with the majestic though judgmental Son of Man riding high in his return. The Second Coming is merely the undoing of what never was. The idea that it is "sure as God" reflects the same content as in the already quoted statement: "...the outcome is as certain as God" (text, p. 52; T-4.II.5:8). The return of sanity is a parallel to the idea that the Second Coming is the return of sense, as we just saw in the text.

It is a part of the condition that restores the never lost, and re-establishes what is forever and forever true. It is the invitation to God's Word to take illusion's place; the willingness to let forgiveness rest upon all things without exception and without reserve.

When the Course talks about the Word of God, as it does here and in many other places, the term has a different meaning from its usage in traditional Christianity. Traditionally the Word of God has always been equated with Jesus, as in the famous "Logos" in the prologue to John's gospel:

> In the beginning was the Word [Logos]; and the Word was with God and the Word was God (Jn 1:1).

If we understand the Word of God as the one Christ, then we all must be part of Christ and therefore no different from Jesus. However, in the Course "Word of God" connotes neither Jesus nor Christ, but rather represents God's answer which corrects the belief in separation. Thus "Word" can be taken at varying times to reflect the plan of the Atonement, forgiveness, or the Holy Spirit. It is God's Word of healing, within our split minds, that corrects the ego's word of separation. We can therefore think of the Holy Spirit as the Voice for God that speaks to us within the dream of separation, and He "speaks" the Word of God that corrects our mis-thoughts.

Q: Traditional Christianity also states that the Bible is God's Word. And don't Catholics say that after the reading of the Gospel, "This is the Word of the Lord"?

A: Yes, they do. In a somewhat similar and broader sense, *A Course in Miracles* can also be thought of as the Word of God, although it never actually states this. It is implied, however, in the idea that the Course carries forth the Atonement message of forgiveness, and therefore embodies in form the Atonement principle of the Holy Spirit, as did Jesus in his life on earth.

The earlier passage I read about the Second Coming restoring what was never lost, and re-establishing what is forever true, affirms the idea that the Second Coming does not do anything except correct the mistake. As we shall see later on, it is really the awakening from the dream.

It is the all-inclusive nature of Christ's Second Coming that permits it to embrace the world and hold you safe within its gentle advent, which encompasses all living things with you. There is no end to the release the Second Coming brings, as God's creation must be limitless. Forgiveness lights the Second Coming's way, because it shines on everything as one. And thus is oneness recognized at last.

The phrase "all living things" occurs frequently in the Course, and seems to suggest that the Sonship of Christ embraces not only humanity but all of what we refer to as living things: animals, plants, etc. There can be no exception; all people, all living things, are one. On another level, however, as we have already commented, nothing is living here in the world of form. And so we must again understand that Jesus is using terms that speak to us within the illusory world we believe is real. Within our level of experiential understanding, therefore, he is asking us to exclude no one (or no thing) from our forgiveness. In truth, of course, there is nothing outside our minds—living or dead, animate or inanimate—but simply the projections of thoughts within ourselves. It is these projections without that must be forgiven, as they reflect what is unforgiven within. *All* of our thoughts must be healed and brought together. Only then can the ego's thought system be undone, the Atonement completed, and the Second Coming ushered in. And so forgiveness is the choice we make individually, completing our unique Atonement path. As each of us completes his or her part in the plan, the Second Coming's way becomes more illuminated.

The Second Coming ends the lessons that the Holy Spirit teaches, making way for the Last Judgment, in which learning ends in one last summary that will extend beyond itself, and reaches up to God. The Second Coming is the time in which all minds are given to the hands of

Christ, to be returned to spirit in the name of true creation and the Will of God.

The process described in this passage remains within the world of illusion. In the context of our image of the carpet, the minds of the entire Sonship are healed and have accepted the Atonement, thus reaching the very end of the carpet. All ego thoughts have been undone and we are a split second away from being home. Hence the sequence is that the collective Sonship accepts the real world (the consummation of forgiveness), then follows the Second Coming (the collective healing—"all minds are given to the hands of Christ"), which makes way for the Last Judgment, after which God takes the last step.

The Second Coming is the one event in time which time itself can not affect. For every one who ever came to die, or yet will come or who is present now, is equally released from what he made.

The Second Coming occurs within time but is also beyond it, since it stands at time's end reflecting the idea that time is not linear. Healing occurs at once and therefore embraces all aspects of the hologram, be they in the past, present, or future.

Q: Isn't this passage referring to the Second Coming as a personal, individual experience instead of it being a collective release?

A: No, it isn't, for it refers to "every one" being "equally released" from the illusory world that was made.

Q: Does the idea that the Second Coming and the Last Judgment are a collective experience, something that will not happen to any of us until each of us has reached the real world, deny the statement in the manual which says that the whole relationship between the Father and the Son lies in Jesus?

A: The idea that the relationship of the Father and Son is in Jesus means that he has no ego, because that relationship is without ego barriers. The Second Coming itself is a collective event. Jesus has transcended his ego and the individual path, and in terms of our image of the carpet this means that he is standing at the carpet's end, "at the finish line" as it were. In this sense he holds the key to the completion of the Atonement path because he showed us that there is no death, and therefore no separation. He becomes the model who helps us make that same choice.

Q: In this view of time that we are learning, Jesus is understood to be at the place where we are already with him and have made that choice for the Second Coming and for the Last Judgment. Could these ideas of the Second Coming and the Last Judgment have two levels of meaning? We each have our own individual second coming, our individual last judgment, but they also are collective in the sense that as we reach the point where Jesus is, we are in touch with that collective pool in which we have all made that choice. Is that what you are saying?

A: The words are used first of all within a linear context of time, and refer specifically to the end of the world. Both of those stages, the Second Coming and Last Judgment, refer to the point when the world is going to end, which means that we all have healed our minds. The individual expression would be the acceptance of the Atonement or the attainment of the real world.

Q: I would say that the Second Coming cannot be individual because the Course talks about the fragmentation happening over and over again, and since we left as one we have to go back as one; the fragmentation has to be healed. The Second Coming is the total healing of that fragmentation. And isn't it also true that no one else's choice can keep me from experiencing the unity of what is there, since the separation has not really occurred?

A: Yes; for example, Jesus is not suffering because of our choices. Once again, the phrases "Second Coming" and "Last Judgment" refer to a collective level when everyone has accepted the Atonement: that is the Second Coming, the collective awakening. In the Bible, the Second Coming is understood to signify the end of the world, and *A Course in Miracles* uses this term the same way. However, the Course is saying that the world will end differently; with mercy rather than with punishment. The next line reflects this collective rejoining:

In this equality is Christ restored as one Identity, in Which the Sons of God acknowledge that they all are one. And God the Father smiles upon His Son, His one creation and His only joy.

In the opening section of Chapter 18, "The Substitute Reality," we find a discussion (quoted earlier: see above, p. 19) of the fragmentation of the Sonship in which the unity of Christ seemed to split. Those seeming fragments need to be gathered back again, and the consummation of that gathering is the Second Coming. What had thus been separated is now unified. On an individual level, that undoing of the ego is already accomplished in Jesus and other ascended masters, anyone who completes his or her path. But the idea of separation remains in the split mind. From Jesus' point of view there is no separation, but the Sonship, still within the dream of time and space, has not yet accepted that truth.

Q: The end of the ego's rule and the healing of the mind still is part of time. There is one point in time where we are all in that place. We all have already made that decision. I think as we individually make that choice we enter into that place. That is how I would see it.

A: That is true. In that sense, just as the revelation that the Father and the Son are one has already occurred, the Second Coming has already occurred as well. Part of the problem is that we are dealing with an illusory system at this point. But within the model of chart 3, the Second Coming occurs when everyone who is an observer suddenly stands up and turns off the set. Individual people have already done that. But at the point when everyone completes the Atonement, the collective healing occurs that the Course refers to as the Second Coming.

Now comes a beautiful passage:

Pray that the Second Coming will be soon, but do not rest with that. It needs your eyes and ears and hands and feet. It needs your voice. And most of all it needs your willingness.

This theme of the holy use of the body occurs many, many times—there are more than ten such references in the Course—and perhaps the loveliest of these is where Jesus says the same thing of himself:

> For this alone I need; that you will hear the words I speak, and give them to the world. You are my voice, my eyes, my feet, my hands through which I save the world (workbook, p. 322; W-pI.rV.in.9:2-3).

The Second Coming thus needs us, which is really another way of saying that the plan of the Atonement needs us. As two workbook lessons state: "My part is essential to God's plan for salvation" and "Salvation of the world depends on me" (workbook, pp. 177,342; W-pI.100; W-pI.186). We all have to do our part, since the Second Coming cannot be completed until each last seemingly separated fragment of the Sonship has healed its mind. Thus, our bodies become the instruments the Holy Spirit uses to extend His forgiveness. Though illusory, our eyes, ears, hands, feet, and voices nonetheless can serve this holy purpose. Above all, the Holy Spirit needs our little willingness to join with His great Love, that we may accept His Atonement at last, and choose in accord with Him rather than with the ego.

Let us rejoice that we can do God's Will, and join together in its holy light. Behold, the Son of God is one in us, and we can reach our Father's Love through Him.

Reaching our Father's Love is the final step, and the way we pass through the final veil is by reuniting the separated Sonship. Forgiveness, in the last analysis, is all we need accomplish and accept, for by recognizing the Son of God in each other, we come to recognize Christ's face shining in ourselves and in all the Sonship as one. This vision of the face of Christ allows the memory of our Father's Love to dawn upon our minds, completing the Atonement. The Second Coming is now here, making way for the Last Judgment.

Chapter 11

THE LAST JUDGMENT

Our discussion of the Last Judgment will follow along the same lines as our discussion of the Second Coming. Before we turn to the passages in the Course which deal with the Last Judgment, we shall begin with two passages from the Bible which set the stage for seeing how *A Course in Miracles* reinterprets this significant concept. In traditional Christian thinking the Last Judgment has been a very frightening idea: the people who followed the ways of Jesus and God would be saved, while those who did not would burn in everlasting damnation. The first section I shall read is perhaps the most famous one of all, the parable of the Last Judgment from Matthew's gospel:

> When the Son of Man [Jesus] comes in his glory, escorted by all the angels, then he will take his seat on his throne of glory. All the nations will be assembled before him and he will separate men one from another as the shepherd separates sheep from goats. He will place the sheep on his right hand and the goats on his left. Then the King [Jesus] will say to those on his right hand, "Come, you whom my Father has blessed, take for your heritage the kingdom prepared for you since the foundation of the world. For I was hungry and you gave me food; I was thirsty and you gave me drink; I was a stranger and you made me welcome; naked and you clothed me, sick and you visited me, in prison and you came to see me." Then the virtuous will say to him in reply, "Lord, when did we see you hungry and feed you; or thirsty and give you drink? When did we see you a stranger and make you welcome; naked and clothe you; sick or in prison and go to see you?" And the King will answer, "I tell you solemnly, in so far as you did this to one of the least of these brothers of mine, you did it to me." Next he will say to those on his left hand, "Go away from me, with your curse upon you, to the eternal fire

> prepared for the devil and his angels. For I was hungry and you never gave me food; I was thirsty and you never gave me anything to drink; I was a stranger and you never made me welcome, naked and you never clothed me, sick and in prison and you never visited me." Then it will be their turn to ask, "Lord, when did we see you hungry or thirsty, a stranger or naked, sick or in prison and did not come to your help?" Then he will answer, "I tell you solemnly, in so far as you neglected to do this to one of the least of these, you neglected to do it to me." And they will go away to eternal punishment, and the virtuous to eternal life (Mt 25:31-46).

Clearly, those who feel even the least bit of guilt, which includes all of us, would have to feel as they read this passage that *they* are the ones who are going to be sent away to eternal punishment. No matter how much they tried to keep the commandments of the Church and to follow Jesus' teachings as presented in the Bible, their own unconscious guilt would tell them that no matter what they did, they would still find themselves condemned by God for not having done enough. Psychologically this means that Christians hearing these passages would have to feel real dread that their own sins would be punished, and that they would inevitably be condemned to hell.

Overlooking the main road approaching a well-known monastery stands a crucifix, where the slain and suffering Jesus says to all who come that way: "This is what I did for you. What have you done for me?" It would take a Christian whose mind was healed of all thoughts of sin and guilt to read those words and be able to smile at the idea that Jesus would actually talk to his beloved brothers and sisters in that tone.

The second rendering of the Last Judgment is from John's gospel. This is not a parable, but Jesus speaking directly:

> I tell you most solemnly, the hour will come—in fact it is here already—when the dead will hear the voice of the Son of God, and all who hear it will live. For the Father, who is the source of life, has made the Son the source of life; and,

because he is the Son of Man, has appointed him supreme judge. Do not be surprised at this, for the hour is coming when the dead will leave their graves at the sound of his voice: those who did good will rise again to life; and those who did evil, to condemnation (Jn 5:25-28).

Perhaps the most frightening of all the passages in the Bible are from the book of Revelation, which we will not read now. The previous two selections are enough to give the idea of what the Course is attempting to correct. The Last Judgment, as it has been portrayed to us, expresses the horrifying thought which is the rock bottom of the ego system: God will punish us for our sins. The manual elaborates on this kind of thinking:

> Who usurps the place of God and takes it for himself now has a deadly "enemy." And he must stand alone in his protection, and make himself a shield to keep him safe from fury that can never be abated, and vengeance that can never be satisfied (manual, p. 43; M-17.5:8-9).

Here, in *A Course in Miracles,* Jesus takes the same term and shows us, as he has done with many other traditional Christian terms, a totally different way of looking at the Last Judgment.

Let us begin with "The Meaning of the Last Judgment," the final section in Chapter 2 (text, p. 29; T-2.VIII).

One of the ways in which you can correct the magic-miracle confusion [a distinction mentioned earlier in the text between the ego's and the Holy Spirit's means of undoing sin] is to remember that you did not create yourself. You are apt to forget this when you become egocentric, and this puts you in a position where a belief in magic is virtually inevitable. Your will to create was given you by your Creator, Who was expressing the same Will in His creation. Since creative ability rests in the mind, everything you create is necessarily a matter of will. It also

follows that whatever you alone make is real in your own sight, though not in the Mind of God.

It is important to note here, again, the Course's distinction between making and creating: making is of the separated mind, and creating of the spirit. Crucial for our understanding the Course's discussion of the Last Judgment, to be talked about in the next sentence, is recognizing that we believe that the body and material universe we made are real. Because we believe we have made them, and as the Course teaches elsewhere (workbook, pp. 403,415; W-pII.3.2:1; W-pII.5.4:5) we believe we have made them to attack God and love, then the body and world become the great symbols of our guilt. Further, since guilt demands punishment, as long as we believe that what we made is real we must also believe our attack on God is real. Thus, God's vengeful counterattack is inevitable. This brings us to the next idea:

This basic distinction leads directly into the real meaning of the Last Judgment.

Therefore, though the traditional meaning of the Last Judgment is that God will punish us because of our sinfulness, *A Course in Miracles* teaches us that what we believe we made is not real. The world and our experiences here are but part of a dream, acceptance of which is the meaning of forgiveness: our seeming sin against God never happened. If it has never happened, then God will not punish us. Hence, the true meaning of the Last Judgment is that God is not vengeful. His Final Judgment, as we shall see presently, is that He simply loves us as He always did. Nothing has changed:

> God is not angry. He merely could not let this happen [the ego's triumph over God's Love]. You cannot change His Mind (text, p. 320; T-16.V.12:7-9).

The changelessness of God's Love for His children is the Course's reinterpretation of the Last Judgment.

The Last Judgment is one of the most threatening ideas in your thinking. This is because you do not understand it. Judgment is not an attribute of God. It was brought into being only after the separation, when it became one of the many learning devices to be built into the overall plan.

Clearly, judgment involves judging between perceived differences. Whether judging between "right" and "wrong" actions, or between "good" and "bad" people, we are reflecting the split or separated mind. The One-mindedness of God or Christ cannot judge, and thus God's only judgment is not a judgment at all. It does not discriminate between His children, for it is all-inclusive. God's judgment is simply the fact of His total Love for His beloved Sons.

Judgment came into being only when the separation occurred. The ego's use of judgment, obviously, is to separate and attack. Within our split minds, the only judgment the Holy Spirit recognizes as real is judging between expressions of God's Love, or calls for it (text, pp. 200-202,273; T-12.I; T-14.X.7:1). In His judgment there is no need to punish, simply to correct. Thus, the Holy Spirit's form of judgment is simply a way to reunify the seemingly separated Sonship. This is the "learning device" that was built into the overall plan. The culmination of this right-minded judgment is the Final Judgment, which is, as we will see, the final recognition that "what is false is false, and what is true has never changed" (workbook, p. 445; W-pII.10.1:1).

Just as the separation occurred over millions of years, the Last Judgment will extend over a similarly long period, and perhaps an even longer one.

No one likes that sentence. Incidentally, in this particular context "the Last Judgment" is really a synonym for "the plan of the Atonement." In general, "the Last Judgment" is the Course's term for the final step of the Atonement. In this particular passage, however, Jesus is talking about the overall process. This sentence is a very good one to keep in mind when encountering those students of *A Course in Miracles* who maintain that within the illusory dream the Atonement can end in an instant, which speaking on Level One, Jesus does say in many places. This passage, however, makes it very clear that within the illusion of time, undoing the belief in separation will take long indeed. The tremendous amount of fear that is present in our minds seems to ensure that this is the case. Yet there is hope as well:

Its length, however, can be greatly shortened by miracles, the device for shortening but not abolishing time. If a sufficient number become truly miracle-minded, this shortening process can be virtually immeasurable. It is essential, however, that you free yourself quickly, because you must emerge from the conflict if you are to bring peace to other minds.

This relates back to the function of the miracle we had considered in Part II. In this passage Jesus is urging us to choose miracles rather than our grievances. The more quickly we can make this choice, the more quickly our minds can be healed; thus the more quickly Jesus can heal other minds through our own. This, of course, is the idea behind the plan of the Atonement. Now Jesus turns to the Last Judgment.

The Last Judgment is generally thought of as a procedure undertaken by God. [This was evident in the Gospel passages we read earlier.] Actually it will be undertaken by my brothers with my help.

Again, God cannot be involved in the Last Judgment because it is a correction for an error which He does not even know about. The workbook tells us twice that "God does not forgive because He has never condemned" (workbook, pp. 73,99; W-pI.46.1:1; W-pI.60.1:2). We are the ones who made the wrong judgment initially by turning away from the Holy Spirit's Atonement principle and identifying with the ego's insane concept of atonement with sacrifice. Therefore we are the only ones who can correct this mistake, by now rejoining with that principle, manifested in the dream by Jesus. This is the reason behind Jesus' emphasis in the Course on joining with him.

It is a final healing rather than a meting out of punishment, however much you may think that punishment is deserved. Punishment is a concept totally opposed to right-mindedness, and the aim of the Last Judgment is to restore right-mindedness to you. The Last Judgment might be called a process of right evaluation. It simply means that everyone will finally come to understand what is worthy and what is not.

With the advent of the Second Coming the Sonship finally awakens from the dream. At this final awakening we stand at the threshold of Heaven and look back at all the things we thought had been real, the entire span of time and space. We realize at last that everything we have made is false, and all that remains is the truth as God created it. That is the Final Judgment. In a sense, it is the summation of all the little judgments that the Course asks us to make continually—judging between the truth of the Holy Spirit and the illusions of the ego. Once again, as we saw in the previous chapter, when the entire Sonship reunites, the Second Coming occurs. So too is the Last Judgment accomplished by the one Son.

After this, the ability to choose can be directed rationally. Until this distinction is made, however, the vacillations between free and imprisoned will cannot but continue.

This passage implies, in distinction from what we have been saying, that the Last Judgment is a process. Thus we again can see how loose Jesus is with his terms: in one passage the Last Judgment is seen as the culmination of the Atonement process of learning to judge rightly; in another, as here, it is the process itself; and still elsewhere it is equated with the

Atonement. The content behind all of these references remains the same, however, and this reflects the ultimate teaching lesson that we pay attention to the content—the meaning of any particular passage—without rigidly holding on to the specific form in which it is expressed.

The individual process of learning right-minded judgments is what is referred to here. As this is learned and we each accept the Atonement for ourselves, the vacillations between the ego and the Holy Spirit cease, so that our judgments are only those of the Holy Spirit. This of course ensures that we are "directed rationally," the condition of living in the real world. When we all have attained this state, the Second Coming and actual Final Judgment are ushered in.

Q: This presents quite a different view of rationality, doesn't it?

A: Absolutely. It is similar to the later discussion in the text on the subject of reason, which is analogous to the right-minded thinking of the Holy Spirit. This naturally has nothing to do with rationality or reason as the world judges them. Incidentally, the Course distinction between the right and wrong mind has nothing to do with the current popular classification of right and left brain. The rational versus intuitive processes reflected in this latter typology can reflect either right- or wrong-minded thinking, depending on whether these abilities are directed by the Holy Spirit or the ego.

The first step toward freedom involves a sorting out of the false from the true. This is a process of separation in the constructive sense, and reflects the true meaning of the Apocalypse.

The reference here is to Revelation, the last book of the Bible. It is sometimes called the "Apocalypse," a term which means "secret or revealed writings." Jesus here reinterprets the final sorting out as not the separation of the sheep from the goats, the good from the evil, but rather the distinguishing of the true from the false—the falsity of the ego's teachings sorted out from the truth of God.

Everyone will ultimately look upon his own creations and choose to preserve only what is good, just as God Himself looked upon what He had created and knew that it was good. At this point, the mind can begin to look with love on its own creations because of their worthiness. At the same time the mind will inevitably disown its miscreations which, without belief, will no longer exist.

This first sentence is based upon the statement in Genesis (1:31) that God looked on His creation and saw that it was good. Jesus obviously is paralleling what we should do with our creations—the extension of our Identity as Christ—with what the biblical God did with His. These creations are therefore only of spirit, and have no referent in the material world. Their reality, however, is reflected by our joining with each other in forgiveness, which extends the Holy Spirit's truth in our split minds.

Our "miscreations" refer to everything of the ego world, thoughts as well as the projections of these thoughts into form. These include everything relating to the physical world, the body, and all aspects of the ego thought system: guilt, fear, specialness, attack, death, etc. We are thus asked once again to judge between the truth of God's and Christ's reality as spirit, and the ego's illusory world of materiality.

The term "Last Judgment" is frightening not only because it has been projected onto God, but also because of the association of "last" with death. This is an outstanding example of upside-down perception.

The "Last Judgment" is frightening not only because we believe God is going to punish us, but also because we associate the word "last" with death. Since we identify ourselves with our physical bodies, then the end of our lives, our physical and psychological existence, must also mean the end of us. To the ego, our physical death is directly equated with punishment by God. This thought has found its clearest statement in the Adam and Eve myth, where the two "sinners" are punished by God for their disobedience by beginning their "lives" in pain, then suffering the length of their days, and dying: "For dust you are and to dust you shall return" (Gn 3:16-19).

If the meaning of the Last Judgment is objectively examined, it is quite apparent that it is really the doorway to life.

The Course's understanding of the Last Judgment is that it is the instant when we make that final judgment separating out the illusions of the ego from the truth of God, and there thus remains nothing left to hinder our return home. The "doorway to life" is open and we simply let God take His final step.

Q: In that sense, someone like Jesus has already completed that process, right? It happens for everyone at the same moment, though; is that also correct?

A: Right. Jesus, having completed the process, knows the false from the true, and stands in that borderland—the real world—between this world and Heaven, holding the door to Heaven open for us. As he says in this moving passage:

> Christ is at God's altar, waiting to welcome His Son. But come wholly without condemnation, for otherwise you will believe that the door is barred and you cannot enter. The door is not barred, and it is impossible that you cannot enter the place where God would have you be. But love yourself with the Love of Christ, for so does your Father love you. You can refuse to enter, but you cannot bar the door that Christ holds open. Come unto me who holds it open for you, for while I live it cannot be shut, and I live forever (text, p. 187; T-11.IV.6:1-6).

Within the holy instant we all have already accepted the Atonement and are with him at Heaven's gate. In time, however, we have yet to make, and therefore accept, that choice.

Q: Returning to the previous passage, it is an interesting sentence because it says "objectively examined." How can people possibly objectively examine this idea if they have been brought up to believe in a theology which stresses condemnation and a harsh last judgment? It is very hard to step out of that mindset, if you really believe it, and then objectively examine any kind of evidence.

A: That is of course what Jesus is really saying here. In fact, the very next line addresses this point:

No one who lives in fear is really alive.

Living in fear is tantamount to identifying with the ego thought system which is, of course, the denial of life. Therefore, no one who is afraid is truly alive, for the Love that is the Source of our life has been denied. Similarly, as the above passage about Jesus holding the door open for us states, anger (or condemnation) serves the same ego purpose of "protecting" us from the Love and life of God. Therefore, we can state that the Course is actually teaching us how to be objective, which means free from all thought and perceptual distortions that inevitably come from choosing the ego's defenses of fear and anger. We choose again, and are healed by letting go of guilt in the context of personal relationships. The diminution of this guilt automatically diminishes our fear of God's punishment.

Your own last judgment cannot be directed toward yourself, because you are not your own creation. You can, however, apply it meaningfully and at any time to everything you have made, and retain in your memory only what is creative and good.

This passage reflects the idea that we cannot truly heal our own egos. As the text teaches, regarding our attempts to undo guilt by ourselves:

> Remember you made guilt, and that your plan for the escape from guilt has been to bring Atonement to it, and make salvation fearful. And it is only fear that you will add, if you prepare yourself for love. The preparation for the holy instant belongs to Him Who gives it....Never approach the holy instant after you have tried to remove all fear and hatred from your mind. That is *its* function. Never attempt to overlook your guilt before you ask the Holy Spirit's help. That is *His* function. Your part is only to offer Him a little willingness to let Him remove all fear and hatred, and to be forgiven (text, pp. 356f; T-18.IV.6:3-5; T-18.V.2:1-5).

The real judgment of ourselves is God's, as we shall see presently. In other words, we really cannot look at ourselves and make that loving judgment of who we are as God's Son. Our repressed fear of God's Love is so powerful that it prevents us from objectively examining the truth. But when we project this unconscious guilt and fear onto other people, and have the little willingness to reconsider our decision, we can listen to the Holy Spirit teaching us to forgive. We cannot forgive our guilt by ourselves, but through forgiving others with the Holy Spirit's help, our own guilt is undone.

Q: What I understood from this passage is that the last judgment cannot be directed toward ourselves because there can be no last judgment about who we really are. What we can judge, though, are the egos we have made. Who we really are is completely apart from judgment. Is this a valid way of interpreting this passage?

A: Yes it is. Strictly speaking, the "Self" in "yourself" should be capitalized because God created us and not ourselves. So the last judgment is directed toward the ego world, where it is needed. To quote once again the introduction to the text:

> The course does not aim at teaching the meaning of love, for that is beyond what can be taught. It does aim, however, at removing the blocks to the awareness of love's presence (text, intro.; T-in.1:6-7).

Our true Self does not need to be judged, but our illusory ego self needs to be judged as false, thereby clearing the way for the memory of our Identity as Christ to return to us.

This is what your right-mindedness cannot but dictate. The purpose of time is solely to "give you time" to achieve this judgment. It is your own perfect judgment of your own perfect creations. When everything you retain is lovable, there is no reason for fear to remain with you. This is your part in the Atonement.

Elsewhere in the Course we are taught that the purpose of the world is to correct our belief about the reality of space and time (text, p. 11; T-1.VI.3:5-4:1). Similarly, the purpose of time is to "give us the time" to make the final judgment. Here, "perfect judgment" would not refer to the Last Judgment, which corrects the ego's judgment, but rather is similar to God's judgment of love. Finally, when we forgive everything in this world, thereby forgiving ourselves, there will be no fear. The guilt that demands fear of God's punishment would be gone: without its *cause* (guilt), the *effect* (fear) must disappear. And this undoing of guilt and fear through forgiveness constitutes our role in the Atonement.

Let us go back to the fourth paragraph in section IV of Chapter 9 (text, p. 158; T-9.IV.9:2):

Do not fear the Last Judgment, but welcome it and do not wait, for the ego's time is "borrowed" from your eternity.

Jesus is telling us again that we do not have to be afraid of the Last Judgment, but simply have to welcome the love that is its true meaning. Moreover, there is no need for us to wait for the Last Judgment, since our waiting in time was our ego's choice, taken from the eternal nature of our reality as God's loving Son. It is only this judgment of love that we need accept.

Now we will move on to the section called "The Borderland," paragraph four, in Chapter 26 (text, p. 508; T-26.III.4):

Nothing the Son of God believes can be destroyed. But what is truth to him must be brought to the last comparison that he will ever make; the last evaluation that will be possible, the final judgment upon this world. It is the judgment of the truth upon illusion, of knowledge on perception: "It has no meaning, and does not exist."

Truth to us is the ego's illusory and insane thought system, based upon our belief that what does not exist is really here, and the Heaven that is truly here does not exist:

> When you made visible what is not true, what *is* true became invisible to you (text, p. 217; T-12.VIII.3:1).

It is thus this ego's thought system we must finally look at with the Holy Spirit's help and judge against. His judgment— illusory perception has no meaning and therefore does not exist—is an application of the first principle of miracles that there is no order of difficulty among them. Every illusion is exactly the same as every other one. Each does not exist and therefore has no meaning. We give it whatever meaning it has, and our projected meaning is always based on the past, as the workbook tells us in the early lessons.

Q: The Course sometimes refers to "spiritual sight." Would this be an example of that?

A: Yes, this final judgment is based upon spiritual sight, or what the Course more usually refers to as "vision."

This [final judgment] is not your decision. It is but a simple statement of a simple fact. But in this world there are no simple facts, because what is the same and what is different remain unclear.

The truth of this final judgment does not rest upon our decision. Our free will, as we have seen earlier, cannot decide what is real and what is not. We are free only to choose between what we *believe* is real and what is not. As Jesus frequently reminds us, what can be simpler? Thus, near the end of the text:

> How simple is salvation! All it says is what was never true is not true now, and never will be. The impossible has not occurred, and can have no effects. And that is all. Can this be hard to learn by anyone who wants it to be true?...How hard is it to see that what is false can not be true, and what is true can not be false? (text, p. 600; T-31.I.1:1-5,7)

"Complexity is of the ego" (text, p. 289; T-15.IV.6:2), and so it is the ego that made up a complex world, with a complex body and complex set of laws whose sole purpose is to obscure the simplicity of the law of truth. The ego attempts to combine truth and illusion, spirit and body, Heaven and this world, so that we can no longer tell what is true from what is false. It now remains for the Holy Spirit to teach us this distinction so that we can ultimately reach the point when we are able to make that final judgment.

The one essential thing to make a choice at all is this distinction. And herein lies the difference between the worlds. In this one, choice is made impossible. In the real world is choosing simplified.

In this world, choice becomes impossible because we do not really understand what we are choosing between. We think we are really making a choice when we choose between different illusions. In the real world, which is the herald of the Last Judgment, we realize that what we are choosing between is everything that the ego made, which is false, as opposed to everything that God created, which is reflected to us through the Holy Spirit's teaching. Therefore, within the ego system we are really choosing between nothing and nothing, which of course renders the whole process meaningless.

Recognizing and accepting this meaninglessness of the ego's choosing is the end of the process of attaining the real world. Thus, again, we learn finally to choose against the ego's thought of *separation* from others through attack, sickness, pain, or guilt. We now transcend these ego barriers and *join* with others through realizing that we are all one and the same. Once we have made that one choice, the only one truly possible in this world—i.e., once we have answered the last unanswered question (text, pp. 430-33; T-21.VII)—all choosing ceases as the Holy Spirit's correction tapes have erased the ego's. Nothing now remains to be corrected, or chosen between. Our minds now simply follow the guidance of Love. Again: what could be simpler?

Now let us turn to the workbook, the summary "What is the Last Judgment?" (workbook, p. 445; W-pII.10):

Christ's Second Coming gives the Son of God this gift: To hear the Voice for God proclaim that what is false is false, and what is true has never changed. And this the judgment is in which perception ends.

Clearly Jesus is telling us here that when we can make this final judgment—"what is false is false" (everything of the ego) and "what is true has never changed" (the truth of God and Christ)—at that moment the entire world of perception ends. It is the awakening and reuniting of the seemingly dreaming and fragmented Son of God in the Second Coming that sets this next "step" in motion:

At first you see a world that has accepted this as true, projected from a now corrected mind. And with this holy sight

[Christ's vision], perception gives a silent blessing and then disappears, its goal accomplished and its mission done.

The Final Judgment on the world contains no condemnation. For it sees the world as totally forgiven, without sin and wholly purposeless. Without a cause, and now without a function in Christ's sight, it merely slips away to nothingness.

"At first" refers to the attainment of the real world, when our minds have been healed. When all of us have accomplished this step, the Second Coming, the unified mind of the Sonship—filled only with the Love of the Holy Spirit—projects out and we perceive through Christ's vision. (The use of the word "projected" here is another example of how the Course is not strictly consistent in its language, as typically the word "projection" is reserved for the ego and "extension" for spirit.) If the cause of the world, which is the belief in sin, is gone, then the world must disappear. This is so because the only purpose of the world is to keep sin real. Therefore, when we let go of our investment in sin, which is the meaning of forgiveness, then the world "merely slips away to nothingness."

There [in that nothingness] it [the world] was born and there it ends as well. And all the figures in the dream in which the world began go with it. Bodies now are useless, and will therefore fade away, because the Son of God is limitless.

The "figures in the dream" refer to the bodies and forms in the physical world. Sections such as "The Dreamer of the Dream" and "The Hero of the Dream" in Chapter 27 discuss the body's role in the various dreams that we have made, all of which have to do with maintaining the belief in the reality of the world of form, change, and death. The body's world is one of limitation, which defends against our true reality as God's limitless Son. Thus we understand, still again, the essential metaphysical teaching of the Course that the entire world of time and space exists only to reinforce the ego's belief that the separation from God is real. When that belief is no longer there, the world no longer has a purpose and must disappear. The physical world does not exist beyond our minds, as we discussed in Part I. So if that mind changes its belief—from sin to forgiveness—the world correspondingly changes as well.

You who believed that God's Last Judgment would condemn the world to hell, along with you, accept this holy truth: God's Judgment is the gift of the Correction He bestowed on all your errors, freeing you from them, and all effects they ever seemed to have.

The "gift" is the Holy Spirit, and its specific expression is the principle of the Atonement. That is the "Correction" spoken of here. If you think back to the diagram in chart 2, the Holy Spirit's correction is represented by the bottom part of the dual highway. Thus, at each step along the way—all of which happened in that one instant when the ego chose its errors and repeated them over and over again—each of those specific errors was corrected by the Holy Spirit. These errors constitute the painful effects of the cause, the original belief that the sin of separation occurred and the "tiny, mad idea" was taken seriously.

To fear God's saving grace is but to fear complete release from suffering, return to peace, security and happiness, and union with your own Identity.

As long as we believe in sin and guilt we must believe God will punish us. Thus, the only way we can attain happiness and peace is to accept God back into our minds as our loving Creator. Since the ego teaches us that to accept God back into our minds is our destruction, we become fearful of accepting His Love. Anything, therefore, that speaks of "peace, security and happiness" must be fearful to the ego. This is the basis of our fear of love and "God's saving grace."

God's Final Judgment is as merciful as every step in His appointed plan to bless His Son, and call him to return to the eternal peace He shares with him. Be not afraid of love. For it alone can heal all sorrow, wipe away all tears, and gently waken from his dream of pain the Son whom God acknowledges as His.

The ego has taught us, again, that we should be afraid of God's Love, because if we get too close to it we will be destroyed. Our guilt demands our suffering and sacrifice, which means that within the ego's strange religion it is a sin to be without suffering. It is a sin to be happy, and it is a sin to be at peace:

> To the ego, *the guiltless are guilty.* Those who do not attack are its "enemies" because, by not valuing its interpretation of salvation, they are in an excellent position to let it go....I [Jesus] have said that the crucifixion is the symbol of the ego. When it was confronted with the real guiltlessness of God's Son [Jesus here refers to himself] it did attempt to kill him, and the reason it gave was that guiltlessness is blasphemous to God. To the ego, the *ego* is God, and guiltlessness must be interpreted as the final guilt that fully justifies murder (text, p. 224; T-13.II.4:2-3; 6:1-3).

The workbook reference "wipe away all tears" comes from the Bible (Isaiah and Revelation), and Jesus is asking us, as long as we believe we are still guilty, to consider belief in a loving God who would wipe away our tears of suffering and sacrifice. This is accomplished by letting go of the guilt that demands our punishment by a vengeful Father. So over and over again we return to the Course's basic teaching that the way we return to Heaven and God's Love is through forgiveness, for only then can the cause of our problems be undone.

Be not afraid of this [of love]. Salvation asks you give it welcome. And the world awaits your glad acceptance, which will set it free.

This is God's Final Judgment: "You are still My holy Son, forever innocent, forever loving and forever loved, as limitless as your Creator, and completely changeless and forever pure. Therefore awaken and return to Me. I am Your Father and you are My Son."

This is one of the lovelier passages in *A Course in Miracles,* and needs little comment except to mention that it reflects a total shift from everything that the ego believes about God and His Son. This lovely truth waits patiently for us until we are able to give it welcome.

Chapter 12

GOD'S LAST STEP

Now we will move on to the final step in the Atonement plan, what *A Course in Miracles* calls "God's last step." To begin with, as we shall see presently, Jesus explains that in truth God does not take any steps. Moreover, His taking steps implies our having been on a journey. Yet we have already remarked several times that such a journey is illusory since we never left home. As quoted earlier, we are on "a journey without distance to a goal that has never changed" (text, p. 139; T-8.VI.9:7). In reality, therefore, the term "God's last step" is merely a figure of speech or metaphor that follows upon the basic metaphor of a journey. Because our experience of time is linear, and that we are indeed returning home, Jesus talks to us on the level we can understand. Thus we are told that the journey ultimately ends with God's taking the last step for us.

Basically then the "last step" is a way of talking about the end of our dream, the culmination of Christ's Second Coming and the Last Judgment. When we finally heal our minds and make that ultimate choice between truth and illusion, the world disappears, and we "return" to the God we never truly left. This is God's last step, a poetic rendering of our completed awakening.

We begin with the last paragraph of the section in Chapter 7 called "The Last Step" (text, p. 105; T-7.I.7):

God does not take steps, because His accomplishments are not gradual. He does not teach, because His creations are changeless. He does nothing last, because He created first and for always.

This is the only place in *A Course in Miracles* where this concept is stated so clearly. Jesus is talking about "the last step," but, to state it again, he does not mean it literally. There are no gradations in God, and so there can be none in His Son. Nothing need be taught to Christ because He is as perfect and whole as His Father, and therefore has no split mind that can or needs to learn. However, within the dream of separation God's Son believes he is on a journey of time, and therefore he must learn within its context.

This usage of the language of the dream is a helpful example, like many others we have already considered, to remind us not to take certain statements in the Course literally. The *meaning*, on the other hand, should always be taken literally. For example, as we have already seen, when Jesus speaks of God weeping over His separated Sons, or His loneliness, he is really using poetic metaphors to express God's Love for us. Similarly, the phrase "God's last step" refers to the end product of the illusory journey of awakening. It is not referring to something that truly happens. Considered in the context of chart 3, the last step is the awakening from the dream that we seem to be living through in our video tapes.

It must be understood that the word "first" as applied to Him is not a time concept. He is first in the sense that He is the First in the Holy Trinity Itself. He is the Prime Creator, because He created His co-creators [our true Selves]. Because He did, time applies neither to Him nor to what He created.

As discussed at the beginning of Chapter 1 (see above, p. 8), this is a very clear example of the Course's use of words within a temporal and spatial context, even though that context is illusory. These words are thus used to help us who believe that reality is temporal and spatial. But, again, the words themselves are not to be taken as expressing literal truth. For example, as we can see here, the word "first" obviously implies a second, third, etc., that will come in the future. But since God is beyond time, such a term as "first" cannot truly apply to Him.

The "last step" that God will take was therefore true in the beginning, is true now, and will be true forever. What is timeless is always there, because its being is eternally changeless. It does not change by increase, because it was forever created to increase. If you perceive it as not increasing you do not know what it is. You also do not know Who created it.

What is "changeless" and "does not change by increase" is spirit, although the word "spirit" does not actually appear in this section. The spirit of God created Christ, whose spirit in turn created the creations of Christ. The increase does not change spirit, certainly an understanding different from the world's sense of increase, which clearly implies a quantitative change. When we increase anything of the material world, there is more of it: we add to our bank account, the amount of food we eat, the number of books we own, etc. Clearly, then, "increase" here implies no quantitative change, a phenomenon that is not understandable in this world. This changelessness of increase is described in this beautiful passage from the workbook:

> As Heaven's peace and joy intensify when you accept them as God's gift to you, so does the joy of your Creator grow when you accept His joy and peace as yours. True giving is creation. It extends the limitless to the unlimited, eternity to timelessness, and love unto itself. It adds to all that is complete already, not in simple terms of adding more, for that implies that it was less before. It adds by letting what cannot contain itself fulfill its aim of giving everything it has away, securing it forever for itself (workbook, p. 185; W-pI.105.4).

Q: Would this correlate in this world to giving: if you do not see that you are gaining by giving, then you are not understanding the process?

A: Yes. The parallel here is that when you "give away" love in this world you are non-quantifiably increasing the love you "have," and nothing really changes. Love is qualitative, not quantitative. Thus, there can be no loss when we extend love to others. For example, if we believe in increase or decrease in terms of material quantity, and then attempt to apply this understanding to spirit, we will surely confuse ourselves and effectively block our comprehension of Heaven. We thus will never know God, but *will* know the ego. The ego world of materiality is quantitative, where everything, including love, is measured as is a pound of potatoes. Belief in this world's reality, therefore, with all its changes—loss and increase— becomes a very powerful defense against God.

God does not reveal this to you because it was never hidden.

This is a subtle correction of the more traditional idea that God gives revelations, and that He gives them only sometimes and to some people. The world's belief is that those who have been given revelations of truth have been chosen by God, clearly implying that God has an ego that judges who is worthy of a revelation and who is not. Jesus' teachings in *A Course in Miracles* are totally different. God is always extending His truth to all. The problem—our problem—is that we do not usually accept God's ongoing revelation of Himself. Those who do—who have dropped their ego barriers to the truth—are the ones who have visionary or revelatory experiences.

Thus "revelation" is not something that God does, just as the "last step" is not something He does. The *experience* of revelation is the effect of a decision we have made. God's Love, like a lighthouse shining into the blackened sea, is passive insofar as it simply shines its light, yet does not actively do anything. We are therefore like the boats who have wandered away from the light, and who now must choose to come back to this home of light in our minds. Thus, God's Love does not call to us in the usual sense of the word, but rather shines out as a beacon of truth that holds out its loving welcome, patiently "waiting" our return. In summary, then, God does not hide His truth, anymore than He reveals it to us. His Love simply is.

Q: In the very beginning of the text Jesus talks about how he is in tune with the revelation readiness of his brothers, and that he can bring down upon us more than we can. So God cannot do anything. He simply is. But is it that Jesus can help us open up to that experience?

A: Yes, that is the idea. Jesus' role is not to give us the revelation, because that is always there; but he helps us remove the interferences to it. The crucial thing is that God does not do it, just as we have seen that the Last Judgment is not something God does. Jesus actually, being an expression of God's Love, does not really do anything either. As the Holy Spirit is the memory of God's Love in our dreams, simply being there, so too is Jesus simply there, as the manifestation of this Love in form. We experience his love as calling to us, helping us here, but in reality it remains quietly within our minds. Like the lighthouse, again, his light-filled presence "passively" serves as the reminder of who we truly are as children of the Light.

A helpful analogy is to consider the sun rising and setting each day. Not one person fails to experience this phenomenon, and often with awe and great pleasure. However, almost all of us understand that it is really the earth that moves, while the sun is stationary. This is a clear example of how our sensory apparatus plays tricks on us, distorting the facts of our physical world. Similarly, our experience of the Holy Spirit's or Jesus' activity distorts the truth that their love remains "stationary," while it is our minds that have wandered off, and must therefore return.

His light was never obscured, because it is His Will to share it. How can what is fully shared be withheld and then revealed?

The same point is reiterated. Traditionally it has been taught that God sometimes withholds His Love, bestowing it upon certain people at certain times. Jesus is teaching us here very clearly that God does not "think" that way: He has not obscured His light, nor withdrawn Himself, as many mystics have experienced. What has really happened is that *we* have withdrawn ourselves into a world of shadows. Thus, the purpose of the Course is to teach us to remove these shadows. All that God has done is "extend Himself" into the dream through our memory of His Love. That extension is the Holy Spirit, and it is the Holy Spirit's function to help us remove those shadows so that we can see the light that has always been there. Even though, to state it once again, we are speaking about God's last step, it is really not a step that God takes. The "step" is really one that we take.

Let us move now to Chapter 13 of the text, the third paragraph of the section "From Perception to Knowledge" (text, p. 241; T-13.VIII.3). It is in that middle ground between perception and knowledge that we find the real world, the Second Coming, the Last Judgment, and then finally God's last step. At the beginning of the paragraph the term "perfect perception" is used. This is another version of the Course's more commonly used term, "true perception," which is the perception of this world cleansed of our projections of guilt and sin.

Perfect perception, then, has many elements in common with knowledge, making transfer to it possible.

True perception contains no ego barriers, and has many elements in common with Heaven such as the fact that it does not exclude. In Heaven there is no exclusion; since there is no separation, everyone is one. Christ is unified with Himself and with His Father. Within the dream of the world this unity is partially reflected in those who have true perceptions and live in the real world. This is living through the vision of Christ, with no guilt separating them from anyone else. The love these people experience comes from the Holy Spirit and embraces all others, who are no longer perceived as different.

Before continuing, let us turn to the last paragraph in section I in Chapter 5 (text, p. 68; T-5.I.7). This is the specific reference for what I just mentioned. It describes the parallels between true perception (even though that term is not used here) and the state of the Kingdom. Basically, three characteristics are talked about. The first is that in true perception, again, everything is universal; there are no exclusions, everyone is included. That is the exact opposite of specialness, and reflects the state of unity in Heaven where there can be no exclusion. Second, in the state of true perception—living in the real world—there is no attack. Since there is no remaining sin or guilt, there is nothing within the mind that can be projected in the form of attack. The state of Heaven is love, the complete opposite of attack. The third characteristic, which follows, speaks of true perception:

> Finally, it points the way beyond the healing that it brings, and leads the mind beyond its own integration toward the paths of creation (text, p. 68; T-5.I.7:5).

That is the pathway that leads to the complete re-integration of the Sonship, paralleling the unity of the Sonship in Heaven. True perception thus represents the end of the process of undoing the interferences to our remembering this unity, pointing beyond the correction to the experience of unity of Christ within Himself, His creations, and with His Creator.

We return now to where we were in Chapter 13 (text, p. 241; T-13.VIII.3):

Yet the last step must be taken by God, because the last step in your redemption, which seems to be in the future, was accomplished by God in your creation.

Basically, Jesus is saying that despite the seeming linearity of time expressed through the use of the words "first" and "last," the beginning and end are really the same. The so-called "last step" God takes is merely our total undoing of the seeming steps that we placed between the First and the Second Coming. This is another example of how *A Course in Miracles* comes within the world of illusion and yet speaks to us of the truth beyond illusions. This reference is similar to the biblical statement of Jesus that he is the Alpha and the Omega, the beginning and the end, the first and the last (Rv 1:8,21:6,22:13).

The separation has not interrupted it. Creation cannot be interrupted. The separation is merely a faulty formulation of reality, with no effect at all.

This is a reflection of the principle of the Atonement which says that the separation never truly occurred, depicted in charts 5 and 6 where it seems as if the dip and spiral had broken the line. In reality the line of eternity has not been affected at all. The same idea is expressed in this passage: our seeming sin against the unity of creation has had no effect. Creation's love has not been changed by our distorted perceptions of its seemingly fragmented reality.

The miracle, without a function in Heaven, is here. Aspects of reality can still be seen, and they will replace aspects of unreality. Aspects of reality can be seen in everything and everywhere.

The miracle has no place in the world of Heaven, because there is nothing in Heaven that has to be corrected. It is here in the world of separation that the miracle has its function. There are several places in the Course which speak of the separated parts of the Sonship as "aspects" (e.g., text, pp. 38,

234, 290; T-3.IV.3:7; T-13.VI.6:4; T-15.V.2:3). At other times Jesus refers to them as "parts" (e.g., text, pp. 29, 209, 290; T-2.VII.6:2-7; T-12.IV.6:8; T-15.V.2:2;3:1). Both are objective or neutral words to describe the seemingly personal individuality of God's Sonship. The aspects of reality that we can still see here are the face of Christ that we see in each other, the sparks of the light of Christ that reflect our inherent innocence:

> In many only the spark remains, for the Great Rays [of Christ] are obscured. Yet God has kept the spark alive so that the Rays can never be completely forgotten. If you but see the little spark you will learn of the greater light, for the Rays are there unseen. Perceiving the spark will heal, but knowing the light will create. Yet in the returning the little light must be acknowledged first, for the separation was a descent from magnitude to littleness. But the spark is still as pure as the great light, because it is the remaining call of creation. Put all your faith in it, and God Himself will answer you (text, p. 175; T-10.IV.8).

These "aspects of reality" replace the aspects of unreality, or the faces of guilt and sin that we projected from within ourselves onto each other. The face of Christ can be seen in everyone, everything, and everywhere, because the innocence of our Identity as Christ remains within our minds. This reflects the principle that we find in the workbook: "God is in everything I see because God is in my mind" (workbook, p. 47; W-pI.30). If we identify with the image of Christ that is our true Identity, this reality will be extended through us and therefore will be what we shall see all around us.

Yet only God can gather them [aspects of reality] together, by crowning them as one with the final gift of eternity.

Here we see again God's "final step," which is really the re-awakening in the mind of the separated Son to his oneness as Christ. It is not really a crowning that God does, but rather an accomplishment we have brought about with the Holy Spirit's help: the acceptance of God's eternity as reality.

Now we will move on to Chapter 30, section V, paragraph three (text, p. 591; T-30.V.3). The title of this section is "The Only Purpose," and it deals with the only purpose that this world has: forgiveness. A good part of this section deals with the real world, but in the passages we shall read now God's final step is the focus.

Not yet is Heaven quite remembered, for the purpose of forgiveness still remains. Yet everyone is certain he will go beyond forgiveness, and he but remains until it is made perfect in himself. He has no wish for anything but this.

As long as we are still here in the world of the body, we are saying that we have not totally forgiven ourselves, the world, or God. Therefore the memory of God is still dim and His Voice obscure. Yet within us is the yearning to return home, and thus despite the ego's raucous shrieking, the decision maker in our minds will yet turn away from this voice and do the "*one* perfect thing and make [the] *one* perfect choice" (text, p. 493; T-25.VI.5:1). Our making this choice is certain, and in our right minds this is all we desire.

And fear is dropped away, because he is united in his purpose with himself. There is a hope of happiness in him so sure and constant he can barely stay and wait a little longer, with his feet still touching earth. Yet is he glad to wait till every hand is joined, and every heart made ready to arise and go with him. For thus is he made ready for the step in which is all forgiveness left behind.

I am reminded here of something Jesus had told Helen in the early weeks of the Course's scribing. He referred to a statement the famous psychic Jeanne Dixon had made about his standing with his feet touching the ground and his hands reaching up to Heaven, representing his role of bridging the gap between our egos and Heaven. In the text it reads this way:

> You stand below me and I stand below God. In the process of "rising up," I am higher because without me the distance between God and man would be too great for you to encompass. I bridge the distance as an elder brother to you on the one hand, and as a Son of God on the other (text, p. 5; T-1.II.4:3-5).

Therefore, our role in this world, like Jesus', is to manifest the Holy Spirit's function of bridging time and eternity, remaining in the real world as He directs, our feet on the earth while our hands reach to Heaven. We are thus to become like Jesus, or those ascended masters who have completed their particular lessons. These teachers remain just a sliver away from Heaven, though they have its awareness, so that they help everyone else attain what they have learned. "Yet is he glad to wait till every hand is joined" refers to the Second Coming and the Last Judgment which is what makes "ready for the step [God's last step] in which is all forgiveness left behind."

What is a little tricky in all this is that the Course is talking about something that really does not exist. Again, Jesus is segmenting out different phases of an inherently unreal process. These terms are therefore simply a poetic means of reaching our very literal and concrete separated minds. And so Jesus speaks of the vision of Christ, true perception, real world, Second Coming, Last Judgment, and the last step. This passage is thus a touching and poetic description of the idea that those parts of the Sonship who have accepted the Atonement for themselves cannot wait to return home, but yet still choose to remain and help everyone else.

The final step is God's, because it is but God Who could create a perfect Son and share His Fatherhood with him. No one outside of Heaven knows how this can be, for understanding this is Heaven itself.

Thus the final step is really the first, because it is only God who could create a perfect Son who is always one with Him. And thus the first and the last are one, with no intervening steps of separating and re-uniting. Then Jesus continues, in effect saying that even though I am trying my best to explain this fact of Heaven to you, you will not really be able to understand it anyway. How can it be that the first step is the last step and the last step is the first step? With regard to Jesus, since he is the manifestation of the Holy Spirit, God's Voice, in that sense he shares in the unknowable truths of Heaven and does understand. Only a mind that has transcended the ego thought system can know the reality that lies beyond the split mind.

Even the real world has a purpose still beneath creation and eternity. But fear is gone because its purpose is forgiveness, not idolatry. And so is Heaven's Son prepared to be himself, and to remember that the Son of God knows everything his Father understands, and understands it perfectly with Him.

The real world still falls short of this, for this is God's Own purpose; only His, and yet completely shared and perfectly fulfilled.

The purpose of the real world, of course, is forgiveness, and its extension through the mind of the Sonship. This passage thus tells us something about the real world. It is not Heaven, for its purpose is not the creation that is the function of God and Christ. Yet, it paves the way for the return of this function to the mind that had chosen fear instead of love. Thus is the ego's perception exchanged for the knowledge of Heaven. Again, the goal of *A Course in Miracles* is not Heaven and the return of our function of creation. Rather, its purpose is the real world, attained through the completion of our function of forgiveness.

The real world is a state in which the mind has learned how easily do idols go when they are still perceived but wanted not. How willingly the mind can let them go when it has understood that idols are nothing and nowhere, and are purposeless. For only then can guilt and sin be seen without a purpose, and as meaningless.

The final chapters of the text discuss idols, another term for the specialness that is the ego's god. An idol is defined as a substitute for God, a false image for His reality, and obviously this replacement of God is the purpose of all special relationships. When idols go, what remains is the true Love of God that was always there, but not experienced. But to accomplish this change, we first must recognize the idols of specialness we had chosen in our insanity to serve the ego's purpose of "protecting" us from God's Love. Guilt and sin are the ego's principal allies in this strange plan, and as we recognize the insanity of this plan, the purpose of these allies drops away and we are able at last to share in the innocence and love of the real world.

Thus is the real world's purpose gently brought into awareness, to replace the goal of sin and guilt. And all that stood between your image of yourself and what you are, forgiveness washes joyfully away. Yet God need not create His Son again, that what is his be given back to him. The gap between your brother and yourself was never there. And what the Son of God knew in creation he must know again.

So once again, we see that God does not do anything (He "need not create His Son again"). The last or final step in the Atonement path is really the same as the first. The sin and guilt that seemed to intervene is gently washed away through forgiveness, and so this gap disappears back into its own nothingness. Incidentally, "gap" is also a term which appears primarily in the final chapters of the text, and is another word for the belief in separation.

Now we will skip to paragraph eight:

How light and easy is the step across the narrow boundaries of the world of fear when you have recognized Whose hand you hold! Within your hand is everything you need to walk with perfect confidence away from fear forever, and to go straight on, and quickly reach the gate of Heaven itself.

The "step across the narrow boundaries of the world of fear" can be understood as the attainment of the real world. The hand we hold is the hand of our special love or hate partner, who represents Christ since in truth we are all one. It is the hand of Christ that is found in the hand of those we forgive. "Reaching the gate of Heaven" is the completion of the Atonement process, the culmination of the real world that leads to the last step, lifting us into the Heaven we never truly left.

For He Whose hand you hold was waiting but for you to join Him. Now that you have come, would He delay in showing you the way that He must walk with you? His blessing lies on you as surely as His Father's Love rests upon Him. His gratitude to you is past your understanding, for you have enabled Him to rise from chains and go with you, together, to His Father's house.

This reflects the scriptural idea of arising and going to our Father's house. What is important here, as it always is in *A Course in Miracles*, is to remember that what enables us to return to our Father's house is forgiveness. Our forgiveness of each other undoes the barriers of guilt and attack that appeared to separate us, not only from each other, but from our true Self Who resides in God. We remember the Christ that is our true Identity by not excluding that Self from each other. Thus, our chains of guilt that bind us to the ego's world of separation are undone through understanding that we are one. Holding each other's hand symbolizes this recognition and acceptance.

An ancient hate is passing from the world. And with it goes all hatred and all fear. Look back no longer, for what lies ahead is all you ever wanted in your heart.

You may recall earlier in this chapter the mention of "an ancient hate that has come into the world through the ego." The "ancient hate [that] is passing from the world" is our self-hatred and guilt, and this passes from the world as we learn to forgive. "Look back" is a reference to the Old Testament story in which Lot's wife disobeyed God's injunction by looking back, and thus was turned into a pillar of salt. Thus we can say that if we look back to the past, making the ego's world of separation real, we inevitably will end up believing that we are indeed pillars of the ego: sinful, guilty, and fearful selves.

Give up the world! But not to sacrifice. You never wanted it. What happiness have you sought here that did not bring you pain? What moment of content has not been bought at fearful price in coins of suffering? Joy has no cost. It is your sacred right, and what you pay for is not happiness. Be speeded on your way by honesty, and let not your experiences here deceive in retrospect. They were not free from bitter cost and joyless consequence.

The traditional way of giving up the world was to deny oneself the so-called pleasures of the flesh. As we have seen in many other places, this kind of denial does not loosen our hold on the world. To the contrary, it attaches us still further to the world. In order to escape from our experienced pain here, we need but realize that the way to give up the world is to remember that it is not our true home.

The "coins of suffering" is a reference to the thirty pieces of silver, which was the price of Judas' recorded betrayal of Jesus. Jesus is teaching us here that to settle for the few crumbs that the world holds out to us as salvation is betraying the Christ in us. We are not asked to sacrifice the pleasures of the world—the world holds no pleasure—but rather are asked to realize that by embracing the world as the idol that would replace God's Love, we are in fact sacrificing the peace and joy that can come only from accepting our reality as God's child. It is this acceptance that undoes the ego's belief in sacrifice, for only then can we attain true happiness, joy, and peace. If we truly looked at anything in this world, we would realize that what we thought had given us happiness and joy was really filled with pain. As Jesus reminds us early in the text:

> All real pleasure comes from doing God's Will. This is because *not* doing it is a denial of Self (text, p. 12; T-1.VII.1:4-5).

Now we will turn to the workbook, Lesson 168, the third paragraph (workbook, p. 313; W-pI.168.3):

Today we ask of God the gift He has most carefully preserved within our hearts, waiting to be acknowledged. This the gift by which God leans to us and lifts us up, taking salvation's final step Himself. All steps but this we learn, instructed by His Voice. But finally He comes Himself, and takes us in His Arms and sweeps away the cobwebs of our sleep.

This gift is the final step. As we saw earlier (see above, p. 48), Lesson 157, "Into His Presence would I enter now" (workbook, p. 289; W-pI.157), expresses the same idea: the final vision, just prior to our being lifted up by God, is not learned. Our learning, through the Holy Spirit, encompasses the removal of the obstacles that allows this vision to emerge and the "final step" to occur. Forgiveness, the only learning the world can offer us, removes these obstacles.

This passage also reinforces the idea that the Son of God merely fell asleep and dreamed of his separation from God. This dream is the interval between the First Coming, God's

creation of Christ, and the Second Coming, which is the re-
awakening from that sleep. This passage thus refers to the
point in the process when we have reawakened from the nightmare with just a few cobwebs remaining. Then God wipes
them away. In the words of the Bible, occasionally quoted in
the Course and cited above, God wipes away our tears, and
then we are gently lifted back unto Himself.

**His gift of grace is more than just an answer. It restores all
memories the sleeping mind forgot; all certainty of what
Love's meaning is.**

God's grace, His Love that is experienced as we awaken
from the dream, is "given to us" as we let go of all remaining
remnants of this dream. It is the final stage, which is really the
unlearned experience that follows forgiveness.

Q: This passage, as well as others in the Course, is reminiscent of some of the mystic literature. Obviously, some of those
men and women had genuine experiences of God, and yet they
spoke as if God would give them the grace of an experience of
Him, which He would then take away as a means of helping
them learn what they still had to learn. How come, even
though the experiences seem genuine, they would use that
kind of expression, "God took this away from me"? Why
would they say that God would "deprive" them of the joy of
His presence?

A: What you are referring to is another example of the important distinction that *A Course in Miracles* makes between form
and content. These great mystics of the Church, I am sure, had
experiences of God and the love of Jesus. This is what the
Course refers to as the "content." It is an experience, similar
to experiences we might have in this century, to which we
might give an entirely different interpretation. The different
interpretations are what we call "form," and of course that is

what theology is: the attempt of the rational mind to explain something that cannot really be understood.

There is the famous example of St. Thomas Aquinas, who wrote the definitive theological tracts of the Church. Near the end of his life he had a mystical experience in which he said, "All that I have written seems to me as straw compared to what has now been revealed to me."[16] He believed at that point that his theological work was as worthless as straw, because once one has a true and authentic experience of God's Love, then one has no need to theologize about it. Shortly after this, while riding on his horse he hit his head against a branch, a blow from which he eventually died. His life evidently had become complete in his experience.

Therefore, the experiences of these saints and mystics may very well have been authentic (content), but the way that they interpreted them was through the theology of their time (form). This theology of the Church, as we know, taught that God leads us back to Him through our acceptance of a life of suffering and sacrifice. And certainly, *A Course in Miracles* goes to great lengths to help us understand that a loving God would never think that way. But that was how the traditional Church thought, and so it made perfect sense to them that the dark night of the soul—St. John of the Cross' evocative phrase depicting the period of darkness that precedes the mystic illumination—would express God's loving activity that withdraws His Love from us as the final step in our purification. And then all of a sudden He returns to us in a blinding light, and we experience union with His Love. But clearly the Church's basic teaching was that God allowed this pain to come into our lives as proof of His Love, and as a means of leading us back to Him.

---

16. Weisheipl, James A., O.P., *Friar Thomas D'Aquino: His Life, Thought, and Works* (Washington: The Catholic Univ. of America Press, 1983). For further discussion see my *Love Does Not Condemn*, pp. 11f. Consult Related Material at the end of this book for additional information.

Q: Do you think that was a subtle way of our egos coming in and saying, "I really do not want to have to take the painful steps of letting go of my special relationships"?

A: That is a tempting way to look at it, and I think the basic teaching of the Course would suggest that. However, it is important not to forget that from the point of view of the Church's mystical theology, the teaching of the Course would be mistaken. They represent different paths. But again, there is no question that *A Course in Miracles* would teach that those experiences would be ways of reinforcing the belief that guilt demands punishment through suffering and sacrifice.

God loves His Son. Request Him now to give the means by which this world will disappear, and vision first will come, with knowledge but an instant later. For in grace you see a light that covers all the world in love, and watch fear disappear from every face as hearts rise up and claim the light as theirs. What now remains that Heaven be delayed an instant longer? What is still undone when your forgiveness rests on everything?

This is a very beautiful portrait of what happens at the end. The "means" referred to is forgiveness, our expressing "the little willingness" to forgive. This makes possible the vision that "comes" to us, after which is God's last step and the knowledge of Heaven.

It is a new and holy day today, for we receive what has been given us. Our faith lies in the Giver, not our own acceptance. We acknowledge our mistakes, but He to Whom all error is unknown is yet the One Who answers our mistakes by giving us the means to lay them down, and rise to Him in gratitude and love.

The "He's" and "Whom's" refer to God. It is this kind of passage which could, I think, really confuse people, leading them to the mistaken idea that all they need do is this particular lesson, and they will be one step away from Heaven and God's last step. Clearly, this cannot be the case since this is only Lesson 168, with all those wonderful lessons still to come. It is important to understand another explanation for passages such as these; namely, that Jesus is doing what he frequently does in the Course: suddenly shifting the dimension of time to a vision of what will happen at the end. And since from the point of view of *A Course in Miracles* time is an illusion anyway, this shift merely reflects the sudden shift from the ego's video tapes of time to those of the Holy Spirit's that reflect eternity.

Thus it would be a mistake for people to have the expectation of all of a sudden being able to let go of all investment in the ego's thought system, and totally adopt the Holy Spirit's. We all know from our own personal journeys, and all we have been talking about so far, that the undoing of the ego takes a great deal of hard work over a long period of time.

And He descends to meet us, as we come to Him. For what He has prepared for us He gives and we receive. Such is His Will, because He loves His Son. To Him we pray today, returning but the word He gave to us through His Own Voice, His Word, His Love:

> *"Your grace is given me. I claim it now. Father, I come to You. And You will come to me who ask. I am the Son You love."*

The basic idea of course is that we do our work by forgiving. God cannot do it for us; as we were the ones who disclaimed God's Love, we are the ones who must now claim it. Undoing our guilt removes the barriers that kept us separate from God, and thus we come to Him as He completes the process by meeting us.

******

Thus we are now at the last step: the Sons of God have all awakened from the dream, made the final judgment about the illusory nature of the world, and God has lifted us up to Himself, or just about. As it is a beautiful summary of the journey and its culmination, leaving us one brief step from Heaven, I shall read the Epilogue to the "Clarification of Terms," at the very end of the teacher's manual.

I shall read this lovely section straight through, as the conclusion to our study of time. However, I should first like to make a few comments about what we will hear. Most sections of the manual do not contain biblical references. Here suddenly, in little over a page, there are at least five of them. Part of the reason for this is that this section was written in December, during Advent, the liturgical season of preparation for Christmas. Thus there are a number of Christmas references, as well as Jesus speaking about himself. The phrase "be not afraid" that occurs in the third paragraph is taken from Isaiah, and also is found in a number of places in the gospels where Jesus seeks to comfort his followers. We have commented on some of these earlier. An obvious Christmas reference occurs on the bottom of the page, which speaks about the "newborn world" and Christ being "reborn." The phrase "morning star," taken from the book of Revelation, has been traditionally used as a reference to Jesus: the morning star who shines away the darkness of the night.

Finally, throughout *A Course in Miracles* there are a number of references to Gnosticism, where specific Gnostic language is used. We find a clear example here at the beginning of the second paragraph, "You are a stranger here." The idea that this is an alien world in which we do not belong is very Gnostic. Lesson 160—"I am at home. Fear is the stranger here"—is probably the clearest reference to this Gnostic thought that we who are strangers in this alien world can never find true peace here. Another common Gnostic phrase is "to find rest," which occurs frequently in the Course, as in the beautiful Lesson 109, for example, "I rest in God." The end of the Epilogue does not actually use the word "rest," but it does express the same idea: "The Son is still, and in the quiet God has given him enters his home and is at peace at last." Thus does the wearying journey end.

Incidentally, the conclusions of all the books—text, workbook, manual for teachers, and now the "Clarification of Terms"—are poetically written and very, very moving. This Epilogue is certainly on the same level of beauty and inspiration as the others.

> Forget not once this journey is begun the end is certain. Doubt along the way will come and go and go to come again. Yet is the ending sure. No one can fail to do what God appointed him to do. When you forget, remember that you walk with Him and with His Word upon your heart. Who could despair when Hope like this is his? Illusions of despair may seem to come, but learn how not to be deceived by them. Behind each one there is reality and there is God. Why would you wait for this and trade it for illusions, when His Love is but an instant farther on the road where all illusions end? The end *is* sure and guaranteed by God. Who stands before a lifeless image when a step away the Holy of the Holies opens up an ancient door that leads beyond the world?

> You *are* a stranger here. But you belong to Him Who loves you as He loves Himself. Ask but my help to roll the stone away, and it is done according to His Will. We *have* begun the journey. Long ago the end was written in the stars and set into the Heavens with a shining ray that held it safe within eternity and through all time as well. And holds it still; unchanged, unchanging and unchangeable.

> Be not afraid. We only start again an ancient journey long ago begun that but seems new. We have begun again upon a road we travelled on before and lost our way a little while. And now we try again. Our new beginning has the certainty the journey lacked till now. Look up and see His Word among the stars, where He has set your name along with His. Look up and find your certain destiny the world would hide but God would have you see.

Let us wait here in silence, and kneel down an instant in our gratitude to Him Who called to us and helped us hear His Call. And then let us arise and go in faith along the way to Him. Now we are sure we do not walk alone. For God is here, and with Him all our brothers. Now we know that we will never lose the way again. The song begins again which had been stopped only an instant, though it seems to be unsung forever. What is here begun will grow in life and strength and hope, until the world is still an instant and forgets all that the dream of sin had made of it.

Let us go out and meet the newborn world, knowing that Christ has been reborn in it, and that the holiness of this rebirth will last forever. We had lost our way but He has found it for us. Let us go and bid Him welcome Who returns to us to celebrate salvation and the end of all we thought we made. The morning star of this new day looks on a different world where God is welcomed and His Son with Him. We who complete Him offer thanks to Him, as He gives thanks to us. The Son is still, and in the quiet God has given him enters his home and is at peace at last (manual, pp. 87-88; C-ep).

APPENDIX

Chart 1

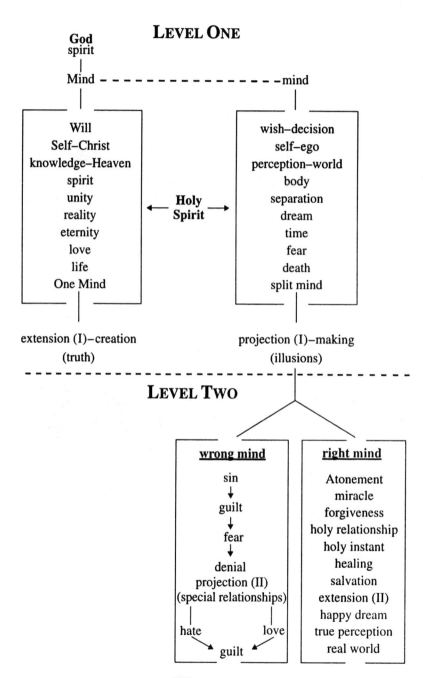

327

Chart 2: The Carpet of Time

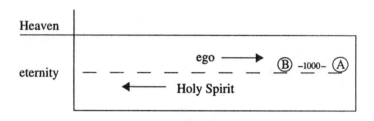

Chart 3: TV - Kaleidoscope - Hologram

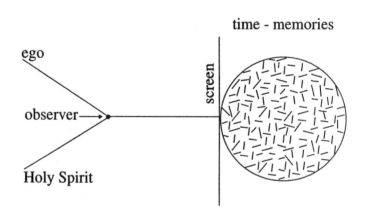

Chart 4: The Two Holograms

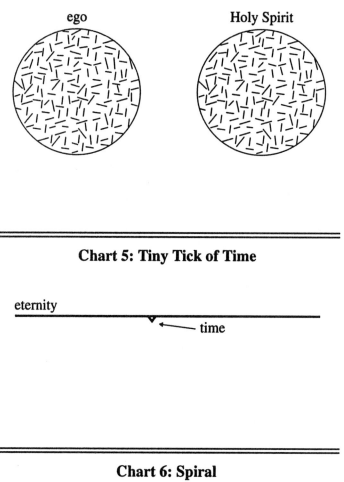

ego

Holy Spirit

Chart 5: Tiny Tick of Time

eternity

time

Chart 6: Spiral

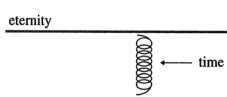

eternity

time

Index of *A Course in Miracles* References

First Edition	Second Edition	A VAST ILLUSION
	text	
intro	T-in.1	14-15
intro	T-in.1:1-5	31
intro	T-in.1:5	130
intro	T-in.1:6-7	195, 293
1	T-1.I.6	60
1-2	T-1.I.13	141
2	T-1.I.15	143
4	T-1.I.47	146
4	T-1.I.48	145
5	T-1.II.3:10-4:1	151
5	T-1.II.4:3-5	311
5	T-1.II.4:7	118
6	T-1.II.6	145-48
6	T-1.II.6:1-3	216
6	T-1.III.1:1	271
10	T-1.V.2:1-5	149-50
11	T-1.VI.3:5-4:1	293
12	T-1.VI.5:4	114
12	T-1.VII.1:4-5	316
13	T-1.VII.4:1	138
14	T-2.I.2:1	44
16	T-2.II.1:11-13; 2:1-3,5	99
16-17	T-2.II.5-6	151-54
18	T-2.III.3:3	15, 151
18	T-2.III.4:1-4	170
20-21	T-2.IV.5	144
22	T-2.V.5:1	245
25	T-2.VI.1:3	149
25	T-2.VI.4:1-4	219
27	T-2.VI.9:14	11, 22
27	T-2.VII.1:8	142

First Edition	*Second Edition*	*A VAST ILLUSION*

text (continued)

First Edition	Second Edition	A VAST ILLUSION
29	T-2.VII.6:2-7	309
29	T-2.VII.7:8-9	241
29	T-2.VII.7:9	149, 178
29-31	T-2.VIII	283-91, 293
29	T-2.VIII.1	271
30	T-2.VIII.2:5	146
32	T-3.I.1:5,8; 2:2-3	172
32	T-3.I.1:8	238
33	T-3.I.3:11	211
38	T-3.IV.3:7	308-309
39	T-3.IV.7:12	126
39	T-3.V.2	271
40	T-3.V.6:3,5	95
41-44	T-3.VI	201
42	T-3.VI.3:1	187
42	T-3.VI.3:1-3	167
44	T-3.VI.10:2	119
44-46	T-3.VII	201
47	T-4.in.3:1	163
49	T-4.I.6:3	254
49-50	T-4.I.9:3	271
52	T-4.II.5:8	129, 212, 272
53	T-4.II.8:1,4	109
53	T-4.II.8:6	243
53	T-4.II.8:8	53
54	T-4.II.11:8	42, 243
54	T-4.III.1:12-13	159
54	T-4.III.1:12-2:2	214
55	T-4.III.4:6	217, 258
58	T-4.IV.10:1-4	270-71
68	T-5.I.5:5-7	224

First Edition	*Second Edition*	*A VAST ILLUSION*

text (continued)

First Edition	Second Edition	A Vast Illusion
68	T-5.I.7:5	307
70	T-5.II.7:1-5	108
73	T-5.III.6:3	8
73	T-5.III.6:5	116
76	T-5.IV.8:1-4	107
79-80	T-5.VI.1-3	217-21
80	T-5.VI.3:5-4:3	25
81	T-5.VI.12:1-6	222-23
88	T-6.I.19:1	228
90-91	T-6.II.10-11	212-17
92	T-6.IV.1:1-2	25
100	T-6.V-C.1	150
105	T-7.I.7	301-306
105	T-7.I.7:4-7	8
106	T-7.II.4:1-5	227
121	T-7.VIII.3:9-11	209
132	T-8.III.4:1-7	240
139	T-8.VI.9:7	39, 84, 163, 301
140	T-8.VII.2:2	228
153	T-9.II.3	150
158	T-9.IV.9:2	293
158	T-9.IV.9:3-4	271
164	T-9.VII.4:5,7	220
166	T-9.VIII.2:8-9; 4:5	220
168	T-10.in.1:1-4	155-56
169	T-10.I.2:1	44, 69, 164
171	T-10.III.2:6	228
175	T-10.IV.8	309
178	T-10.V.14	157-60
187	T-11.IV.6:1-6	290
196	T-11.VIII.2	150

First Edition	Second Edition	A VAST ILLUSION

text (continued)

First Edition	Second Edition	A VAST ILLUSION
200-202	T-12.I	285
209	T-12.IV.6:8	309
211	T-12.V.8:3	103
217	T-12.VIII.3:1	294
220	T-13.in.2:2-3; 3:1	226
221	T-13.I.3:2	151
221-22	T-13.I.3-5	161-66
222-23	T-13.I.7-9	167-70
224	T-13.II.4:2-3; 6:1-3	299
229	T-13.IV.4-5	198-201
229	T-13.IV.4:2-5	59
229	T-13.IV.6:6	203
229-30	T-13.IV.7-9	204-209
230	T-13.IV.7:5	116
231	T-13.V.3:5	207
234	T-13.VI.4-6	171-76
234	T-13.VI.6:4	309
240	T-13.VII.17:6-7	9
241	T-13.VIII.3	306-309
250	T-13.XI.8:1	228
255	T-14.III.4	61
255	T-14.III.4:1	81
262-64	T-14.V	112, 240
273	T-14.X.7:1	285
280	T-15.I.1-2	177-79
280	T-15.I.2:1	112
280-81	T-15.I.3-7	206
283	T-15.I.15	180-82
289	T-15.IV.6:2	295
290	T-15.V.2:2; 3:1	309
290	T-15.V.2:3	309

First Edition	Second Edition	A VAST ILLUSION

text (continued)

306	T-15.XI.10:11	138
313	T-16.IV.1:1	198
315	T-16.IV.6:1-2	28, 195
317	T-16.V.1:1	198
320	T-16.V.12:7-9	284
322	T-16.VI.8:8	78
328	T-17.II.1:1-3,6-7; 2:1-2	105
333	T-17.IV.2:3	246
337	T-17.V.2:5	39
338	T-17.V.7:9	78
339	T-17.V.11:7-8	93
344	T-17.VII.10:2	78
347-48	T-18.I.4-5	277
347-48	T-18.I.4:1-3; 5:2-6	19
348	T-18.I.7:1	230
355	T-18.IV.1-5	134
355	T-18.IV.2:4-6	161
356	T-18.IV.6:3-5	292
357	T-18.V.2-3	134
357	T-18.V.2:1-5	292
359	T-18.VI.1:6	7
359	T-18.VI.4:7-8	92
362	T-18.VI.14:6	262
362	T-18.VII	84
362	T-18.VII.3:1	181
362-63	T-18.VII.4:4-5; 5:1-2; 6:3-4,6-8	124
363	T-18.VII.4:6-11	131
363	T-18.VII.4:10-11	215
363	T-18.VII.6	130, 132-34
364	T-18.VIII.1:7	29

•

First Edition	Second Edition	A VAST ILLUSION

text (continued)

364	T-18.VIII.3:3-4	45
364	T-18.VIII.4:1-2	67, 243
365-66	T-18.VIII.8:4,6-7; 9:1-4,8	141
377	T-19.III.3:3-7	94
385	T-19.IV-B.5:3-4; 8:3	165
392	T-19.IV-D.6:1-3	265
392	T-19.IV-D.7:1-4	183
393-95	T-19.IV-D.8-21	84
402	T-20.IV.1:1	155
404	T-20.IV.8	241-43, 247
413	T-20.VIII.8:1,6	42
415	T-21.in.1:1	207
415	T-21.in.1:7-10	140
415-17	T-21.I	70, 88
418	T-21.II.2:3-5	24
418	T-21.II.5:1-5	98
430-33	T-21.VII	296
431	T-21.VII.3:7-14	192
440	T-22.II.8:5-8	182-83
441	T-22.II.10:2	155
449	T-22.VI.9:2-5	182
452	T-23.I.1:1	110
452	T-23.I.2:7	100
455-60	T-23.II	155
455	T-23.II.1:1,4-7	199
455	T-23.II.1:1-5	28
455	T-23.II.2:1-2	135
457-58	T-23.II.13:3	156
459	T-23.II.19:1-6	264
464	T-24.in.2:1	53
471	T-24.III.8:13	109

First Edition	*Second Edition*	*A VAST ILLUSION*

text (continued)

479	T-24.VII.6:1	97
484	T-25.I.7	27
484	T-25.I.7:1,4-5	58
487-89	T-25.III	91
487-88	T-25.III.4:1; 5:1	193
488	T-25.III.6:1-5	184
493	T-25.VI.4:1; 6:6	96
493	T-25.VI.5	232-33
493	T-25.VI.5:1	310
493	T-25.VI.5:3-11	185-86
508-509	T-26.III.4	294-95
509-10	T-26.IV.1:1; 2:1,3-5	257
510	T-26.IV.6:1	60
511-13	T-26.V	57-84
511	T-26.V.3:5	45
515-16	T-26.VII.7:3-4	156
518	T-26.VII.17:1	115, 238
519	T-26.VIII.1	186-88
519	T-26.VIII.1:1; 3:1-2	112
519	T-26.VIII.3:1-2	189
519	T-26.VIII.3:7	189
520	T-26.VIII.6:1-2	189
521-22	T-26.IX	114
521	T-26.IX.4:1	9
522	T-26.IX.6:1	84
522	T-26.IX.8:4-5	139
535	T-27.V.1:1-7	112
537	T-27.V.10:1-2	112
537	T-27.V.10:4-6	149
539-43	T-27.VII	297
539-46	T-27.VII-VIII	53

First Edition	Second Edition	A VAST ILLUSION

text (continued)

First Edition	Second Edition	A VAST ILLUSION
540	T-27.VII.6:4-5	104,140
541	T-27.VII.7:3-4	91
542	T-27.VII.13:3-5	15
543-46	T-27.VIII	297
544	T-27.VIII.6:2	8
544	T-27.VIII.6:3	8
544	T-27.VIII.6:4	45
544	T-27.VIII.6:4-5	8, 108
544	T-27.VIII.7:1	8
545	T-27.VIII.9:1-5	230
545	T-27.VIII.10	185
545-46	T-27.VIII.11	233
547-50	T-28.I	85-119
550-53	T-28.II	53
551	T-28.II.4:2-4	229
552	T-28.II.9:3	85, 145
553	T-28.III.1:2	153
554	T-28.III.5:2-4	10
558-59	T-28.V.5:3-4,6-7	66
559-60	T-28.VI.2:1	66
563-65	T-29.I	119
572	T-29.VI.2	264-67
573	T-29.VII.1:9	166
576	T-29.VIII.6:2-6	44
578	T-29.IX.6:2-3	191
584	T-30.I.14:3-5,7-9	202
585	T-30.II.1:8; 2:1-5,8-9; 3:4-5; 4:4-5	159
587-88	T-30.III.6:1-2,4; 10:1-2	68
589	T-30.IV.2:1-2; 3:5-6; 4:3-6	191
589	T-30.IV.4:6-11	191

First Edition	*Second Edition*	*A VAST ILLUSION*

text (continued)

591-92	T-30.V.3-6	310-13
592	T-30.V.8-9	314-15
600	T-31.I.1:1-5,7	295
600-601	T-31.I.3:1-4; 4:3-5	211
601	T-31.I.5:1,5	158
607-10	T-31.IV.2:1-11; 9:3; 10:4-5; 11:3-4,6-7	62
609	T-31.IV.8:4-5	62
610	T-31.V.2:6	90
622	T-31.VIII.11:4-5	240

workbook for students

1	W-in.4:1	138
6	W-pI.4.1:4-7; 2:3-6	96
11	W-pI.7.2:1	37
47	W-pI.30	309
73	W-pI.46.1:1	286
99	W-pI.60.1:2	286
99	W-pI.60.1:5	160
118	W-pI.70.2:1-2	155, 239
174	W-pI.99.4:1-6:1	227-30
177	W-pI.100	278
185	W-pI.105.4	303
189	W-pI.107.2:1-3:1	48
191	W-pI.108	148
193-94	W-pI.109	321
227-28	W-pI.128	157
229-30	W-pI.129	157
230	W-pI.129.7:5	158
231-32	W-pI.130	157
236	W-pI.132.3:1-2	116

First Edition	Second Edition	A VAST ILLUSION

workbook for students (continued)

First Edition	Second Edition	A VAST ILLUSION
237	W-pI.132.6:2	243
237-38	W-pI.132.12:3-4	158
246	W-pI.135.11	231-32
247-48	W-pI.135.17-20	233-36, 238-40
252	W-pI.136.13-14	190-92
254-56	W-pI.137	84, 112, 176
258	W-pI.138.7:1-2	192-93
284	W-pI.155	95
289	W-pI.157	316
290	W-pI.157.9	48
291	W-pI.158.2:8	14
291	W-pI.158.2:8-4:5	37-41
291	W-pI.158.2:8-9	15
291	W-pI.158.4:1	11, 147
291	W-pI.158.4:5	53, 128
295-96	W-pI.160	321
312	W-pI.167.9	43-44
313-14	W-pI.168.3-6	316, 317, 319, 320
315	W-pI.169.1:1-2	54
315-16	W-pI.169.4-9	45-53
316	W-pI.169.8:1-2	15
316	W-pI.169.10	27
322	W-pI.rV.in.9:2-3	278
331	W-pI.182.3-4	75
337	W-pI.184.9:1-4; 11:1-2	212
338	W-pI.184.12:1-3; 13:2-3; 14:1	160
339	W-pI.185.1:1-2	126
342	W-pI.186	278
345-46	W-pI.187.6:3-4	230
347	W-pI.188.1:1	23, 178
357-59	W-pI.193	226

First Edition	Second Edition	A VAST ILLUSION

workbook for students (continued)

359	W-pI.193.13:6-7	93
360	W-pI.194	142, 242
360	W-pI.194.4	27
360	W-pI.194.4-5	193-95
360	W-pI.194.4:1-2	58
360	W-pI.194.4:3-5	58
403	W-pII.3.2:1	284
403	W-pII.3.2:1-4	86
409	W-pII.4.5:2	191
415	W-pII.5.1:1-4	180
415	W-pII.5.4:5	284
433	W-pII.8	253-59
435	W-pII.294	97
439	W-pII.9	272, 274, 275, 277-79
440	W-pII.302.2	154
443	W-pII.308.2	116
445	W-pII.10	296-300
445	W-pII.10.1:1	285
463	W-pII.13	136-40
469	W-pII.14.3:7	192
477	W-ep.1:1	130

manual for teachers

3	M-1.1:1	125
3	M-1.1:1-2	126
3	M-1.2	125-27
3	M-1.4	128-29
3	M-1.4:4-5	102, 140, 195
4	M-2.2-4	27-28, 30-32, 34-36
8-10	M-4.I.3-8	39

First Edition	Second Edition	A VAST ILLUSION

manual for teachers

First Edition	Second Edition	A VAST ILLUSION
10	M-4.I.6:11	167
13	M-4.VIII.1:6	237
16	M-5.I.1:1-2,7	42
24	M-8.6:1-4	231
25	M-9.1:1-2,4	246
30	M-12.1:1	150
30	M-12.3:3	127
31	M-12.5:6-7	179
32	M-13.1:2	49, 115, 198
35	M-14.1:1-5	259-60
35	M-14.2:8-3:4	261-62
35	M-14.4:1-3	263
43	M-17.5:8-9	283
43	M-17.6:2	64
43	M-17.7:12-13	161
51	M-21.1:7	47
51	M-21.1:9-10	111
61	M-26.4:1-2	162
64	M-27.7:1-5	267
67	M-29.2:6	132

clarification of terms

First Edition	Second Edition	A VAST ILLUSION
73	C-in.1:1-2	59
73	C-in.3:1-3	246
79	C-3.1:3-4	80
81	C-4.4:5	266
82	C-4.6:1,7-10	254
85	C-6.2:2	271
86	C-6.5:5	76, 84, 164
87-88	C-ep	323

First Edition	*Second Edition*	*A VAST ILLUSION*

"Psychotherapy: Purpose, Process and Practice"

5	P-2.II.4:4	125
7	P-2.III.2:1-4,6; 3:3-5	208
8	P-2.IV.1:7	62
20	P-3.II.8:5	39

"The Song of Prayer"

16	S-3.II.1:8-2:2	180

Foundation for "A Course in Miracles"
Academy ✦ Retreat Center

Kenneth Wapnick received his Ph.D. in Clinical Psychology in 1968 from Adelphi University. He has been involved with A COURSE IN MIRACLES since 1973, writing, teaching, and integrating its principles with his practice of psychotherapy. In 1982, with his wife Gloria, he began the Foundation for "A Course in Miracles," and in 1988 they opened an Academy and Retreat Center in upstate New York. The following is their vision of the Foundation and description of the Center.

In our early years of studying *A Course in Miracles,* as well as teaching and applying its principles in our respective professions of psychotherapy, and teaching and school administration, it seemed evident that this was not the simplest of thought systems to understand. This was so not only in the intellectual grasp of its teachings, but perhaps more importantly in the application of these teachings to one's personal life. Thus, it appeared to us from the beginning that the Course lent itself to teaching, parallel to the ongoing teachings of the Holy Spirit in the daily opportunities within our relationships, which are discussed in the early pages of the manual for teachers.

One day several years ago while Helen Schucman and I (Kenneth) were discussing these ideas, she shared a vision that she had had of a teaching center as a white temple with a gold cross atop it. Although it was clear that this image was symbolic, we understood it to be representative of what the teaching center was to be: a place where the person of Jesus and his message in *A Course in Miracles* would be manifest. We have sometimes seen an image of a lighthouse shining its light into the sea, calling to it those passers-by who sought it. For us, this light is the Course's teaching of forgiveness, which we would hope to share with those who are drawn to the Foundation's form of teaching and its vision of the Course.

This vision entails the belief that Jesus gave *A Course in Miracles* at this particular time in this particular form for several reasons. These include:

1) the necessity of healing the mind of its belief that attack is salvation; this is accomplished through forgiveness, the undoing of our belief in the reality of separation and guilt.

2) emphasizing the importance of Jesus and/or the Holy Spirit as our loving and gentle Teacher, and developing a personal relationship with this Teacher.

3) correcting the errors of Christianity, particularly where it has emphasized suffering, sacrifice, separation, and sacrament as being inherent in God's plan for salvation.

Our thinking has always been inspired by Plato (and his mentor Socrates), both the man and his teachings. Plato's Academy was a place where serious and thoughtful people came to study his philosophy in an atmosphere conducive to their learning, and then returned to their professions to implement what they were taught by the great philosopher. Thus, by integrating abstract philosophical ideals with experience, Plato's school seemed to be the perfect model for our teaching center.

We therefore see the Foundation's principal purpose as being to help students of *A Course in Miracles* deepen their understanding of its thought system, conceptually and experientially, so that they may be more effective instruments of Jesus' teaching in their own particular lives. Since teaching forgiveness without experiencing it is empty, one of the Foundation's specific goals is to help facilitate the process whereby people may be better able to know that their own sins are forgiven and that they are truly loved by God. Thus is the Holy Spirit able to extend His Love through them to others.

A teacher is defined in the Course as anyone who chooses to be one, and so we welcome to our Foundation all those who wish to come. We offer lectures and workshops for large groups as well as classes for smaller groups that would facilitate more intensive study and growth.

* * * * *

The Foundation, about 120 miles from New York City, is situated on ninety-five acres surrounding beautiful Tennanah Lake in the Catskill Mountains. Its country location and comfortable accommodations provide a peaceful and meditative setting in which students may carry out their plans for prayer, study, and reflection.

RELATED MATERIAL ON *A COURSE IN MIRACLES*

By Kenneth Wapnick, Ph.D.

Books and Pamphlets

CHRISTIAN PSYCHOLOGY IN *A COURSE IN MIRACLES*. Second edition, enlarged. Discussion of the basic principles of the Course in the context of some of the traditional teachings of Christianity. Includes a new Preface and an Afterword.
ISBN 0-933291-14-0 • #B-1• Paperback • 90 pages $4.
Audio tape of the first edition of the book, read by Kenneth Wapnick
#B-2 $5.

A TALK GIVEN ON *A COURSE IN MIRACLES*: An Introduction. Fifth edition. Edited transcript of a workshop summarizing the principles of the Course; includes the story of how the Course was written.
ISBN 0-933291-16-7 • #B-3 • Paperback • 160 pages $4.

UN CURSO EN MILAGROS: UNA INTRODUCCIÓN BASICA. Spanish translation of A TALK GIVEN ON *A COURSE IN MIRACLES*: An Introduction. Includes a glossary of some of the more important terms used in the Course.
ISBN 0-933291-10-8 • #B-3S • Paperback • 152 pages $4.

BETRACHTUNGEN ÜBER *EIN KURS IN WUNDERN*. German translation of A TALK GIVEN ON *A COURSE IN MIRACLES*: An Introduction. Order from: Greuthof Verlag und Vertrieb GmbH • Herrenweg 2 • D79261 Gutach i. Br. • Germany • Tel. 07681-6025 • FAX 07681-6027.
ISBN 0-933291-12-4

GLOSSARY-INDEX FOR *A COURSE IN MIRACLES*. Fourth edition, revised and enlarged. A study guide: summary of the Course's theory with a listing of all major terms; glossary of 139 terms and index of most important references; index of more than 800 scriptural references as found in *A Course in Miracles*, cross-referenced to the Bible. The book is keyed to both the first and second editions of the Course.
ISBN 0-933291-03-5 • #B-4 • Hardcover • 734 pages $20.

FORGIVENESS AND JESUS: The Meeting Place of *A Course in Miracles* and Christianity.   Fourth edition.   Discussion of the teachings of Christianity in the light of the principles of the Course, highlighting the similarities and differences; the application of these principles to issues such as injustice, anger, sickness, sexuality, and money.
ISBN 0-933291-13-2 • #B-5 • Paperback • 355 pages $16.

THE FIFTY MIRACLE PRINCIPLES OF *A COURSE IN MIRACLES*. Third edition. Combined and edited transcript of two workshops; line-by-line analysis of the fifty miracle principles, with additional material.
ISBN 0-933291-15-9 • #B-6 • Paperback • 115 pages $8.

AWAKEN FROM THE DREAM. Gloria and Kenneth Wapnick. Presentation of the Course's major principles from a new perspective. Includes background material on how the Course was written.
ISBN 0-933291-04-3 • #B-7 • Paperback • 133 pages $10.

THE OBSTACLES TO PEACE. Edited transcript of tape album; line-by-line analysis of "The Obstacles to Peace"—sections central to the Course's theory—and related passages.
ISBN 0-933291-05-1 • #B-8 • Paperback • 295 pages $12.

LOVE DOES NOT CONDEMN: The World, the Flesh, and the Devil According to Platonism, Christianity, Gnosticism, and *A Course in Miracles*. An in-depth exploration of the non-dualistic metaphysics of *A Course in Miracles*, and its integration with living in this illusory world.
ISBN 0-933291-07-8 • #B-9 • Hardcover • 614 pages $25.

ABSENCE FROM FELICITY: The Story of Helen Schucman and Her Scribing of *A Course in Miracles*. Discussion of Helen's lifetime conflict between her spiritual nature and her ego; includes some of her recollections, dreams, letters, and personal messages from Jesus—all never before in print; an account of her own experiences of Jesus, her relationship with William Thetford, and the scribing of the Course.
ISBN 0-933291-08-6 • #B-11 • Paperback • 521 pages $16.

OVEREATING: A Dialogue. An Application of the Principles of *A Course in Miracles*. Pamphlet presenting the Course's approach to issues such as food addiction and preoccupation with weight. (Edited and slightly expanded version of the tape "Overeating.") ISBN 0-933291-11-6 • #B-12 • Paperback • 35 pages $3.

Video Tape Albums

SEEK NOT TO CHANGE THE COURSE. Reflections on *A Course in Miracles*. Talk given by Gloria and Kenneth Wapnick, including questions and answers, on some of the more common misunderstandings about the Course.
#V-1 135 mins. VHS $30 PAL (non-U.S.) $40
Audio tape version $15.

FOUNDATION FOR "A COURSE IN MIRACLES" Conference and Retreat Center. Gloria and Kenneth Wapnick speak about the Course's beginnings, the origin and purpose of the Foundation, and their vision of its development in the future. A visual and verbal portrait of the Center.   #V-2 24 mins.
VHS $10 PAL (non-U.S.) $20.

Audio Tape Albums
Classes and Workshops

CHRISTIAN PSYCHOLOGY IN *A COURSE IN MIRACLES*. Audio tape of first edition of book of the same title, read by Kenneth Wapnick. #B-2 1 tape $5.

THE SIMPLICITY OF SALVATION. Intensive overview of the Course. The two levels of discourse in the Course; in-depth summary of the major principles; comparison of the Course and Christianity; the story of how the Course was written.
#T-1 8 tapes $65.

HOLY IS HEALING. Psychotherapeutic applications of the Course. Workshop weaving together the theory of *A Course in Miracles* with psychotherapeutic and personal examples offered by participants. #T-2 8 tapes $65.

ATONEMENT WITHOUT SACRIFICE: Christianity, the Bible, and the Course. Workshop exploring the relationship between *A Course in Miracles* and the Judaeo-Christian tradition, with special emphasis placed on the role of sacrifice and suffering. #T-3 2 tapes $15.

THE END OF INJUSTICE. Overview of the Course. The thought systems of the ego and the Holy Spirit; application of principles to problems involving sex, money, injustice, and sickness. #T-4 6 tapes $45.

THE EGO AND FORGIVENESS. Introductory overview of the Course. The ego's thought system of sin, guilt, fear, and special relationships, and its undoing through the Holy Spirit's thought system that includes forgiveness and holy relationships. (Album consists of first two tapes of "The End of Injustice.") #T-5 2 tapes $15.

THE FIFTY MIRACLE PRINCIPLES OF *A COURSE IN MIRACLES*. Line-by-line commentary on the fifty miracles principles which begin the text; introduces students to the central concepts of the Course: Atonement, miracles, healing, time, forgiveness, the Holy Spirit. #T-6 3 tapes $24.

THE WORLD ACCORDING TO *A COURSE IN MIRACLES*. The Course's theory of the world and its role in the ego's plan to usurp God's function and substitute a world of its own for the creation of God. #T-7 3 tapes $24.

THE OBSTACLES TO PEACE. Line-by-line commentary on the "Obstacles to Peace" sections of the text, focusing on the ego's attraction to guilt, pain, and death, and the fear of God's Love, and the undoing of these obstacles through forgiveness. #T-8 6 tapes $48.

SPECIAL RELATIONSHIPS—PART 1. Line-by-line commentary on sections discussing specialness; explains the unloving nature of most relationships, and how to transform them. #T-9 8 tapes $65.

SPECIAL RELATIONSHIPS—PART 2. Continuation of Part 1, developed through commentary on later chapters in the text including "The Healed Relationship," "The Treachery of Specialness," "The Forgiveness of Specialness." #T-10 6 tapes $48.

TIME ACCORDING TO *A COURSE IN MIRACLES.* The metaphysics of time—its holographic though illusory nature; the relation of time to the role of the miracle in the plan of the Atonement; the end of time. #T-11 6 tapes $48.

JESUS AND *A COURSE IN MIRACLES.* Discussion of passages in the Course in which Jesus refers to himself: as the source of the Course; his historical teaching example as the manifestation of the Holy Spirit, and perfect model of forgiveness; and his role as our teacher, without whom the undoing of the ego's thought system would be impossible. #T-12 5 tapes $40.

CAUSE AND EFFECT. The importance of this principle in understanding how forgiveness undoes the ego's thought system of guilt and punishment; line-by-line analysis of text sections on our dreams of suffering and victimhood. #T-13 8 tapes $65.

PSYCHOTHERAPY: PURPOSE, PROCESS AND PRACTICE. Line-by-line commentary on the companion pamphlet to the Course, scribed by Helen Schucman from Jesus. #T-14 7 tapes $56.

THE GIFTS OF GOD. A discussion of the inspired poetry of Helen Schucman, scribe of the Course; includes personal reminiscences about Helen. #T-15 3 tapes $24.

SEEK NOT TO CHANGE THE COURSE: Reflections on *A Course in Miracles.* Gloria and Kenneth Wapnick. Audio version of video tape of the same name. #T-16 2 tapes $15.

LOVE DOES NOT OPPOSE. Gloria and Kenneth Wapnick. The importance of non-opposition as the basis of forgiveness in special relationships. #T-17 8 tapes $65.

THE SONG OF PRAYER. Line-by-line commentary on the companion pamphlet to the Course, scribed by Helen Schucman from Jesus; the role of prayer as a reflection of the process of our acceptance of the true meaning of Jesus' presence in our lives; Jesus' relationship with Helen as the model for understanding the nature of prayer. #T-18 10 tapes $80.

THE ORIGIN OF *A COURSE IN MIRACLES*. The story of the scribing of *A Course in Miracles*; reflections on Helen Schucman and William Thetford. #T-19 1 tape $6.

I WILL BE STILL AN INSTANT AND GO HOME. A collection of two talks and a meditation by Kenneth Wapnick, and one talk by Gloria Wapnick and Kenneth—given at various Sunday services. #T-20 1 tape $6.

JESUS AND THE MESSAGE OF EASTER. The Course's view of Jesus, and the meaning of his crucifixion and resurrection. #T-21 8 tapes $65.

THE AUTHORITY PROBLEM. The authority problem with God and its reflection in our everyday life. #T-22 5 tapes $40.

OUR GRATITUDE TO GOD. Our gratitude to God, Jesus, and to each other; the obstacles and resistances to this gratitude. #T-23 5 tapes $40.

SICKNESS AND HEALING. Discussion of the cause and purpose of sickness in the ego thought system; analysis of healing as occurring in the mind—the healing of the belief in guilt, by turning to the Holy Spirit and forgiving. #T-24 8 tapes $60.

WHAT IT MEANS TO BE A TEACHER OF GOD. Discussion of the ten characteristics of a teacher of God; also includes discussion of magic and healing. #T-25 6 tapes $48.

OVEREATING: A DIALOGUE BASED UPON *A COURSE IN MIRACLES*. The ego dynamics involved in food addictions and weight problems; forgiveness through the Holy Spirit as the solution. #T-26 1 tape $6.

TO JUDGE OR NOT TO JUDGE. The Course's teachings on judgment; the process of recognizing our need to judge, and letting Jesus or the Holy Spirit judge for us. #T-27 4 tapes $32.

HEALING THE UNHEALED HEALER. The characteristics of the unhealed healer; healing through joining with Jesus in understanding all forms of sickness and problems as calls for love. #T-28 8 tapes $65.

THE REAL WORLD: OUR HOME AWAY FROM HOME. A discussion of our true home in Heaven, the ego's home in the world, and the Holy Spirit's correction of the ego's world: the real world. #T-29 8 tapes $65.

TRUE EMPATHY: THE GREATER JOINING. The world's version of empathy contrasted with the Holy Spirit's true empathy. #T-30 8 tapes $65.

JESUS: THE MANIFESTATION OF THE HOLY SPIRIT. A discussion of Jesus and the Holy Spirit in the context of the difference between appearance and reality, and the importance of Jesus as our guide in leading us out of the dream; includes a discussion of the relationship of Jesus to Helen Schucman and to *A Course in Miracles*. #T-31 5 tapes $40.

THE LAWS OF CHAOS: OUR WAR WITH GOD. An in-depth exploration and discussion of the five laws of chaos that form the foundation of the ego's thought system, and powerfully express the ego's defenses against the Love of God. #T-32 12 tapes $85.

"THERE MUST BE ANOTHER WAY." The words that led to the birth of *A Course in Miracles* provide the theme of this workshop which discusses forgiveness as the "other way"—rather than specialness—of relating to ourselves, each other, and to God. #T-33 1 tape $6.

THE METAPHYSICS OF SEPARATION AND FORGIVENESS. Summary of the teachings of *A Course in Miracles*, specifically showing how the principle that the thought of separation and the physical world are illusions becomes the foundation for the understanding and practice of forgiveness in our daily lives. #T-34 1 tape $6.

THE WORKBOOK OF *A COURSE IN MIRACLES*: ITS PLACE IN THE CURRICULUM—THEORY AND PRACTICE. Discussion of the metaphysical principles underlying the lessons, the mind-training aspects of the workbook, Jesus' gentle teaching method, and students' common misuses of the workbook. Two charts and an annotated outline of the workbook included. #T-35 8 tapes $65.

MAKING THE HOLY SPIRIT SPECIAL: THE ARROGANCE OF THE EGO. Presentation of the major Course teachings on the role of the Holy Spirit—and Jesus as His manifestation—and the importance of Their Presence in our lives. Discussion of the contrasting attitudes of arrogance and humility in asking help of the Holy Spirit, as well as what it means to hear His Voice. The idea that the Holy Spirit acts in the world is shown to rest on misunderstandings of the principles and language of the Course, as well as on our unconscious desire for specialness. #T-36 7 tapes $56.

THE MEANING OF JUDGMENT. Discussion based on "The Forgiving Dream" from the text, centering on four forms of judgment: 1) the dream of judgment against ourselves; 2) looking with Jesus at this ongoing judgment of guilt without further judgment; 3) judging all things in accord with the Holy Spirit's judgment; 4) joining with Jesus in the judgment of God's Love that is the only reality. #T-37 1 tape $6.

New Releases

THE WEB OF SPECIALNESS

DUALITY AS METAPHOR IN *A COURSE IN MIRACLES*

"RULES FOR DECISION"

See next page for ordering information

Ordering Information

For orders *in the continental U.S. only*, please add $2.00 for the first item, and $1.00 for each additional item, for shipping and handling.

For orders to *all other countries* (SURFACE MAIL), and to *Alaska, Hawaii*, and *Puerto Rico* (FIRST CLASS MAIL), please add $4.00 for the first item and $1.00 for each additional item.

New York State residents please add local sales tax. (New York law now requires sales tax on shipping and handling charges.)

VISA and MasterCard accepted.

Order from:

Foundation for A COURSE IN MIRACLES
951-296-6261 • www.facim.org
41397 Buecking Drive
Temecula, CA 92590

* * * * *

A COURSE IN MIRACLES and other scribed material
may be ordered from:

Foundation for Inner Peace
Box 1104
Glen Ellen, CA 95442
(707) 939-0200

A COURSE IN MIRACLES, Second edition:
Hardcover: $30 Softcover: $25

PSYCHOTHERAPY: PURPOSE, PROCESS AND PRACTICE: $3.00

THE SONG OF PRAYER: PRAYER, FORGIVENESS, HEALING: $3.00

THE GIFTS OF GOD: $21.00

Additional copies of this book may be ordered from:

F   *Foundation for A COURSE IN MIRACLES*
951-296-6261 • *www.facim.org*
41397 Buecking Drive
Temecula, CA 92590

Send a check or money order (in US funds only) for $12.00 plus shipping: please see preceding page for shipping charges.